The
Fortune
Cookie
Chronicles

The *Fortune Cookie* Chronicles

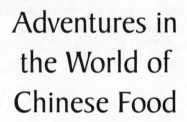

Adventures in
the World of
Chinese Food

Jennifer 8. Lee

TWELVE

NEW YORK   BOSTON

Twelve
Hachette Book Group USA
237 Park Avenue
New York, NY 10017

Visit our Web site at www.HachetteBookGroupUSA.com.

Twelve is an imprint of Grand Central Publishing.
The Twelve name and logo is a trademark of Hachette Book Group USA, Inc.

Printed in the United States of America

First Edition: March 2008
10 9 8 7 6 5 4 3 2 1

Library of Congress Cataloging-in-Publication Data
Lee, Jennifer 8.
    The fortune cookie chronicles: adventures in the world of Chinese food / Jennifer 8. Lee.—
1st ed.
        p. cm.
    Summary: "A woman's search for the world's greatest Chinese restaurant proves that egg rolls are as American as apple pie"—Provided by publisher.
    ISBN-13: 978-0-446-58007-6
    ISBN-10: 0-446-58007-4
    1. Chinese restaurants—United States. 2. Food in popular culture—United States. 3. Food in popular culture—China. 4. Cookery, Chinese. 5. Food habits—United States. 6. Chinese Americans—United States—Social life and customs. 7. Gastronomy. I. Title.
    TX945.4.L44 2008
    641.5951—dc22   2007033432

Book design by Giorgetta Bell McRee

For Mom and Dad,
who left their homeland so their children
could follow their passions,
and for all the other moms and dads
who have done the same

Do the Chinese eat rats? This has always been a mooted question. Geographies contain the assertion that they do, and an old wood-cut of a Chinaman peddling rodents, strung by the tails to a rack which he carried over his shoulders, is a standard illustration of the common school atlases of 10 years ago. A large portion of the community believe implicitly that Chinamen love rats as Western people love poultry.

—**New York Times,**
August 1, 1883
"Mott Street Chinamen Angry.
They Deny They Eat Rats."

Contents

The
Fortune Cookie
Chronicles

 **PROLOGUE**

March 30, 2005

t's the same televised routine twice a week, Wednesdays and Saturdays, at 10:59 P.M. central time. And on March 30, 2005, everything was as always. The host introduced the drawing. The white balls, air-popped, rolled out one by one from the machine: 28, 39, 22, 32, 33. The final ball, red, from another machine, plopped down and slowly spun to a stop: 42. The six balls took fifty-six seconds to appear, fifty-six seconds that sent shocks through the lottery system across the country.

After the drawing, with the cameras turned off, Sue Dooley, a former preschool teacher, helped maneuver the two machines back into the vault. Sue was one of the two Powerball staff members who took turns overseeing the drawings. One of the frontline soldiers of the Powerball security, she'd been hired, in part, because working with children had made her good at bossing people around. She was the one who'd dropped the balls into the wispy churn of the machines that night, climbing up onto a milk crate because, at five foot two, she needed help to reach that high.

Lotteries live and die by their integrity. Fraud and scandal have led to crackdowns on American lotteries in two waves of moralistic prohibition—once before the Civil War and again before the turn of the twentieth century. In an infamous case, in 1823 Congress created a lottery to raise money to beautify Washington; the organizers ran away with the money. By the late nineteenth century, Congress had passed a restriction on transporting lottery tickets across state lines, which to this day hinders the creation of a national lottery.

But in the late 1980s, increasingly dependent on lotteries to avoid raising taxes, states figured out a way around the national ban. They found they could legally form coalitions of state lotteries to form megalotteries, whose larger jackpots would attract greater ticket sales, as long as the states sold only state-branded tickets within their borders. Lotteries were akin to insurance companies—taking in lots of little flows of money that would statistically cover big payouts at some profit to the institution. Megalotteries are somewhat analogous to reinsurance firms, in that the states can spread the risk of large payouts among one another. The megalotteries proved to be so popular, raising billions of dollars for education and infrastructure, that by 2005 only a handful of states abstained from either Powerball or its chief rival, Mega Millions.

With billions of dollars depending on the security of Powerball, there were numerous precautionary measures in place. At every drawing officials waited until the last minute before they decided which two of the four Powerball machines they would use. Copies of the ticket sales data were kept in multiple locations. The vault housing the machines was padlocked twice and secured with numbered plastic seals that could be used only once. Two keys were needed to open the vault, kept separately by the Powerball staff and by an auditor.

Satisfied that everything was secure, Sue put the vault key

into her purse and drove the five-mile stretch of empty Des Moines highway from the studio to wait for the results. The Powerball headquarters had been located in the Des Moines area in part because it was neither the East nor the West Coast. "No one cares if it's located in Iowa. No one's feelings are hurt," one Powerball administrator explained. Iowa is as inoffensive as it is flat.

That night had been a low-key, uneventful drawing, and Sue figured she could be in bed by midnight. The jackpot was only $84 million. Once, that figure would have generated some excitement, but Powerball administrators had discovered the phenomenon of jackpot fatigue: players needed ever-larger jackpots to entice them into buying tickets in large numbers. The threshold for an attention-grabbing megajackpot had once been $10 million; it now stood at $100 million. The $84 million jackpot had generated only $11 million in ticket sales, on the modest end of a normal lottery. Based on the ticket sales, officials expected to get three or four second-place winners—people who'd picked the first five of the six numbers correctly—and perhaps one jackpot winner.

Around 11:15 P.M., Sue pulled up to the Powerball headquarters, which was tucked into an anonymous office complex in a stretch of grass off Interstate 35. It was hard to believe that the low-slung bland strip mall contained a twelve-person office that oversaw some $3 billion a year in annual sales—enough that if those sales belonged to a publicly traded company, it would be in the Fortune 1000. The staff had kept the office purposely nondescript, with none of the glitzy logos and neon lights that often marked state lottery headquarters. In fact, the office had originally lacked any sign whatsoever indicating that it served as Powerball headquarters, but when senior citizens in search of nearby medical suppliers had kept coming in to ask for respirators and medications, the staff had stuck four small letters on the front door: MUSL, the contrived abbreviation for "multistate lottery."

Sue turned on her computer and waited for the results to come in from the various states. Before the prizes could be doled out the next morning, all the numbers had to be checked and rechecked.

This can't be right, she thought as she saw the first tallies trickle in. Statistically they had expected only 3.7 second-place winners, but the states were reporting huge numbers, so large that no one had ever seen anything like this in the history of American lotteries.

Arizona: 11
Pennsylvania: 13
South Carolina: 14
Tennessee: 12
Indiana: 10

Against the odds, states that normally had almost no second-place winners were coming in with more than had been predicted for the entire drawing.

Rhode Island: 5
Minnesota: 4
Connecticut: 4

Even Montana, with its sparse population of 900,000, had a winner. Across all the states there were 110 winners. Sue checked to see if they were concentrated in any way, but the tickets had been sold by different vendors from different computer systems across different states. None of the tickets had been computer-generated, meaning the players had independently chosen the numbers themselves.

What was going on? She grabbed the phone.

• • •

Chuck Strutt, the Powerball director, was a mild-mannered man who wrote poetry in his spare time. But sometimes he lost momentum. His last book of published poetry had included a number of blank pages, in jest.

Chuck was sitting at home when his phone rang; when he heard what was happening he felt a shiver. Occasionally, Powerball would get four or five times the number of expected second-place winners, and once they'd even had seven times the predicted figure. But their accountants and statisticians had calculated the odds and found that these occurrences were flukes of chance; distributions could sometimes put you in those ranges. Nearly thirty times the number of expected winners, however, was well outside any statistical probability.

Not only that, but 104 of the 110 winners had picked the same sixth number, 40, instead of the Powerball number of 42. It would have been better had the winners all matched the final Powerball number of 42. In that case, under the lottery's fine-print rules, the jackpot would simply have been split among the 110 people. But Powerball's second prize and under were all fixed amounts, meaning their liability was theoretically unlimited: the more winners, the more Powerball had to pay out. Foreseeing this, Powerball had legally protected itself in scenarios that could generate an outlandish number of winners. For example, the most popular sequence played in Powerball was 1, 2, 3, 4, 5, 6, followed by 5, 10, 15, 20, 25, 30. If the winning numbers resembled either of those, there would be thousands upon thousands of lower-place winners, as had happened in the Massachusetts Lottery once when the numbers 1, 2, 3, 4, 6, and 10 were drawn. There would also have been thousands of winners if 9, 1, 1 had come up in any of the pick-3 lotteries in the days after September 11. So on the back of each Powerball ticket, written in small print, are the words "In unusual circumstances, the set prize amount may be paid on a pari-mutuel basis, which will be lower than the published prize amounts." Powerball also kept a reserve fund of $25 million, of which $20 million would be drained by the unexpectedly high number of $100,000 and $500,000 winners in that night's drawing.

Chuck and Sue brainstormed about possible causes. An episode of *Lost*, the hit ABC television show, had featured a lottery number that had simultaneously brought jackpots and misfortune to its winners. Sue, a lifelong fan of *The Young and the Restless*, recalled that a recent plotline had involved a $1 million Powerball ticket dispute between Kevin and Michael. Perhaps one of the widely syndicated lottery columnists had suggested those numbers.

That night, Chuck barely slept. *What if this is fraud?* he wondered. *Had someone managed to game the system?*

Some seven hundred miles away, in Nashville, the next morning, Rebecca Paul came to work puzzled by the unusual spike in Powerball winners. Rebecca had run four state lotteries, including her current position as the head of Tennessee's. She was intrigued by the number of winners in Tennessee alone: not only did they have the jackpot winner, they also had twelve second-place winners.

With more than twenty years of experience under her belt, Rebecca was one of the most respected veterans and one of the first women in the insular, tight-knit community of state lottery officials. Her office wall featured a collection of different magazine issues through the years—all with her photo on the cover.

She had started down the path of state lotteries as a beauty pageant queen when, as Miss Indiana, she had placed in the top five in the Miss America pageant with a gymnastics tumbling routine. That honor had led to a job as a part-time weather girl on a local television station, which she later parlayed into a position in sales and marketing. In 1985, she got a call from the Illinois governor, James Thompson, who asked her to start the state lottery. She had no experience with lotteries, she said; he told her he wanted her anyway. She knew how to sell things, and lotteries were in essence about marketing—selling people their dreams. Even as a lottery official, she retained one prominent vestige of her beauty pageant days: her hair, which could be best described by the word "bouffant."

Rebecca sat down at her desk with a Powerball form and colored in the winning numbers with a purple felt-tip pen to see if any patterns emerged—a cross or a diagonal or a diamond—but none did. She contacted the head of security of the Tennessee Lottery with instructions to start looking for any evidence of fraud.

But at 8:30 A.M., Tennessee already had a winner waiting for the prize office to open its doors, a great-grandfather named James Currie who worked the night shift as a system operator at Pinnacle Foods, the parent company of the Duncan Hines and Aunt Jemima brands. He had made the two-hour drive from Jackson, Tennessee, with his sister, Sherion; he dreamed of buying a Cadillac with his money.

The staff, as was customary, asked how he had selected his winning numbers.

"From a fortune cookie," he replied. He had always used birthday and anniversary dates, but he'd realized that they weren't getting him anywhere. So a few months earlier he'd switched to a fortune cookie number he had obtained from a Chinese takeout restaurant near his home called Dragon 2000. He'd had a good feeling about those numbers and had been playing them for three months.

In Idaho at 11:18 A.M. another winner reported using a fortune cookie number. Same with Minnesota at 12:06 P.M. and

Wisconsin at 12:09 P.M. One winner had even kept the original fortune: "All the preparation you've done will finally be paying off." On the bottom were the numbers that so many Americans had taken an inexplicable faith in: 22, 28, 32, 33, 39, 40.

The ritual of Chinese food in America had sent the twenty-nine-state Powerball on a collision course with fortune cookies. The fortune cookies had prevailed.

CHAPTER 1

American-Born Chinese

There are some forty thousand Chinese restaurants in the United States—more than the number of McDonald's, Burger Kings, and KFCs combined.

Tucked into exurban strip malls, urban ghettos, and tiny midwestern towns that are afterthoughts for cartographers, Chinese restaurants have spread nearly everywhere across America—from Abbeville, Louisiana, to Zion, Illinois, to Navajo reservations, where, in a distinction shared with only a handful of businesses, they're exempted from tribe-member ownership. Old restaurants, clothing stores on Main Streets, and empty storefronts have been reborn as Chinese restaurants. The Washington, D.C., boardinghouse where John Wilkes Booth and his accomplices planned Abraham Lincoln's assassination is now a Chinese restaurant called Wok n Roll.

Chinese restaurants have long been a weekly or monthly ritual for many Americans.

As far back as 1942, chop suey and chow mein were added to

the U.S. Army cookbook. Jonas Salk, while developing the polio vaccine in the early 1950s, would eat his lunch at Bamboo Garden on Forbes Avenue, near the University of Pittsburgh, nearly every day. He always ordered the same thing: a bowl of wonton soup, an egg roll, rice, and chicken chow mein made with homegrown bean sprouts—all for $1.35.

Chinese restaurants are sought out for special events, too. In 1961, before the Freedom Riders left for the first fateful bus ride through the Deep South to protest segregation, a number of that company met for dinner at a Chinese restaurant in Washington. "Someone referred to this meal as the Last Supper," said John Lewis, then a young theology student from rural Georgia, later a congressman. In October 1962, emissaries for John F. Kennedy and Nikita Khrushchev met secretly at Yenching Palace in the Cleveland Park neighborhood of Washington to work out a solution to the Cuban missile crisis. Chinese restaurants were neutral territory.

Nearly everyone has a go-to Chinese restaurant. Dwight Eisenhower ordered his chicken chop suey from Sun Chop Suey Restaurant on Columbia Road in Washington, D.C., for decades. When he became president, the FBI investigated every employee at the restaurant (just as a precaution). Likewise, Peking Gourmet Inn outside Falls Church, Virginia, had to install a bulletproof glass window near table N17. That is where the Bushes, both father and son, sit at their favorite Chinese restaurant.

It's not surprising that the Powerball officials heard the same tale repeated over and over again across the twenty-nine states, from coast to coast. The stories were different. The stories were the same. It was takeout. It was sit-down. It was an all-you-can-eat buffet. It happened years ago, months ago, earlier that day. It was dinner. It was lunch. It was where they ate every week with coworkers. It was on a family vacation to a neighboring state. The number had been in a fortune cookie they had cracked open themselves. The number had been on a fortune found while cleaning a car or waiting at a convenience-store counter. But the one thing all those stories had in common was the starting point: a meal from a Chinese restaurant that had ended with a fortune cookie.

The lottery story ran in *AM New York,* the commuter daily I picked up one morning to read on the New York City subway. The one-paragraph article said the March 30 Powerball had been pummeled with an unusually large number of winners, 110 in all, largely because of fortune cookies.

I perked up.

I am obsessed with Chinese restaurants. Like many Americans, I first discovered them in my childhood. I grew up during the 1980s on the Upper West Side of Manhattan, where Broadway is sometimes called Szechuan Alley for the density of Chinese restaurants along it. My parents had first settled in the area when my father was studying for his Ph.D. at Columbia University; because my mom never learned to drive, our family never moved out of the city. As a result, I was raised not too far in time and place from many of the changes that revolutionized Chinese food in the United States.

My siblings and I are known as ABCs, American-born Chinese. We're also known as bananas (yellow on the outside but white on the inside) and Twinkies (which has more of a pop-culture but processed ring to it). There are a lot of inside jokes among immigrant families. My family even has one embedded in the children's names. My parents named me Jennifer; my sister is Frances; my brother is Kenneth. If you string together our first initials, you get JFK, which, my parents tease, is the airport they landed at when they first came to America.

My parents arrived in the United States courtesy of the Immigration Reform Act of 1965, which opened the doors to educated and skilled workers like my father and dramatically shifted the balance of immigration away from Europe. Countries like Taiwan, South Korea, and India stood ready to offer the best products of their meritocratic educational systems.

My mom took care of the home and did most of the cooking, while my father worked on Wall Street. But like many families in our area, we'd order Chinese takeout when she was too busy to cook. As a girl I would run down to the neighborhood Chinese restaurant with a crisp twenty-dollar bill in my pocket. Barely tall enough to see past the counter, I'd solemnly order dishes from the big white menu, using the Chinese names that my mom had carefully taught me. (Without exception, the vocabulary words that Chinese-American kids—and immigrant kids in general—know best are almost always related to food.)

Then I'd lug home my treasure: a plastic bag of steaming, generously stuffed trapezoidal white cartons. Our family gathered around the table as we pulled out the boxes, each one bursting with the potential of anonymity. Out came chopsticks, the little clear packets of black soy sauce, and crunchy fortune cookies. Each untucking of the lid released a surge of aroma and a sight to spark the appetite. Would it be the amber-colored noodles of roast pork lo mein? The lightly sweetened crispiness of General Tso's chicken nestled in a bed of flash-cooked broccoli? Or the spicy red chili oils of mapo tofu? Virginal white rice would be doused with steaming sauces, the mingling of simmered soy sauce, piquant vinegar, slivers of ginger, and fragrant garlic. The Chinese food begged to be mixed together: sweet, sour, salty, and savory flavors layering upon one another. They tasted even better the next day when the leftovers were reheated. We'd break open the fortune cookies for the message inside, rarely eating the cookie. The cheerfully misspelled, awkwardly phrased, but wise words of the Chinese fortune cookie sages gave me comfort.

My parents' bookshelves were lined with Chinese philosophical classics like Confucius's *Analects* and the *I Ching*. For a girl who could not untangle the thicket of Chinese characters in those opaque and mysterious books, the little slips of insight represented the distillation of hundreds of years of Chinese wisdom.

Then came a shocking revelation.

Fortune cookies weren't Chinese.

It was like learning I was adopted while being told there was no Santa Claus. How could that be? I had always believed in the crispy, curved, vanilla-flavored wafers with the slips inside.

It was through reading *The Joy Luck Club* by Amy Tan when I was in middle school that I first became aware of the mass deception. In one tale, two Chinese women find jobs in a San Francisco fortune cookie factory, where one is utterly perplexed when she learns that the cookies and their cryptic messages are considered Chinese.

I asked my mom if she had known all along that fortune cookies weren't Chinese. She shrugged. She said when she first got to the United States from Taiwan, she'd assumed they were from Hong Kong or mainland China. China is a large and fractured place. She had never been to mainland China. Neither had I.

The Americanness of fortune cookies hit home a few years later, in a 1992 front-page story in the *New York Times* with the headline "A Fortune Will Greet You in an Endeavor Faraway." The article announced that Brooklyn-based Wonton Food was to sell fortune cookies in China. It added that in Hong Kong, the cookies were already being marketed as "genuine American fortune cookies."

The Americanness of fortune cookies should have served as a hint for what else I was to learn about Chinese food. Only now, looking back, do I find it obvious. As a child, I never considered it strange that the food we ordered from Chinese restaurants didn't quite resemble my mom's home cooking. My mom used white rice, soy sauce, garlic, scallions, and a wok. But she never deep-fried chunks of meat, succulent and soft, then drenched them with rich, flavorful sauce. She cooked with ingredients that were pickled and dried and of strange shapes and never appeared on the take-out menu. Her kitchen was filled with jars and bags of all sorts of unusual things—white fungus, red beans, pungent black mushrooms, porous lotus roots. She used pre-served foods: eerily translucent thousand-year-old eggs, spicy pickled bamboo shoots, vinegared mustard greens. Her dishes involved bones and shells—sweet-and-sour ribs, boiled garlic shrimp, chicken feet.

At the open seafood storefronts of Manhattan's Chinatown, my parents would pick through the bins of live crabs, sluggish but still menacing to a wide-eyed six-year-old girl. We would haul the writhing creatures back home in thin plastic bags and deposit them in the kitchen sink. We would steam the life out of them in my mother's decade-old wok, their waving pincers grad-ually slowing to a halt as their bodies became progressively red and orange. The Chinese holistic approach to crab was not the sanitized, edited version of Red Lobster. Our crabs burst forth with weird colors and textures. The goopy orange paste, called *gao,* was the best part, my mom told me.

My parents were always annoyed when we went to the "real Chinese restaurants" in Flushing, Queens, and I asked for my favorite dishes, beef with broccoli and lo mein. They inevita-bly ordered dishes that had eyeballs, like steamed whole fish with ginger and scallions. For a girl who was more familiar with the pleasantly geometric fish-fillet sandwiches of her elementary school cafeteria, the piscine servings were unnerving. Instead of eating this fish that had been merrily swimming in the tank just minutes before, I turned my chopsticks to the comforting crisp green broccoli, tender slices of beef, and soft amber noodles. My siblings and I turned up our noses at the bitter hot tea. We either added sugar or insisted on having cups of ice water. My parents were exasperated. They had thrown their children into a pool of cultural heritage in America: Chinese Saturday school, Chinese camp, Chinese chorus, Chinese martial arts, and Chinese folk dancing. (Perhaps 90 percent of all Chinese-Americans girls have twirled a silk ribbon at some point in their lives.) Yet on the issue of food, our taste buds were firmly entrenched. They groused about our inability to appreciate "real Chinese food."

I never really understood what "real Chinese food" meant until I went to China. Years of study in Chinese Saturday school, daily classes in college, and a semester in Taiwan had opened up the world of the dense opaque characters of my mother's books. China was a foreign country to me, but one where I happened to speak the language. Ostensibly I spent my fellowship year studying at Beijing University, but in reality I was educating myself by traveling cross-country from the deserts of Inner Mongolia to the lakes of Sichuan to the peaks of Tibet. Alongside the Coca-Cola, McDonald's, and KFCs that have penetrated China's core, I encountered a variety of cuisines that were more akin to my mom's cooking than the ones of America's Chinese restaurants: more vegetables, less meat, less oil. I began spitting bones out onto the table and drinking watery soup after a meal to wash it all down. I even drank hot tea—no fortune cookies to be found. I began to roll my eyes at the take-out Chinese food I had grown up with; it wasn't authentic.

But as interesting as the local food was to me, I was interesting to the locals. You could see their minds processing: She looks perfectly Chinese. She speaks Chinese perfectly. But something is amiss. Perhaps it was the way I moved, the way I laughed, the way I dressed. I wasn't, they felt, of China. Hong Kong? Taiwan? they asked.

"I'm American," I explained.

Their reply: "No, you're Chinese. You were just born in America."

I was not an American to them. I was an American-born Chinese. Maybe the same thing was true of Chinese food back home: It's Chinese. It just happened to be born in America.

Or maybe the truth was closer to this: It's American. It just looks Chinese.

That morning, as I read about the Powerball winners on the subway, people swarmed around me as usual. I looked at them and thought about how many of them had eaten Chinese food in the last week, how many had read their fortunes and added "in bed," how many kept a favorite fortune folded in their wallet. How many might have played the lottery with their lucky numbers? I had never played the lottery, but I was entranced by the idea that so many people took the same leap of faith and played the identical numbers from a fortune cookie. Right there on the subway, I decided to follow those fortune cookies back to their source—from the winners back to the restaurants, back to the factory and the people who write the fortunes, back to the very historic origins of fortune cookies. Following the Powerball fortune cookie trail, I believed, was something that would help me unravel the nagging mysteries of Chinese food in America. For the story of the Powerball trail was the story of Chinese food in reverse. I'd fallen into an obsession with Chinese food—in a way that my friends and parents actually found rather worrisome, given my hyperrational nature. Charitably, you could describe me as "passionate" about Chinese food. Passions seem lively and motivating, while obsessions sound dark and vaguely deviant. But the line between passion and obsession is a wobbly one. Obsessions pick us more than we pick them. They control us more than we control them. Why do people become obsessed with bird-watching, solving mathematical proofs, making money? Maybe they're trying to complete themselves, to fill a void, whether it be through beauty, truth, or security.

Within hours, I identified one of the Powerball restaurants, Lee's China, in Omaha, Nebraska. I looked up the number online and dialed. A woman picked up.

I started out by introducing myself in Mandarin Chinese.

I received the telephone equivalent of a blank stare.

I switched to basic Cantonese.

More blankness.

I tried English.

The woman cut me off. "We're Korean," she said in a thick accent. Then she hung up.

Over the next year I compiled a list of the Powerball restaurants and winners, drew up an itinerary, and began a consuming journey that crisscrossed the country. By the end, I had visited forty-two states, with nearly all of the Powerball states among them. I had driven cars until bugs had splattered across my windshield like egg whites dropped in soup. I'd taken red-eye flights, pulled all-nighters driving on interstate highways, stewed on buses for twenty-three consecutive hours, and crashed in the relative air-conditioned comfort of Amtrak trains.

I must pause to acknowledge my Garmin GPS machine, which is one of the best dollar-for-dollar investments in happiness I have ever made. If you simply have faith in it, you can let go of your worries. You may not understand why it is telling you to do whatever it is telling you to do, but you trust that it will get you to your final destination. Like religion.

If you don't own a Chinese restaurant, you can get in on the action by investing in the stock PFCB—P. F. Chang's China Bistro, a publicly traded Chinese restaurant chain. The Chinese chain Panda Express may have more restaurants nationwide, but it is privately held. P. F. Chang's, which brings in an astounding $5 million each year per restaurant, is headquartered in the expansive desert, in an adobe-style complex tucked among the cactuses and lush golf courses of Scottsdale, Arizona.

I was brought to the original P. F. Chang's in Phoenix by an affable Chinese restaurant owner named Jim Ye, who once worked as a wok cook in P. F. Chang's. Jim was an owner of the Chinese Gourmet Buffet in Chandler, Arizona, where the Cobbs family got the fortune cookie that made them winners in the fateful March 30 Powerball. Years ago, in trying to learn about upscale Chinese restaurants, he'd taken a job at P. F. Chang's. The other employees were surprised to see him. Wow! Finally, a Chinese person! A real Chinese cook! That's because your average cook in P. F. Chang's is more likely to speak Spanish than Chinese. The entire top management team has nary a Chinese face. The executive chef is named Paul Muller; he's originally from Rosedale, Long Island.

In the early days before P. F. Chang's became known as a national chain, customers would genially ask how Mr. Chang was doing. There is no Mr. Chang. The "P. F." in P. F. Chang stands for Paul Fleming, one of the creators of the Outback Steakhouse and the founding visionary for the Chinese chain. The "Chang" derives from the surname of Phillip Chiang, the consultant for the restaurant's Chinese cuisine, who was the son of Cecilia Chiang, the famed San Francisco restaurateur who owned the upscale Mandarin restaurant in Ghiradelli Square. In naming the restaurant, the management dropped the i from Chiang. "We took the i out so the signage could be a little bigger," explained Richard Sullivan, one of the original partners of the chain. That conveniently left them with Chang. "Chang: it's like Smith in America. It sounds Chinese, and we wanted something that people could pronounce," he said. The idea for the restaurant came about when Fleming moved to the Phoenix area and was disappointed in the choices for high-quality Chinese food there. He wanted to combine a Chinese menu with upscale service. P. F. Chang's sees itself in the same category as the Cheesecake Factory, so much so that the companies trade real estate tips with each other.

It's an American restaurant with a Chinese menu. P. F. Chang's exists because Chinese food has ceased to be ethnic, Sullivan explained. "People consider it ethnic when it's new to them and they don't understand," he said. But this is no longer true for an American society raised on beef with broccoli.

You can recognize any P. F. Chang's by its signature icon: gargantuan terra-cotta warriors—the severe-looking soldiers from the tombs of the Qin Shi emperor in the ancient Chinese capital of Xi'an. The emperor had been dead for some two thousand years before the tombs were discovered in 1976, by a peasant digging a well. (I saw the peasant some twenty-four years later at the tombs, sitting at the gift shop, signing autographs.) The outside of the restaurant is flanked by two gigantic terra-cotta horses wearing Christmas wreaths. "You will find in our restaurants an Asian influence, be it through the terra-cotta warriors to the horses to our mural," Brian Stubstad, the director of design and architecture for the company, explained to me. There are no dragons or phoenixes. Red and gold are minimal. No Great Walls of China. No pandas. Were it not for the certain Chinese-ish items, the restaurant could be a nice steakhouse.

But not everyone finds the terra-cotta warriors charming. "Chinese people would never put that in a restaurant," Jim told me, pointing at the statues. "It's not lucky. It's something you put in burial site! But in America, they think it's a Chinese thing." From a Chinese perspective, P. F. Chang's is decorated with death.

• • •

Monty McCarrick, a Wyoming truck driver with a long black ponytail and a receding hairline, called his wife, Joyce, from Iowa, where he'd stopped during a trip across the country.

"Are you sitting down?" asked Monty, whose right arm is marked with a tattoo of an American flag and a scar from a bullet wound. (A friend's gun accidentally went off.)

"You wrecked the truck," Joyce said anxiously.

No, he crowed. They'd won $100,000 in Powerball.

"You got to be shittin' me."

Two months earlier they had gone to their favorite Chinese restaurant, Chinatown, located in Powell, Wyoming (population 5,000+), about a half-hour drive from their home. There Monty got the lucky numbers in a fortune cookie; five weeks later he bought the fateful ticket in Council Bluffs, Iowa, on his way to Ohio to deliver a load.

I dropped by the McCarricks' home, a modest one-bedroom apartment they shared with their cat, Coco, who sometimes accompanied Monty on his road trips. Their three rooms were splattered with Elvis Presley memorabilia. As a teenager, Joyce had been a founder and president of Elvis Presley's international fan club. Now in her fifties, she still had framed photos of the two of them together on her living room wall: he with his sultry lips and stiff pompadour and her with a perky ponytail and bangs. She used to visit his family during her summers in Nashville. When he did his military service in Germany, she talked to him once a month. Joyce had fifteen handwritten letters from Presley. "He had horrible spelling and horrible grammar," she recalled. In total she estimates her collection could be worth as much as $100,000. That was the couple's most valuable asset until Monty won the Powerball drawing. They paid off $20,000 in credit card debt built up in four accounts.

In Monty's drives across the country, Chinese restaurants are reliable, accessible eating establishments. "They are pretty much in every town you go to," he said. "It's fairly inexpensive. You get all you want to eat, for anywhere between five and seven dollars." What's nice, he noted, is how predictable they are. "I know it's going to have the stuff that I am going to like," he said. "You get the sweet-and-sour pork and you get the noodles, the lo mein noodles, and the egg foo yong. That is pretty tasty."

"The way they make the food, too, is pretty much the same," he explained. "There is some exceptions, like egg rolls. Some places make them different and better than others. The wontons, the deep-fried wontons, those are pretty much the same. The chicken is pretty much the same." For Monty, the predictability is reassuring. "I don't like a lot of change," he said. "I'm a simple person."

As I drove away from their home, toward South Dakota, Joyce waved good-bye and called out: "Watch out for the moose at the top of the mountains!"

Louisiana had two of the 110 Powerball winners, but, more important, it had Cajun Chinese food. When informed of my quest, a colleague told me that I had to visit Trey Yuen Cuisine of China, a restaurant in Mandeville, outside New Orleans, to try dishes like Szechuan alligator and a soy-vinegar crawfish. Trey Yuen had been serving Szechuan alligator since the late 1970s, shortly after alligator meat became legal, and the dish has remained one of its more popular.

Trey Yuen was owned by five brothers named Wong, whose great-grandfather had taken a boat to San Francisco in the late nineteenth century, seeking work. His sons and grandson followed him and found work in Chinese restaurants. (One of them even married a Chinese woman he'd never met. A live rooster stood in for him at the wedding ceremony back in China.) Eventually the Wong brothers' grandmother established a chop suey restaurant in Amarillo, Texas, along historic Route 66.

The sons traveled across the States, working in Chinese restaurants, until they found the opportunity to open the original Trey Yuen. Their mother used to tell them, "You guys are like my five fingers. Individually you are not very strong. Together"—she would form a fist—"you are solid." Together, the five brothers have owned their restaurants for over thirty-five years.

Trey Yuen's Szechuan alligator dish ended up being light-colored chunks of meat mixed with ginger, garlic, and crushed pepper. The alligator looked like cooked chicken but tasted surprisingly springy and tender. "I call it bayou veal," said Tommy Wong, the fourth of the five brothers, in a Texas twang. "Some people are squeamish about trying alligator, especially people from out of town," he said. Of course, he eventually does tell the people who dine on "bayou veal" the truth—"After they've eaten it."

Tommy showed me a plate of raw chicken side by side with raw alligator. I would not have been able to distinguish them if it weren't for the fact that the alligator meat came in long, pale strips. "See how nice and lean it is, and clean. High in protein," he added. "Most people leave it in big chunks—that's where the mistake is. Because of all the connecting tissues."

Could you get Szechuan alligator anywhere else in the world? Probably not in China, yet this dish in front of me was arguably—even recognizably—Chinese.

A driving force behind Chinese cooking is the desire to adapt and incorporate indigenous ingredients and utilize Chinese cooking techniques, Tommy explained. Chinese cooking is not a set of dishes. It is a philosophy that serves local tastes and ingredients.

That idea continued to reverberate with me as I encountered creations like cream cheese wontons (also called crab Rangoon) in the Midwest, Philly cheesesteak rolls (egg rolls on the outside, cheesesteak inside) in Philadelphia, and the chow mein sandwich in New England. Chinese food, perhaps, does not have to originate in China.

In Rhode Island, home to five of the Powerball winners, I stopped at Chan's Egg Roll and Jazz in Woonsocket, a restaurant with a century-long history. In its latest incarnation, the owner, Jon Chan, had turned it into a nightclub drawing prominent jazz acts from around the country.

This part of New England features the fabled chow mein sandwich, a subject of study for Professor Imogene Lim, a third-generation Canadian who speaks better Swahili than Chinese.

I dragged along my friend Lulu Zhou, a girl whose doe eyes and round cheeks make her appear like a thinly disguised anime character. Though she is Shanghainese and was raised mostly in Hong Kong, Lulu speaks flawless English with the lilting ticks of an American teenager. (For instance, "And then the dragon freaked the guy shitless" was her retelling of a Chinese fable.) Her parents, both lawyers, now live in Beijing, but she had spent most of her academic career in English-language schools—mostly in Hong Kong, as well as a brief period in New York City when her father was at NYU's law school. When she was six years old, she glimpsed her parents' green cards with their photos and RESIDENT ALIEN stripped along the top. At the time, *Star Trek: The Next Generation* was popular, so the idea of extraterrestrials was in her head. "Are my parents aliens?" she thought in shock. That suspicion was exacerbated when her parents snatched the cards away from her.

In college, Lulu developed a fascination with Jewish guys—partially from working on the school newspaper, she believed. In response, I bought her a book called *Boy Vey!*, a tongue-in-cheek guide to dating Jewish men. She read it cover to cover and began sprinkling into her conversations with Jewish guys questions about whether they were Sephardic or Ashkenazi.

When the chow mein sandwiches were set in front of us, Lulu looked at them with a combination of mock horror and genuine fascination. Trapped between two pieces of white Wonder bread was a crunchy pile of fried Chinese noodles slathered in a brown gravy flecked with bits of celery and onion. It was moist and soft and crunchy, all at the same time. Lulu giggled. We weren't sure how to approach it. The gravy had softened the bread, making it too messy to pick up with our hands. I attempted to attack mine with a knife and fork. Lulu plucked the crispy noodles out of the bread. It wasn't bad; the gravy gave the sandwich a lot of flavor, and the textural mix of crunchy noodles, sodden bread, and flavored liquid was quite intriguing. In some other life, we might even have thought it was quite good. But that day, we couldn't get our minds around the concept of a starch-on-starch sandwich.

The trail of the chow mein sandwich then led me to Fall River, Massachusetts, and the Oriental Chow Mein Company, arguably the largest supplier of chow mein mixes in the world, limited market though it is. When I stepped into the brick building, I was embraced by the warm smell of frying noodles, which guides lost customers to the store. Founded in the 1920s, the company had been passed down through the family, and is now largely managed by Barbara Wong and her sons. Barbara was born in Canton, China (before it was known as Guangdong). She came to the states when she was seventeen, following a father she had known only through letters.

At the factory, heavy dough was flattened by continuous rolling into a thin sheet, cut up into strips—they looked like the end products of a corporate paper shredder—steamed, and then fried. Piles of discarded noodles were scattered across the floor. A methodic *swish-chunk* sound streamed through the factory: boxes being sealed. There were stacks and stacks of boxes waiting to be mailed, addressed to Tulsa, Oklahoma; Locust Grove, Georgia; Lake Oswego, Oregon; Dunnellon, Florida. "Everywhere, everywhere, everywhere. My customers are from all fifty states!" Barbara cheerfully explained. Many customers had grown up in the area but had been pulled away.

For many, the chow mein sandwich captured memories of growing up: Mom's home cooking. Hanging out after school. Flirting. First dates. The sandwich evoked both family and friends. Locals even shipped the mix overseas, unleashing the force of the chow mein sandwich on foreign soil. During the first Gulf War, residents sent chow mein mixes to local men who were serving abroad. When I heard this, it reminded me of a phone conversation I'd had after the 2003 Iraq invasion. I was in Washington; a number of my friends had been swept up in the historic journey: cynical journalists, idealistic nation builders, mercenary contractors. Many of them informed me of the two improvised Chinese restaurants that had popped up next to the landing pad of a military hospital in the Baghdad Green Zone, a ten-minute stroll north of Saddam Hussein's palace. The restaurant in the back was slightly more popular because patrons figured it would be less likely to be damaged by an insurgent attack from the street. These Chinese restaurants in Baghdad had neither Chinese nor Arabic on their menus, only English. Though the Chinese restaurateurs had never been to America, they knew how to attract large crowds with American-style Chinese food like sweet-and-sour pork and pan-fried dumplings.

Among those friends of mine deployed was Walter Miller, a foreign service officer who resembles a bookish version of James Dean. We would chat by phone (his cell phone in Baghdad had a 914 area code, as though he were only in Westchester). In one of those conversations, I wondered aloud why the Chinese restaurants were so popular with my friends in Iraq when, after all, in the Middle East diners should indulge in the authentic local cuisine of kebabs and hummus.

"It's a taste of home," Walter said. Even against the whirl of Medevac helicopters, Chinese food had become a beacon for American patriots. "What could be more American than beer and take-out Chinese?"

Favored cuisines become refuges in times of crisis. On September 11, my friend Daniel Hemel and his friends, after their high school classes were canceled and they had learned that their parents were safe, headed to a local Chinese restaurant in Scarsdale, New York, called Chopstix to watch the news and eat stir-fry. Chinese food was comfort food for him and his friends: something predictable and familiar when they needed an anchor in an explosion of uncertainty.

I looked back at my journeys across the numerous Powerball restaurants. American Chinese food is predictable, familiar, and readily available. It has a broad appeal to the national palate. It is something nearly everyone nowadays has grown up with—both young and old. I marveled that on a single day, Chinese food had united so many different people from different parts of the country: a schoolteacher in Tennessee, a farmer-veterinarian in Wisconsin, a research microbiologist in Kansas, a police sergeant from New Mexico, retired septuagenarian snowbirds from Iowa, a bank clerk from South Carolina, a salesman from New Hampshire.

Our benchmark for Americanness is apple pie. But ask yourself: How often do you eat apple pie? How often do you eat Chinese food?

CHAPTER 2

The Menu Wars

In November 1976, Misa Chang, a petite Chinese immigrant and mother of three, opened a Chinese restaurant on the southeast corner of Broadway and West Ninety-seventh Street in Manhattan and waited for customers. A good decade before the gentle currents of gentrification climbed along the northern edges of Central Park's western neighborhood, people were leery of being out much at night. It was cold. It was dark. It was dangerous. Often the staff of four would outnumber their customers. After two frustrating weeks of watching the largely empty tables under the naked fluorescent lights, Misa had a piercing insight that would shift the trajectory of the restaurant industry in New York City. If the customers didn't want to come to her, she would bring the food to them. She would begin a delivery service. Diners had long looked to Chinese restaurants for takeout, but free door-to-door Chinese delivery would be something intriguing. Misa may not have understood English very well, but she understood Americans. She printed up hundreds of white paper menus and walked from apartment to apartment herself, sneaking into buildings to slip the menus under residents' doors.

Two hours after her first tour through the apartment buildings, the phone rang. The order: wonton soup and an egg roll. Misa hadn't hired any Chinese delivery boys yet, so she walked the two blocks through the snow to make the drop herself. A woman answered the apartment door, amused that a five-foot-no-inch-tall Chinese woman had appeared with her order. She handed Misa a one-dollar tip.

At the time, the idea of making food deliveries to people's doors was quixotic. Misa launched her delivery service well before the popularization of ATMs and VCRs. The idea that something—entertainment, food, cash—could be available on a consumer, rather than industry, timetable was startling.

But customers intuitively grasped the idea of delivery. Orders began to trickle in, then to pour in. Misa made the next hire to her staff of four: a delivery boy. Eric Ma, a scrawny sixteen-year-old busboy from a nearby Chinese restaurant, was a student at Norman Thomas High School. For his new job, Eric bought himself a used bicycle for fifteen dollars.

Soon the orders began flooding into Empire Szechuan Garden at an unrelenting pace. The phones wouldn't stop ringing. Misa hired more delivery boys. The bags didn't fit on the tables and had to be lined up on the floor. Eric and the other delivery boys would be sent out with eight orders at a time, perilously balancing the bags on their handlebars. It was a seller's market back then. Empire Szechuan could deliver during the hours and to the geographic region it wanted. Customers were appreciative of the steaming hot food that appeared at their door, tipping generously. When the delivery boys were wet from the rain, they offered them towels.

For a long time, the neighborhood around the original Empire Szechuan was still relatively ragged. But Misa found a new way to deal with the homeless men. With fried rice and noodles, she bribed them to stay away from her front door.

I grew up about a mile and a half north of Misa's restaurant, largely oblivious to its significance but cognizant of its evolution. It gobbled the Blimpie's and a Mexican restaurant, opened a glass-encased outdoor café that later disappeared, and settled into a neon pastel motif in the early 1990s.

By the time I met with Misa, the restaurant's floor space had expanded fivefold. The place still had the *Miami Vice*–era feeling from its last renovation, but the red pillars of the original restaurant remained intact. In person, Misa, now a sexagenarian grandmother of ten, was a chirpy combination of age and energy. She wore oversized jewelry and carried two cell phones. She was always in motion, shuttling from restaurant to restaurant—Empire Szechuan had expanded throughout Manhattan—and to the Fulton Fish Market, so she carried a toothbrush and toothpaste in her purse. "That way I can wake up from a nap in the car, brush my teeth, and be ready to go," she said.

She had a button nose and thinning red-tinted hair, which was cut into what is best described as a double mullet. Two tails of hair trailed down either side of her neck. She said she likes the ease of short hair but the feeling of having long hair. The double mullet was her solution.

In the 1970s, there were only a limited number of ways to earn a living as an immigrant woman in the United States, Misa explained. Opening a restaurant was one of them. She and a few others scraped together $25,000 from their savings and through loans from family and friends.

She was not the first restaurant owner to come up with the idea of hand-delivering food to people's homes. Nor was she even the first Chinese restaurant owner to do so. Before World War II, John Kan's Chinese Kitchen delivered piping hot food around San Francisco. In the late 1930s, Chinese restaurants in New York's Chinatown were using automobiles to bring chop suey to people's doors. Of course, delivery was not always the easy, spur-of-the-moment decision it is now. Even in the 1950s, some restaurants demanded twenty-four hours' notice to bring a three-course meal to your door. But for whatever reason, none of those scattered services catalyzed the delivery frenzy the way Empire Szechuan did.

With delivery powering her business, Misa's restaurant empire quickly expanded. In 1979, Empire Szechuan Gourmet received a one-star rating from the *New York Times,* which was notable given its modest decor and no-nonsense service. The menu appealed to a more sophisticated crowd as yuppies began moving into the Upper West Side. They then added Empire Szechuan Columbus, Empire Szechuan Balcony, and Empire Szechuan Bleecker. Empire Szechuan moved into the West Village, the East Side, Long Island, Miami.

Flush with cash, Misa and her partners started investing in real estate, including the older eight-story building that held the original Empire Szechuan Gourmet. Eric, that first delivery boy, was promoted to a manager. He also married Misa's daughter and became her son-in-law.

Misa herself had not had much schooling, but she'd always had a shrewd intuition for what her customers wanted before they even knew they wanted it. She began delivery at a time when two-career families were starting to become common. Misa hired women as waitresses at a time when Chinese restaurants generally hired only men. "They smile more," she told me. She quickly expanded her menu when she felt that Chinese food was becoming stale. She introduced sushi to her restaurants so that couples wouldn't have to fight about choosing Chinese or Japanese for dinner. She added pad thai to the menu when Thai food started gaining in popularity. She began a bubble-tea café in the restaurant to take advantage of the tapioca drink craze. She added a low-carb diet selection way before Atkins or South Beach hit the national radar. She knew when to upgrade the look of her restaurants away from red and gold to pastel neon, and again to the concrete, exposed brick, and recessed lighting of the turn of the millennium.

With Misa's vision, Empire Sezchuan had a lock on the delivery market early on. Then it slowly dawned on others that there was no reason they could not make deliveries, too. The other Chinese restaurants entered the market—some of them learning from former employees of Empire Szechuan itself. Up and down Broadway, competing Chinese restaurants sprang up almost overnight in formerly shuttered storefronts, almost all with "Hunan" or "Szechuan" in their names: Hunan Balcony. Hunan 94. Hunan Gourmet. Szechuan West. Szechuan Broadway. The deliverymen stuffed brown paper grocery bags with stacks upon stacks of menus, using rags to hide them from the watchful eyes of doormen and neighbors. Then other ethnic restaurants joined in the fray, seemingly in reverse order of the cuisine's distance from China: Thai. Japanese. Indian. Soon it became a free-for-all, an ethnic smorgasbord.

The first signs of trouble appeared in the building entryways. Simple "No Menus" signs metamorphosed into more punctuation-adorned, aggressive postings of "No Menus! Of Any Type! Got It?" The signs were originally written in English, which did little to abate the problem, as the menu men generally weren't literate in English. (As Eric Ma explained it to me, "If they understood English, would they be making deliveries?") So the "No Menu" signs soon became bilingual, with Chinese characters. Next they turned trilingual and even quadrilingual, to combat what had become a multiethnic, multirestaurant siege. Then it wasn't just restaurants anymore. Other businesses piled in: carpet cleaners, nail salons, dry cleaners, and even grocery stores. The flyers were stuffed into mailboxes, piled on lobby furniture, thrown in heaps on lobby floors, and shoved under doors. Residents and landlords argued that the flood of paper engulfing the Upper West Side was a health and safety hazard. They feared that the accumulation of menus would alert burglars to when people were away. And what if it rained and someone slipped on a wet menu? Who would they sue? The menu guys were entering buildings by buzzing bells and cheerfully announcing that they were from UPS. They were propping security doors open with rocks or following residents in. At this point, it wasn't just Empire Szechuan Gourmet that was papering the apartment buildings, but infuriated Upper West Siders felt it was the place at which they could point their fingers. Angry doormen would arrive at Empire Szechuan and dump a month's worth of accumulated menus from their buildings, many of them from other establishments. One building complex in Harlem escorted menu men out in handcuffs, which immediately cut down on the flyer volume there.

The menu wars became violent on both sides, drawing blood in August 1994. One evening, a writer named Philip Carlo walked out of his building on West Eighty-eighth Street and spotted a lanky Chinese man putting menus from a restaurant called China Barbecue in his vestibule, near where a bilingual "No Menu" sign had been placed.

Carlo told the deliveryman to stop and returned the menus to him. The deliveryman put them back down. Carlo picked them up again. The deliveryman put them down again. The back-and-forth over the menus turned into a shoving match, which turned into an exchange of punches that spilled out onto the street. Carlo suffered a bloody nose, but he was evidently the better fighter; the deliveryman had a broken jaw. Carlo was convicted of assault and sent to Rikers Island for sixty days. The charges against the deliveryman were dropped. In a separate incident, a secretary, Jane O'Connor, was punched by an Empire Szechuan deliverer after telling him to stop dropping menus at her West Ninety-sixth Street building. She won a $2,000 judgment.

The local community board also used its political leverage to punish Empire Szechuan. It persuaded the Department of Transportation to oppose the renewal of the outdoor-café license administered by the Consumer Affairs Department.

Upper West Siders being Upper West Siders, they were not afraid to use the legal and judicial process to get their way. The New York State assemblyman for the Upper West Side, Scott Stringer (who would go on to become Manhattan borough president), introduced a bill that would quadruple the fine for distributing menus and other fliers on private properties that explicitly opposed them. But other New York City Council members expressed concerns over freedom of speech.

Misa, too, argued that the menus were little different from the political fliers that were distributed on the streets. Nonetheless, Empire Szechuan and Misa suffered setbacks. In 1994, a landlord named Saul Lapidus sued Empire Szechuan in small-claims court for distributing menus in his two brownstones in the West Seventies. He told Empire Szechuan that he would charge it ten dollars every time he had to clean up the menus. Empire Szechuan responded that the menus were protected by the First Amendment guarantee of free speech and that there was no proof that they'd been left by Empire Szechuan employees anyway. But the judge, Kibbie F. Payne, ruled that because building lobbies were private property, Empire Szechuan had no free-speech protection there. He said there was enough evidence to prove that the menus had been distributed by the restaurant and fined it $447.75 to compensate Lapidus for cleaning up the mess. Meanwhile, Misa had already been thinking ahead. She'd contacted the United States Postal Service to inquire about bulk postage rates. Empire Szechuan would begin distributing the menus by mail.

At lunch, Misa told me she had no regrets, even though her flood of menus had launched an angry backlash among New York City residents. "My workers have to feed their families," she said. "We weren't robbing or stealing from anyone." Distributing menus was fair game, she felt.

Over the past three decades, she boasted to me, tens of thousands of Chinese immigrants have passed through her restaurants. "Sometimes I go traveling, I will meet someone. They know me. They've worked for me," she said. "For a lot of them, they are new immigrants. We give them a chance. They need the money." Many of her former employees had been students who needed a toehold in America. "A lot of people are Ph.Ds. Some have been doctors. One has gone on to be an ambassador," she noted.

I could not quite put my finger on why Empire Szechuan's delivery service had created such a snowball effect. Was it a timing issue? Delivery had existed, in tepid forms, prior to Misa's arrival. Even during the 1970s, scattered pizza parlors and fried-chicken joints in New York City had offered delivery service. Many restaurants, Chinese and otherwise, did takeout. Some restaurants even had paper menus. There were a number of nice sit-down Chinese restaurants on the Upper West Side when the original Empire Szechuan Gourmet first opened: Moon Palace, Great Shanghai, Happy Family. Today all of them are gone. If Misa hadn't come along with her vision of aggressive delivery, would it have occurred to someone else from those restaurants? Or perhaps Misa's success had to do with choosing the right market, introducing delivery in the right New York neighborhood at the right time. The Upper West Side of Manhattan was densely packed with apartment buildings, co-ops, and brownstones. Women were moving into the workplace in larger numbers, and were looking for quick but healthy ways to feed their families when they didn't have time to make home-cooked meals. Young professionals loved the idea that food could come from a phone rather than a stove.

But the more I thought about it, the more the whole situation seemed eerily familiar. A low-cost method of distributing advertising had led to indiscriminate carpetbombing of materials, which had led to copycat marketers, which had led to infuriated customers, which had led to a back-and-forth in judicial and legislative recourse, which had led to new ways to distribute advertising.

This was spam. Miss Chang had succeeded in part because she had understood the power of spam before anyone else. It wasn't just about the service; it was about the marketing. I had met the proto-spammer.

The decision to buy the building on Broadway and Ninety-seventh Street turned out not to be the wisest business move for Misa's partnership. "I know Chinese restaurants. But I don't know real estate," Misa admitted. Managing an aging property, with its upkeep and building inspections, eventually became too much of a headache. She and her partners sold to a landlord who wanted to turn that valuable spot over to Bank of America. Empire Szechuan Gourmet had to find a new home.

Misa decided to move the flagship restaurant to a preexisting spin-off on 100th Street, long nicknamed Empire Szechuan Junior. I watched her haggle, in her broken English, with the owner of a town-car service upstairs. She thought his company's sign was ugly and offered to make him a new one that would fit better with the new Empire Szechuan decor.

The original Empire Szechuan on Broadway and Ninety-seventh Street shut down on October 4, 2005, after nearly twenty-nine years of business. Misa wasn't at the restaurant for the formal closing, because it pained her. The restaurant was disassembled without much fanfare. By the next afternoon, the staff had moved to the new Empire Szechuan restaurant on 100th Street. It was open for business immediately.

The change attracted little attention. By then, neighborhood Chinese restaurants were nothing special. Other places, like the Vietnamese Saigon Grill, had intoxicated Upper West Siders with their exotic new cuisine.

Over time, it became clear that the 100th Street restaurant didn't have the same visibility and traffic as the original location, which had been just a block away from a major crosstown bus line and an express subway stop. Business slowed.

Today, nearly every self-respecting restaurant in Manhattan, from neighborhood diners to high-end establishments, delivers. They have to, in order to survive. Over the years, Chicago, Washington, and Boston also jumped on the delivery bandwagon, though some other cities, like San Francisco, seem stubbornly resistant. Several years ago, many of my friends began murmuring about something called SeamlessWeb. I had never encountered the service. But my friends, particularly those in finance, consulting, and law, swore by it. At work, they could order lunch and dinner over a Web site and never have to see the bill. Even the tip could be set and billed directly to the company. Now it was possible to feed yourself without ever leaving your desk. No more turning in receipts stained with chicken tikka masala. No more struggles with English on the phone. Companies loved it. Accounting departments loved it. My friends loved it. I was horrified and fascinated at the same time. It was just a half step down from (and a half hour slower than) the food replicators in *Star Trek*. You can have a sumptuous $25 sushi dinner in thirty minutes. But the cost: the delicately prepared meal has to be savored while you're slogging through a spreadsheet or proofreading a contract.

"Now you see, everyone does delivery," Misa told me over lunch at the 100th Street Empire Szechuan. She rattled off a list of restaurants within a one-block radius that delivered: pizza, the Indian place across the street, steakhouses, the fried-chicken place. She added in amazement, gesturing across the street, "Even the diner does delivery."

"When you feel like you've done something well, you have a feeling of success," she said. But she added sadly, "Now everyone has caught up." The revolution Misa started had become the norm. The innovator had been overtaken by the popularity of her innovation.

CHAPTER 3

A Cookie Wrapped in a Mystery Inside an Enigma

It was a clash between cities. A battle of cultural legacies. A matter of competing firsts. The identity of an American icon was at stake.

The critical 1983 debate: Who invented the fortune cookie, and where?

The courtroom, located on the fourth floor of San Francisco's City Hall, was filled to standing room only. The media had arrived in full force—local and national, newspaper and television. Bakers sat next to businessmen. A federal judge presided.

On one side was the Los Angeles contingent, which argued that the inventor of the fortune cookie was David Jung, a Chinese immigrant from Canton, the founder of the Hong Kong Noodle Company in Los Angeles shortly before World War I.

On the other side sat the San Francisco contingent, which claimed that fortune cookies had no Chinese origins at all but, rather, were introduced by a Japanese (!) immigrant named Makoto Hagiwara, who'd tended the Japanese Tea Garden in Golden Gate Park, also shortly before World War I.

At one point during the trial, Sally Osaki, a San Francisco city employee who had done research to support the Japanese argument, dramatically pulled out a set of round black iron grills. These irons were originally used by the Hagiwara family to cook the fortune cookies, she announced.

Not only did Osaki have the only physical evidence in a trial based largely on hearsay, but San Francisco had the home-court advantage. The sponsor was itself a local civic booster organization. (An earlier trial by the same court had ruled that the martini had been born in San Francisco, rather than in the nearby city of Martinez—a decision which was later rejected in Martinez by another mock court.) There was at best only the slimmest of chances that San Francisco would lose in a media kangaroo court.

Indeed, Judge Daniel M. Hanlon handed out a ruling that San Francisco, not Los Angeles, was the birthplace of the fortune cookie. The room, full of locals, burst into cheers and applause. The Los Angeles attorney scowled and muttered about an appeal.

But it was an odd split decision. The judge stayed mum on the other, and arguably more interesting, question: whether Japanese or Chinese immigrants had introduced the cookie to the United States. He intoned, "Matters of the East, we should leave to the East."

That question was still unanswered, more than twenty years later, as I began my investigation of the fortune cookie. It gnawed at me: Could fortune cookies have been introduced to the United States by the Japanese? Did Chinese restaurateurs steal the idea of fortune cookies from their fellow Japanese immigrants? If so, why had the Chinese succeeded in making them so popular?

Over the millennia, the Japanese have borrowed many concepts and inventions from the Chinese—written language, soy sauce, even chopsticks. Certain cultures tend to get credit for inventing practically everything, among them the Greeks, the Arabs, and the Chinese. Are fortune cookies an example where the cultural osmosis worked in reverse?

It cannot be denied that the fortune cookie is an odd member of the Chinese dessert family. Traditional Chinese desserts, as any Chinese-American child will tell you, are pretty bad. There is a reason Chinese cuisine has a worldwide reputation for wontons, and not for pastries.

For most of our young lives, my family was baffled by elementary school bake sales, to which we were told to bring in goodies to sell. While other kids arrived bearing brownies, chocolate chip cookies, and apple pies, Chinese families didn't bake. Even today, my Western friends who move to China are bewildered when they find that their apartments don't have ovens. "What do you do on Thanksgiving?" one friend wailed.

By the time I entered fifth grade we had formed our response to the bake sales: handmade fried dumplings—but with ground turkey instead of ground pork (healthier, my mom said). They were always one of the first items to sell out.

The yumminess of desserts is largely dependent on two things: (1) sugar and (2) fat. In contrast, traditional Chinese desserts use little sugar and fat, and a lot of red bean and lotus, peanut and sesame, soy and almond. Even the famous Chinese moon cakes, essential to the Mid-Autumn Festival, taste a bit like the hockey pucks they resemble. I scrutinized other Chinese baked sweets—the almond cookie (which was at least a cookie) and the yellow egg roll (which was rolled, something similar to folding)—for any family resemblance to the fortune cookie. It wasn't out of the realm of possibility, but I felt like a paleontologist trying to justify a hypothesis using only vague evidence from the Cambrian period. If the Chinese had introduced the crispy, curvy, wafer-thin fortune cookie to the United States, where *had* they drawn their inspiration from?

It's fairly easy to trace fortune cookies back to World War II. By the 1940s English-language fortune cookies were already commonplace in Chinese restaurants in San Francisco and southern California. San Francisco was a way station for servicemen to and from the Pacific arena, and the influx of eager, bright-eyed young men during the war helped fuel the rise of the city's flamboyant Chinese nightclubs. Soldiers and sailors flocked to Chinese restaurants, where they were treated with the familiar—chop suey, chow mein, egg foo yong—and the exotic fortune cookies. From California, the cookies made an accelerated postwar journey across the country. Convinced that these San Francisco fortune cookies were part of truly "authentic" Chinese cuisine, servicemen started demanding the treats when they returned home to the Midwest and the East Coast.

Mystified but eager to please their customers, local Chinese restaurant owners placed orders with California cookie makers. As demand around the country grew, local entrepreneurs in major cities set up their own fortune cookie companies—though production still centered in Los Angeles and San Francisco and, eventually, New York. Customized cookies were used to announce engagements. Boxes of fortune cookies were sold on supermarket shelves.

By the late 1950s, Americans were consuming an estimated 250 million fortune cookies a year, and the little folded desserts were becoming part of popular culture. At the 1960 Democratic convention, both Senator Stuart Symington and Adlai Stevenson distributed them as part of their presidential campaign, as did Abraham Beame in his 1965 mayoral race. In 1972, as a prank, someone even presented Chicago's Irish mayor, Richard Daley, with green fortune cookies. Companies were buying custom cookies to hawk everything from airlines to power companies, and from fish sticks to pharmaceuticals. And when Transamerica executives heard of a planned protest to their then-controversial (now-iconic) pyramid-shaped building in San Francisco, they greeted the protestors with fortune cookies filled with custom messages like "Transamerica not square outfit" and "Pyramid protestor miss point." The cookies helped quell the objections.

It is the history of the fortune cookie prior to World War II that is murky. A number of families claim to be its originator, with elements of their stories sharing similar aspects. They all have an Asian immigrant inventor introducing the cookie in California sometime before World War I. All the alleged inventors are long, long dead. Their children and grandchildren are dying off too, so we are left with a matter of "he said, his son said, and his grandson said."

Even the figures in the 1983 fortune cookie trial were disappearing in alarming numbers by the time I began searching for them. David Jung's son was dead. Makoto Hagiwara's grandson was dead. I had no reason to believe that Sally Osaki, who had pulled out the black iron grills at the trial, was still alive. But churning through the public records, I found a number of different listings in the San Francisco area for a Sally Osaki who was in her seventies. How many could there be? I figured. I left messages on her answering machine and waited.

Several days later, on a sleepy afternoon after Christmas, a pleasant-sounding woman returned my call.

"It's Sally Osaki," she said cheerfully. We chatted about the fortune cookies. She still had some documents left over from the trial. Sally, who had been born in California, told me of the fortune cookies from her childhood in central California. Her family and friends used to pass around bags of fortune cookies during drive-in movies when she was a young girl. The little slips of paper inside had originally been written in Japanese back then, she remembered. Only later, she recalled, did the messages appear in English.

"When did they change?" I asked curiously.

"I think they changed by the time we came out of camp."

"Camp" to most Americans conjures up idyllic images of canoeing, bonfires, and good-natured panty raids. My parents sent me, my brother, and my sister to Chinese camp for one week every summer when we were growing up. There, we ostensibly studied Chinese folk dancing and songs, crafts, and martial arts. In reality, we just learned to flirt and sneak around behind our counselors' backs.

Sally, however, was referring to the Japanese internment camps, locations in the interior of the country where the United States government detained 110,000 people of Japanese ancestry—about two-thirds of whom had been born in the United States and were, therefore, citizens. When they were forced from the West Coast in 1942, Japanese-Americans were told that they could bring only as many clothes, toiletries, and other personal items as they could carry. The officials called it "internment," but the barbed wire around the camps made it resemble imprisonment.

"How old were you when you went to camp?" I asked.

"Nine years old."

Type "fortune cookie" into Google today and out spills a virtual cornucopia of fortune cookie products for sale on the Internet. There are chocolate-dipped fortune cookies, white-chocolate-dipped fortune cookies, caramel-dipped fortune cookies. There are fortune cookies available in cappuccino, mint, blueberry, and cherry. One of the most successful companies offering flavored fortune cookies, Fancy Fortune Cookies, was started by a former

Ringling Bros. and Barnum & Bailey Circus clown, who said a message from God told him to go into the fortune cookie business. You can buy custom fortune cookies for ad campaigns. You can buy silver fortune cookie jewelry on eBay. There are giant fortune cookies the size of a football. There are medium fortune cookies the size of a softball. There are Spanish-language fortune cookies. Good Fortunes, a company based near Los Angeles, sells a whole line of clothing called Cookie Couture, which offers a pair of thongs with the fortune cookie tastefully placed just so. There are scandalous X-rated fortune cookies for bachelor and bachelorette parties. To counter them, there are Christian biblical cookies.

Then there is the whole business around the wedding-proposal fortune cookie. You can have a custom fortune with your proposal inserted into a cookie. Or, for more dramatic effect, you can send the engagement ring to a company that will place it inside a cookie. One Web site provides a tip for the poor man's fortune cookie wedding proposal: wrap a fortune cookie in a moist paper towel and put it in the microwave for thirty seconds on high. That will soften the cookie enough so that it can be pried open for the careful insertion of your special message.

San Francisco, as the presumed source of the fortune cookie phenomenon, was the most natural place for me to embark on my research. My first stop was to meet Sally at her son's apartment in Japantown. Once a booming immigrant community with vibrant temples and shops, Japantown has faded to just six square blocks, a quaint cultural shadow of its pre–World War II existence. The Japanese families have largely assimilated into the burbs, so for the most part all that is left is a contingent of older people in neatly tended condos and a smattering of shops. The borders are announced by the sudden transition into green-and-white bilingual street signs. "Sutter Street" was written both in English and in Japanese katakana phonetics. The apartment was decorated in a Zen Japanese style of shades of beige and wood paneling—more Japanese than most Japanese homes I'd seen in Tokyo. Sally's son didn't really speak the language, she explained, but his entire aesthetic was Japanese.

Despite her short graying hair and glasses, Sally could best be described as "cute." As she introduced herself, I found it disconcerting to see an Asian-looking woman my grandmother's age speaking flawless English. On the East Coast, it was rare to find an Asian-American over forty-five who spoke English without an accent. By and large, they were first-generation arrivals to the United States. Only on the West Coast are there considerable numbers of Asian-American families that stretch back multiple generations.

Sally had kept many of the documents from the trial. A few in particular stood out: a letter from a woman named Kathleen Fujita Date (DAH-tay) that gave a hint as to how fortune cookies began to appear in Chinese restaurants and the testimonial letter from George Hagiwara, Makoto Hagiwara's grandson.

Kathleen Fujita Date, of Berkeley, had sent a handwritten letter to Sally during the research period for the trial, with a tale passed down from her parents, Mr. and Mrs. Shizoh Fujita, friends of Makoto Hagiwara's. Sometime in the 1920s, Mrs. Fujita had been having lunch with a group of five Japanese-American women in a Chinese restaurant down a San Francisco alleyway. One of the women had brought a bag of crescent-shaped crackers with little slips of paper inside, called *senbei*. The laughter of the women as they read the fortunes caught the attention of the Chinese restaurant owner, who came over and asked what they were doing. Once shown the *senbei,* the man asked where he could buy some; they told him about a Japanese confectionery shop called Shungetso-do at the corner of Sutter and Buchanan Streets. Later, Mrs. Fujita saw the restaurateur buying a whole box of the cookies there. From then on, she and her friends would often witness Chinese men driving up and buying boxes of fortune cookies. "Sometimes when we went in to buy them, they would tell us, 'Sorry the Chinese already bought them all,' " Ms. Date recalled.

The other letter, from George Hagiwara, said that while his grandfather had come up with the idea for the fortune cookie, the production of it had actually been outsourced to a Japanese confectionery shop called Benkyodo. Benkyodo, now a century old, was still in operation in Japantown, run by the third-generation owners, just across the street from where I met Sally. George has long since passed away, but his daughter, Tanoko Hagiwara, was still living in the area, and she referred me to her son, Douglas Dawkins, the keeper of the Hagiwara family history. I met Doug at his telecommunications consulting company, DRDC, which was located in a converted loft space with an impressive but industrial view of container ships floating through the port of San Francisco. In his forties, Doug has green eyes and salt-and-pepper hair. (His own children are blond-haired and blue-eyed. "When I'm walking on the street with them, people think I'm the nanny," Tanoko joked.)

With the humming of the computer servers in the background, he recounted Hagiwara family history for me. He pulled out a number of boxes that contained documents and family photos, including those of Makoto Hagiwara himself.

The round man in the fading photo had chipmunk cheeks, spectacles, a walrus mustache, and a barrel-chested five-foot-five frame. By all accounts, he had a fierce, outgoing personality. "He was a very go-get-'em kind of guy," Doug told me.

Makoto, Doug's great-great-grandfather, had come to the United States from the Yamanashi region in the central part of Honshu, the main Japanese island. In San Francisco, he dabbled in different businesses, including raising bonsai trees and importing Asian art.

The Japanese Tea Garden was built as part of a World's Fair, the Midwinter International Exposition of 1894. Afterward, it was kept open and Makoto was invited to be the superintendent and live there. The family sold tea to visitors, many of whom were tourists. "They dressed in kimonos when people were around, but when no one was around, they would wear Western clothing," Doug said. To accompany the tea, the family served a variety of *senbei,* including the one that eventually became known as the fortune cookie.

But that all ended in 1942, when the family was removed to an internment camp in Topaz, Utah, which at its peak was the fifth-largest town in the entire state. Their house in the tea garden was destroyed by a wrecking company. "They took it off as junk," Doug said. The exhibit's name was changed to the more innocuous "Oriental Tea Garden." The family would not be released until 1945.

The old Japanese shop Benkyodo is part sweets store, part neighborhood diner, featuring a long counter with stools, where customers order a cup of coffee and stay for hours to catch up on neighborhood gossip. Except for the period around when the family was interned during World War II, the business has operated more or less continuously since 1906, when the present owners' grandfather, Suyeichi Okamura, opened the original store on Geary Boulevard to sell Japanese treats.

The store no longer makes fortune cookies. The owners had no historical records, but they directed me to their aging mother, who lives above the store. I climbed the stairs and found a woman who seemed like a worn photocopy of the pale beauty in the black-and-white photographs in the apartment. Sue had been a teenager when she and her family were sent to the internment camp. There, she was pursued by a boy named Hirofumi Okamura, Suyeichi's son, who was later inducted into the 442nd Infantry Regimental Combat Team, an all-Japanese-American unit sent to fight in North Africa, Italy, southern France, and Germany. It became the most highly decorated unit of its size and length of service in the history of the U.S. Army, with twenty-one recipients of the Medal of Honor.

Despite his time away, Hirofumi successfully made Sue his wife. She recalled her first glimpse of the Benkyodo cookie machine. "It was a nine-foot machine and it was in the basement," she said. "It was circular and it spun around and around in a circle." She had married into the family business, so she helped out with making fortune cookies. When we reached the edge of her memories, her son Ricky suggested that I talk to his cousin in Los Angeles, Gary Ono, about the origin of the fortune cookie. Over the last few years, Gary had done a lot of research into the Okamura family's role in the original fortune cookies. "He's easiest by e-mail," Ricky said. "He's been all over the place." As for himself, he shrugged. "I don't know anything," he told me.

CHAPTER 4

The Biggest Culinary Joke Played by One Culture on Another

To understand what happened on the night of the Powerball lottery of March 30, 2005, you have to understand fortune cookies. To understand fortune cookies, you have to understand chop suey. Were it not for chop suey, there would likely not be any fortune cookies in America today.

Chop suey is the greatest culinary prank that one culture has ever played on another. Even its name is an inside joke of sorts. What Americans once believed to be the "national dish" of China translates to "odds and ends" in Cantonese. But it was decades before Americans began to realize that they had been had. ("Say, where did they get this chop-suey stuff?" wrote Will Rogers, a California mayor (no relation to the actor), in a letter to the *New York Times* during his 1932 visit to China—nearly thirty-nine years after chop suey began its explosion into the American landscape. He added, "I have run the legs off every rick-sha motorman in China, and nobody had ever heard of it.")

It was a deception born less out of humor than a desperate

need to survive. The ruse was so effective that the myths around it survive in history books. Chop suey is a tale—with elements of labor strife, culinary xenophobia, and celebrity tie-ins—that must be told from the beginning.

Before Americans loved Chinese food, you see, they loathed it. Because, in part, they feared the Chinamen on their shores. Then along came chop suey, and that changed everything.

In the late 1800s, Americans were less than enamored of the Chinese and their cuisine. The Chinese, they suspected, ate rats. If not rats, then cats. If not cats, then dogs. This paranoia rose to the level of serious journalistic inquiry. An 1883 *New York Times* article opened with the provocative question "Do the Chinese eat rats?," noting that "a large portion of the community believe implicitly that Chinamen love rats as Western people love poultry." A *New York Times* reporter followed a sanitary inspector on a tour of a Chinese kitchen to investigate charges from a neighbor.

Would he find delicate skeletons? A loose tail or two? A furry carcass?

In fact, he soberly informed his readers, "There was nothing suggestive of rats or cats about the place." Meanwhile, the accused Chinaman had learned a thing or two about the American legal system; he threatened to sue his neighbor for slander.

But we're getting ahead of ourselves. The story begins in China.

An immigrant's decision to pick up and leave his country is often a difficult one, of a type that sociologists break into "push" and "pull" factors. Tumult rippled through nineteenth-century China in the form of overpopulation, wars, rebellion, and natural disasters—all push factors that weakened the bonds between the people and the land. The Qing government's hold on the kingdom, especially in the southern reaches, was attenuating, setting the stage for massive rebellions. Western imperialism swept into China with the Opium War of 1839–42 and the subsequent unequal treaties that opened five ports and demanded indemnities. The costs of the indemnities were passed on to rural peasants through burdensome taxes, thereby exacerbating the consequences of the period's natural disasters.

One single county, Taishan (or Toisan), in Guangdong Province, suffered onslaughts of near-biblical proportions. In a sixty-year period, from 1850 to 1910, it endured fourteen great floods, seven typhoons, four earthquakes, two severe droughts, four epidemics, and five serious famines, plus a twelve-year ethnic war between locals and Hakka transplants. At least 80 percent of the Chinese immigrants to the United States before the 1950s would hail from around this region.

Nature and war ravaged the region, but the financial markets struck a blow as well. A credit crisis in 1847 extended from British banks down to the Chinese warehouses along the Pearl River, shutting down trade in the urban center of Guangzhou and throwing 100,000 men into unemployment.

Then, from seven thousand miles away, came a faint glimmer of hope. On a January day in 1848, James W. Marshall discovered flakes of gold at Sutter's Mill. This catalyzed Yerba Buena, a sleepy bayside California settlement of a few hundred souls, into a boomtown of 30,000, drawing people by land and sea. To a nation that was pre-airplane, pre-highway, pre–*National Geographic,* the Chinese that arrived on the shores of what is today San Francisco were thoroughly otherworldly. They were vaguely human, in the sense that they had the right biological number of arms and legs, eyes and fingers. Other than that, they were as strange then to Americans with European roots as the popular bug-eyed slit-nostriled Area 51 extraterrestrial icons look to us today. The Chinese were commonly referred to as "Celestials"—

a term with connotations that (like E.T.!) they had descended from the heavens. They had long, dark hair worn in a single braid down the back. They spoke in choppy, singsongy tones. They wrote in an alphabetless language that must have seemed as bizarre then as *Star Trek*'s Klingon language does today.

But what struck Americans as unnerving was how these strangers ate. They cooked meats and vegetables of mysterious origins and strange textures, often cut up into itty-bitty pieces, or mashed and doused with exotic sauces. In native Chinese restaurants, reported one disgusted white observer, people were served "pale cakes with a waxen look, full of meats."

Since the country's Puritan and Protestant roots still maintained a tight influence on the popular culture, food was sustenance, not something to be enjoyed. Tempered by religious piety and frontier austerity, American cuisine was dominated by one characteristic: Aggressive Blandness. If there was a second guiding principle, it would be Extreme Saltiness. In much of the country, highly seasoned or fancy foods were regarded with hostility and suspicion, as a form of sensual indulgence. Spicy foods were suspected of something worse than increasing the craving for alcohol: many people shared the notion that they stimulated extreme appetites for sex. Only the southern states—whose complicated settlement history had left them with an amalgam of African, English, French, Spanish, and Italian cooking traditions—escaped with a lively cuisine. They simmered and sautéed and used rich spices, while in the rest of America the cooking vocabulary essentially consisted of baking, boiling, and roasting—quiet, passive activities that more or less encapsulated Americans' attitude toward food. So Americans were suspicious of these foreigners and their animated cooking over large flames. There were too many noises: chopping, clanging, the roar of the fire, chattering over meals.

As one San Francisco magazine writer observed of their ingredients in 1868, "Few western palates can endure even the most delicate of their dishes. Shark's fin, stewed bamboo, duck's eggs boiled, baked and stewed in oil, pork disguised in hot sauces, and other things like these, are the standard dishes of a Chinese bill of fare." The Chinese also seemed willing to consume anything they dredged from the sea: seaweed, abalone, squid, turtles (still available today, live, in many restaurant tanks).

And the things they could do with beans! As one writer noted, "Undisputed ruler, lord of all lesser greens, reigns the almighty bean. Boston has adopted the baked bean, but China had it first. Not only baked but boiled, made into pastes, soups, oil and cheese." Now tofu is available in every suburban supermarket and is a vegetarian staple, but in the eyes of a turn-of-the-century American with European ancestry, it was a bit revolting: "In the window of almost every Chinese grocer is a bilious pyramid of yellow-green cakes of bean cheese." What was this semisolid substance? "Taken alone and reduced to an essence," the journalist jeered, "the result is a feeling, not a flavor."

(For their part, the Chinese, with a largely dairy-free diet, were horrified by cheese. Even today my Chinese friends from China find the springy, gooey, oozing texture of cheese somewhat stomach-turning. Yet cheese and tofu are essentially made by similar processes: a fluid is coagulated until it separates into liquids and solids; the solids are kept, pressed together, and processed. With beans, the solids become tofu. With milk, the curds become cheese.)

Chinese meat products were eyed with suspicion: these animals did not hail from a farm; nor had they been caught by a fishing rod or felled by a bullet from a hunter's rifle. "The meat things served here are strangely barbaric, seen in their uncooked stages in the open meat markets below, which are redolent with articles of diet for which an Occidental butcher would have no name," one journalist remarked, reminiscing about San Francisco's

Chinatown months after the 1906 earthquake had leveled the neighborhood. In addition, there were "giblets of you-never-know-what, maybe gizzards, possibly livers, perhaps toes."

The image of the Chinese as vermin-eating immigrants persisted in the public's imagination. A picture of a rat-eating Chinese man was used in children's textbooks in the late 1800s. An enterprising Jersey City exterminator designed an advertisement for his rat poison, Rough on Rats, that showed an oddly dressed Chinaman devouring a rat and the line "They Must Go!" (This subtly referred to both the rats and the Chinese immigrants.)

Even Mark Twain, while working as a reporter in Virginia City, Nevada, kept his distance. In the 1860s, during a visit to a shopkeeper named Ah Sing at 13 Wang Street, he accepted the hospitality of the merchant's brandy but declined the "small, neat sausages, of which we could have swallowed several yards if we had chosen to try, but we suspected that each link contained the corpse of a mouse."

The Americans were horrified by Chinese table manners. In a culture that judged a man's class by how adroitly he maneuvered a metal knife and fork, eating rice with spindly wooden sticks was emasculating. These eating utensils were even used to make a point in a criminal trial; the lawyer for the white leader of an 1865 race riot defended his client's behavior by informing the judge, "Why, sir, these Chinamen live on rice and, sir, they eat it with sticks!"

To be sure, Chinese cooking did find some fans—the budget-conscious and the adventurous—partially because it provided good food for good value. "The best eating houses in Francisco are those kept by the Celestials, and conducted in a Chinese fashion; the dishes are mostly curries, hashes and fricassees, served in small dishes and as they were exceedingly palatable, I was not curious enough to inquire about the ingredients," wrote William Shaw, a self-identified gold seeker, in 1851. Called "chow chows," Chinese restaurants could be spotted by the triangular yellow flags fluttering outside their doors. They attracted miners and bohemians looking to escape the mundane.

The waves of Chinese continued to wash up on the shores; the immigrants took jobs in manufacturing, agriculture, mining, and railroads. They were willing to work for less, and they were numerous, and they kept coming. The population of what is now the state of Idaho was in the 1870s some one-third Chinese. America had become infested with these creatures, white workers felt. Some of them wanted to make it stop. In their efforts, they littered the coast from Los Angeles to Tacoma, Washington, with the dead bodies of Chinese men.

The embers of culinary xenophobia smoldered. These foreigners' dining habits became a point of attack, a concrete behavior used to differentiate "them" from "us." Samuel Gompers, a hero of the labor movement and the president of the American Federation of Labor, published a pamphlet under the auspices of that organization in 1902: "Some Reasons for Chinese Exclusion: Meat Versus Rice, American Manhood Versus Asiatic Coolieism—Which Shall Survive?" Real men could not live on rice alone.

As white economic anxiety grew, it was unleashed in the form of shootings, arson, mutilation, and lynchings. Across the West, there were numerous impromptu campaigns to purge the country of Chinese. In 1885, an anti-Chinese rally in Seattle set a deadline for all Chinese to be out of Washington Territory by November 1. Two days after the deadline, residents conducted a giant raid against Tacoma's Chinatown, where the merchants, who were less transient than the laborers, had remained. Doors were kicked down, bodies were dragged, people were herded like wayward cattle. About six hundred Chinese were forced to wait for transport to Portland at a railroad station where there was no shelter. During the night a heavy rain fell; some Chinese died. The same year, miners in Rock Springs, Wyoming, conspired to drive their Chinese competition out, attacking their settlement with guns and fire. As the Chinese miners tried to escape the burning wooden shacks, their attackers forced them back into the flames. Some who fled into the mountains were later eaten by wolves. At least twenty-eight people died.

But the most lurid tale was the Snake River Massacre of 1887. The water in Hell's Canyon in Oregon ran red with blood as more than thirty Chinese gold miners were killed and mutilated by a group of white men who had conspired to steal their gold and force the Chinese out. Three killers were brought to trial. Not one was convicted, and the killers kept their souvenirs. A Chinese skull fashioned into a sugar bowl graced the kitchen table of one ranch home for many years.

The economic and political backlash culminated in the Chinese Exclusion Act, passed in stages between 1882 and 1902, which restricted Chinese immigration and prevented Chinese arrivals from becoming naturalized citizens. It would be the only law in American history to exclude a group by race or ethnicity.

But even as the doors slammed shut, some Chinese had already made it to the other side. Were they to be considered lucky or not? They had bought their way to a land of opportunity, but now the opportunities were rapidly shriveling. The Chinese were driven from agriculture, mining, and manufacturing. They were driven eastward, inland. They found themselves stranded in a strange land, thousands of miles and months of sea travel from their hometowns. They had come to make money, to support their families, but now employers were afraid to give them jobs for fear of violent retribution. The jobs slowly dried up.

So what happened?

The Chinese response still dots the American landscape today: restaurants and laundries.

In the half century from 1870 and 1920, the number of Chinese restaurant workers surged from 164 to 11,438, even though the total number of Chinese employed declined. Between 1900 and 1920, in many cities the number of Chinese restaurants doubled. In New York City there were six Chinese restaurants in 1885. Less than twenty years later, in 1905, there were more than one hundred chop suey restaurants between Fourteenth and Forty-fifth Streets and Third and Eighth Avenues. Restaurant workers didn't even appear on San Francisco's 1877 list of the twenty-two top occupations, which included whip makers, stonecutters, and lumbermen. The top occupations were listed as cigarmakers (7,500); merchants, traders, and clerks (5,000); and house servants (4,500). Laundrymen (3,500) appeared just before enslaved prostitutes (2,600). Laundries had long been a domain of Chinese workers, ever since 1851, when Wah Lee first hung up a sign for "Wash'ng and Iron'ng" in San Francisco and drove down the prices for starched collars and hard-boiled shirts. The Chinese had a near lock on laundries on the West Coast, and those continued to grow and thrive.

Why was there suddenly an entrepreneurial explosion of restaurants, and why, of all small businesses, did laundries survive?

Cleaning and cooking were both women's work. They were not threatening to white laborers.

The Chinese did not survive as restaurateurs by selling American diners "waxen meats," "bean cheese," or shark's fin soup. Americans had once sneered at Chinese food, but by the turn of the century they were flocking "zombielike" to Chinese restaurants, which had proliferated across the country. In 1900, the *New York Times* declared that New York City had experienced an "outbreak of Chinese restaurants all over town." Diners were being drawn by something dazzling! Something sophisticated! Something exotic! Something that had taken the country by storm. Something called...chop suey?

In a cooking tradition hostile to excessive spices, sharp flavors, and "foreign" ingredients, chop suey meant new textures. Thin, squiggly white bean sprouts. Crispy, round water chestnuts. Gravy! New York City had gone "chop suey mad." Chop suey parlors lined the streets of downtown Brooklyn, Washington, and Des Moines. Instead of the Yellow Peril, the Chinese-Americans had been transformed into benign restaurateurs selling a saucy vegetable-and-meat concoction.

The dish became a national addiction. Men impressed their dates with their sophistication by taking them out for chop suey, while they themselves could order from the safer, less adventuresome dishes on the "American" side of the menu: hamburgers and grilled pork chops. A fifteen-year-old Chicago girl stole $3,400 from her parents, using fake checks, and spent it on chop suey; she was put on probation by a juvenile court in 1923. Attempts to prove that she had used the money for things other than chop suey failed.

Chop suey even became a government-tracked commodity. In 1920, a dozen Chinese restaurant owners were hauled in front of a Chicago city council committee investigating living costs. They were grilled about the price of the ingredients and their profit margins on every kind of chop suey, from plain to chicken with fine white mushrooms. The aldermen then declared that chop suey prices were too high.

Middle-class women examined newspaper and magazine recipes, trying to make their own brown sauce, vegetables, and rice taste as authentic as that of the chop suey parlors. (The secret, they were told, was soy sauce and sesame oil.) Chop suey, along with chow mein and egg foo yong, were added to the bible of American domesticity: *The Joy of Cooking*.

Chinese restaurants became so common in New York that in 1952 a prominent German restaurant finally caved in and restored to its name the umlaut that had been removed during

World War I. Lüchow's owner had gotten tired of tourists coming in and ordering chop suey and egg rolls.

There was one small point that the restaurateurs were careful not to emphasize to their customers: the dish Americans knew as chop suey was all but unknown in China. In fact, the dish was reported in China decades after it appeared in the States. During World War II and its aftermath, local Chinese cooks hung up "chop suey" signs to attract American soldiers as customers.

The magic behind chop suey was that it was familiar but exotic. Chinese restaurant owners would use this formula again and again—with fortune cookies, with General Tso's chicken, with other dishes.

But where had chop suey come from? And how had it spread so fast?

Two tales are commonly cited, each with variations. In fact, both stories are so firmly accepted that they are repeated in history books, newspapers, and on the Internet, to the point where they have taken on the tenacious quality of historical truth.

In the first tale, white railroad (or mine) workers come to a Chinese restaurant just before (or after) its closing in San Francisco (or the Wild West). They are drunk (or just hungry) and order (or force) the cook to prepare something for them to eat. He takes the scraps (or leftovers) from the kitchen and whips up a random concoction of vegetables, meats, and brown sauce. The workers, of course, love it and ask the poor cook what the dish is called. Since it really doesn't have a name, he makes one up, calling it "chop suey." The workers are satisfied and wander off. Somehow, from that, a craze is born.

The second tale is more historical in nature, tying itself tightly to an 1896 visit to the United States by a prominent Chinese diplomat named Li Hongzhang. The details vary but are very specific in how they vary: Li is a guest (or host) of a dinner in

New York (or Washington, Boston, Chicago, or San Francisco). At the dinner a dish is summarily thrown together by a Chinese cook (or Li himself) because Li has indigestion (or does not like the Western dishes available or the Western guests do not like the Chinese dishes available). When the guests (or newspaper reporters) ask for the dish's name, they are told it is called chop suey. The dinner that is most specifically cited is a banquet at the Waldorf-Astoria in August 1896.

The Li Hongzhang story is cited so often, with so much detail, how could it not be true? But the menu from that Waldorf-Astoria banquet was actually French: consommés and soufflés. After nibbling a bit, Li had his servants bring him a tray of boiled chicken, white rice, and vegetable soup, according to the detailed account provided by the *New York Times*.

The definitive scholarly paper on the origins of chop suey was published some twenty years ago, in 1987, by a then graduate student named Renqiu Yu, in the journal *Chinese America: History and Perspectives,* which I found devilishly hard to track down.

It was a few months before I met up with Ren Yu. We agreed to have lunch at Big Wong King Restaurant one September afternoon; the shops already had their moon cakes on display for the upcoming Mid-Autumn Festival. Ren told me that he first became interested in chop suey when he moved to New York City to earn his Ph.D. at New York University. As a single graduate student, he ate out a lot and noticed that chop suey was on the majority of the menus. He never ordered the dish, but he observed others savoring it.

He spent almost three years doing his research, including a summer in NYU's library scrolling through microfilm of the *New York Times,* looking for any early mention of chop suey. Chop suey was not created from whole cloth, Ren believed. An actual Chinese dish called "chow chop suey" (or "chow chop sui" or "chow chop sooy") was being served among the Chinese themselves by the 1880s and early 1890s; "chow" means to stir-fry and "chop suey" often meant animal entrails—livers, giblets, and the like.

That fit with what I'd found, that there were early mentions of something called "chow chop suey" before the Li Hongzhang visit, a dish described as being made with gizzards. But the new dish had suddenly taken off after Li Hongzhang's visit, in part because of the way it was (deceivingly?) associated with him. "You have a celebrity culture in America," Ren mused. "If it is associated with a name of a celebrity, it will sell very well." He rattled off a list of things: clothes, sneakers, perfumes. "What is wrong with the Chinese practice of an American commercial skill? Selling a dish by attaching his name?

"That's my hypothesis," he said. "There is no documentation."

But there was yet another claim. One night I was scrolling through the newly digitized files of old *New York Times* articles, stretching back to 1851, when something caught my eye. The headline was "Chop Suey Injunction: Len Sem of 'Frisco Here to Allege Copyright Infringement"; it was dated June 15, 1904.

The story unfolded: Chinatown was plunged into gloom, an air of silent preoccupation overhanging the habitués of Mott and Pell Streets. Word had spread of an economic crisis. Earlier in the week, a San Francisco Chinese man had walked into the soaring twenty-six-story St. Paul Building on Broadway. Armed with a sheaf of legal documents, he'd headed into the law offices of Rufus P. Livermore, who ran a distinguished small-time practice just southwest of Chinatown. The San Francisco visitor's name was Lem Sen. He told Mr. Livermore that he was the inventor of chop suey and had the documents to prove it. And in an aggressive, sophisticated assertion of intellectual property rights, he wanted to file an injunction to stop the "manufacturing and serving" of chop suey in New York City.

This claim surprised Mr. Livermore, but it did not come totally out of the blue. He had already sensed that something was amiss with chop suey. Like most Americans, he had long assumed it was the "national dish" of China, but only a few weeks earlier he had heard a story that had cast a seed of doubt. That month, a Chinese envoy to the St. Louis Exposition, Pu Lun, had paid a visit to New York. As Mr. Livermore heard it, one of the guides tried to please Pu Lun during his tour of Chinatown by telling him, "And now, your highness, we will soon be dining on your national dish, chop suey."

"What is chop suey?" the prince asked innocently.

Now in front of Livermore was a man who claimed that chop suey was no more the national dish of China than pork and beans. He asserted that there was not a grain of anything Celestial in it. He said that he'd been employed at an American-owned restaurant when his boss told him to manufacture some weird dish that "would pass as Chinese and gratify the public craze at the time" created by a visit from a high-level Chinese diplomat. In an expression of his humor, Lem Sen christened his dish "chop suey," a term often used in Cantonese for "odds and ends" or "bits and pieces." But then his recipe was stolen, and spread across America. Lem Sen wanted these copycats stopped.

The reporter quoted Lem Sen: "Mellikan makee thousand dollar now. Lem Sen, he makee, too. But me allee time look for Mellican man who stole. Me come. Me find! Now me want papel back, and all stop makee choop soo or pay me for allowee do same."

Was this the answer? Had it been lying in the depths of newspaper archives for all that time, unlocked by the magic of optical recognition? It had appeared several years after the span that Ren, the historian, had examined in the historical record.

Digging through more records, I discovered a brief, four-paragraph wire story describing the Waldorf-Astoria banquet.

The article, which ran across the country, listed "chop suey" as the food that was brought to Li Hongzhang—the first time that name may have appeared in print as such. But the dishes served to him had been, specifically, boiled chicken and rice. I knew enough about how reporters groped through unfamiliar situations to guess that the wire-service reporter might have asked someone what Li Hongzhang had been served, been told "odds and ends" in Chinese, and interpreted it as a name of a single dish.

If so, then Lem Sen's story held a grain of truth. Everything fit: the purposeful myth that connected it to the diplomat Li Hongzhang; the sudden rise in popularity of Chinese restaurants within a decade; why the term "chop suey" appeared in print before 1896 but only as "chow chop suey"; how chop suey later emerged as its own dish everywhere. Had this short wire story spurred a national American demand for something called "chop suey," which Lem Sen then invented so as to have a dish to serve? One that incorporated interesting but not outlandish vegetables, like celery, bean sprouts, and water chestnuts?

I pondered the tale about the bullied Chinese chef who threw scraps together for hungry laborers. That probably did happen somewhere, sometime. In a way, "chop suey" had always existed in the sense of "odds and ends." But how could a recipe like that have spread with such ferocity without some spirited campaign behind it?

"It's an amazing story," Ren wrote back to me in an e-mail, after I gave him the article.

So was the injunction ever filed? Was that sheaf of legal papers that Lem Sen had carried into Livermore's office buried in the bowels of New York City's courthouse system? I couldn't find anything during a visit downtown.

Perhaps Lem Sen was the true innovator. Or perhaps he was

claiming credit while building on work also done by others—like Watson and Crick with Rosalind Franklin's X-ray diffraction images of DNA—especially since the historical evidence seems to point to chop suey first becoming popularized in New York City.

But I wanted to believe his story. I wanted to believe that there was a single figure in history who had come up with the recipe—not simply of a single dish, but the recipe for success at a time when it was desperately needed by Chinese workers in the United States. I wanted to believe that there was an individual who had created one of the earliest gambits of celebrity marketing in the United States.

Maybe it's the writer's weakness, always trying to distill history into simple stories about a single person, a fight, an invention, a small act of civil disobedience. That is why we often say World War I was triggered by the assassination of the Archduke Franz Ferdinand. Or that the American civil rights movement was prompted by Rosa Parks refusing to give up her seat. Perhaps that's also why I felt compelled to seek the true origins of the fortune cookie—whether the creator turned out to be a noodle-maker in Los Angeles or a gardener from Japan. We want a person behind a phenomenon. These symbolic characters make the mess of history more streamlined, palatable, and digestible—not unlike Americanized Chinese food. Against a backdrop of chaos, there is a single pleasant narrative.

Chop suey has done its duty. A century later, the dish is gently fading away from American menus, supplanted by General Tso's chicken, beef with broccoli, and sweet-and-sour pork. It has been kicked out of *The Joy of Cooking*, replaced by more fashionable Chinese dishes. It is still found in some urban Chinese takeouts and in scattered restaurants around the country, but few people order it, restaurant owners tell me. Most Americans now know that chop suey is not real Chinese food. A handful don't care.

Yet it still endures. Chop suey, I discovered, has become an American export. I have found it in Japan, Korea, Jamaica, Guyana, and the Caribbean. In India, "American chop suey" (often made with ketchup!) remains one of the most popular dishes on Chinese menus, a stalwart just across the border from China. In Los Angeles, a Chicano girl who worked at Avis confided to me that her family would sometimes drive four hours to Mexicali, the Chinese-restaurant capital of Mexico, to have chop suey. She added, "You can't get it in the same way in the United States."

CHAPTER 5

The Long March of General Tso

I have traveled thousands of miles, from New York to the Hunan city of Changsha, to pay homage to one of the most prominent Chinese figures known in America.

Undoubtedly, the most famous man to emerge from Hunan, a rural province largely analogous to Arkansas in America, is Chairman Mao Zedong, the megalomaniac Communist leader who led the careening nation through wars and revolutions. His name reverberates with sacred reverence in Hunan. China's aspiring politicians pay visits to his childhood home, sometimes secretly. My driver has Mao's face as his cell phone background.

But rivaling Chairman Mao's stature in the United States is another man, one who plays a more familiar role in our day-to-day lives, a man whose name passes through the lips of thousands of Americans every week. He is the great scholar-warrior Zuo Zongtang, a crusher of rebellions against the imperial Qing court, an elder statesman who held modern Chinese territory together. Outside China, however, he is less often recognized in history books than in cookbooks. Born in 1812 about fifty miles north of Changsha in the small village of Jietoupu, he is also known as General Zuo or, more famously, General Tso. The Chinese respect the general as a vicious and gifted military leader, the equivalent of American Civil War general William Tecumseh Sherman. But millions of Americans know him only for the chicken dish named in his honor. He is the General Tso of General Tso's chicken. Tso Tsungtang—the more modern spelling is Zuo Zongtang—may have died in 1885, but his name lives forever in small towns and big cities across the United States, spoken, even if mispronounced, more often than Chairman Mao's. ("Tso" is commonly said like "So" but is actually properly pronounced halfway between "Zuoh" and "Juoh," something like "Jaw.")

What I discover: in America, General Tso, like Colonel Sanders, is known for chicken, not war. In China, he is known for war, not chicken.

General Tso's chicken is probably the most popular Chinese chef's special in America. What's there not to like? Succulent, crispy fried chicken is drenched in a tangy, spicy sauce and sautéed with garlic, ginger, and chili peppers until it bursts with flavor. Each bite is a rapturous gastronomic journey, beginning with a pleasant crunch that gives way to the tender dark meat, all while your tongue experiences the simultaneous ecstasy of sweetness paired with the kick from the chili peppers.

In my travels, I have encountered chicken belonging to General Gau, General Chau, General Tao, General Tsuo, General Joe, General So, General Chow, and just plain old "General." Then there was my personal favorite, in Wichita, Kansas: General T (perhaps a cousin of Mr.?). The general goes undercover at the United States Naval Academy dining hall, which serves "Admiral Tso's Chicken."

You can taste the general's chicken in all-you-can-eat $4.95 supper buffets along interstate highways, at urban takeouts with bulletproof windows, and in white-tablecloth establishments that have received starred reviews in the *New York Times*. You can sample variations where the sauce is brown and runny, red and syrupy, or yellow and sweet like honey. There are renditions with short squat pieces, long thin pieces, dark meat, white meat, and mysteriously reconstituted mystery meat. There are versions akin to McDonald's Chicken McNuggets, with more bread coating than meat, and others where you cannot tell where the chicken ends and the dough begins.

Hunan Province is famed for producing fiery leaders and spicy dishes. Hunanese locals brag that their cooking—based on simmering, stewing, and steaming—is one of the eight great regional cuisines of China. What the other seven are, few could tell me. (It turns out that China's eight great regional cuisines, like the Ten Commandments and the nine Supreme Court justices, are something that everyone knows the number of, but few can readily name.)

What I found was unsettling. Unlike kung pao chicken, which nearly every self-respecting Chinese chef can make, a request for General Tso's chicken left many cooks, waitresses, and restaurant owners scratching their heads.

The refrain was consistent: "We don't have General Tso's chicken here" or "We've never heard of it." Even after I showed them pictures of the dish on my digital camera, they would frown and look at me blankly, then helpfully suggest another chicken dish, often the local specialty, mala or kung pao. One waitress at a three-hundred-year-old restaurant pressed me to try another dish associated with a famous Hunan personage: "This is what Mao Zedong and his circle ate when they used to come here."

But nothing they offered ever resembled our crispy General Tso's, nor his American cousins: sesame chicken, lemon chicken, sweet-and-sour chicken. In fact, any batter-dipped, stir-fried chicken dish was hard to come by in this urban corner of Hunan.

I set out to find the general's ancestral village in rural Hunan. Perhaps there people would know the story behind the chicken. Hunan may be poor and inland, but it prides itself on having produced a disproportionately high number of warriors, revolutionaries, and political leaders. Aside from Mao Zedong and the general, its august roster includes Liu Shaoqi, once Mao's presumed successor, and Hu Yaobang, the popular Communist leader whose death triggered the 1989 Tiananmen Square protests.

When you ask locals why they have so many newsworthy leaders, they almost universally echo a line used by Mao. It has to do with the spicy food, they say; a lifetime of eating the cuisine generates a revolutionary temperament in the people here.

Our general, the son of peasant farmers, looked to be an early washout after he thrice failed the competitive imperial examinations. He returned to a quiet life in his ancestral home in rural Hunan. But like many men whose fates are caught up in history, his life changed forever with the outbreak of war—in his case, a rebellion led by a Chinese convert who believed himself the younger son of Jesus Christ. The self-declared New Messiah, Hong Xiuquan, and his Taiping Rebellion established the Heavenly Kingdom, which at its peak covered most of southern and central China. Its government abolished private property and gave women equal rights.

Tso, whose political career started when he was thirty-eight, drove the heavenly rebels out of Hunan and continued his ruthless campaign toward the coast. By 1864, he, together with his military mentor, Zeng Guofan, had dethroned the Taiping king and quashed the rebellion at the Third Battle of Nanking, in which some one hundred thousand people were killed. After it was all said and done, the Taiping Rebellion had consumed over twenty million lives, making it the bloodiest civil war in human history. In exchange for his service, our general was rewarded with a promotion to earl and went on to quash rebellions in China's west.

That was the story of General Tso's long march across China. But how did his long march across America come to pass? Perhaps, I thought, those in his village would know.

The journey to the general's birthplace turned out to be a more difficult ordeal than my driver and I had planned on. We knew the name of the town and the direction from Changsha, but my driver never consulted a map. Automobile travel in rural China involves dodging mangy dogs, farmers pulling carts, young motorcyclists, and plump chickens, creating the overall sensation of a live video game—Grand Theft Auto: Rural China. Stopping at red lights is apparently optional. Driving in the countryside also involves a great deal of honking. The sonorous rumbling horns of trucks, the high-pitched beeps of scooters, and the tenor tones of sedans come together in a shrill arpeggio. Honking in America is a punitive action; in China, it's considered a courtesy.

We were soon lost. We stopped to ask an old man with a missing tooth for directions. He gestured wildly and then jumped into the car with us, explaining that he was from near where the general had been born, where hundreds of members of the general's family still lived, where they had their own area called Zuojiaduan, or "Zuo family section." He commanded us to take a right onto a suspicious-looking dusty dirt path that seemed to lead nowhere, but then made a T-shaped intersection with a paved road. The old man got out, waved good-bye, and pointed in the direction opposite from where he was heading.

Shortly thereafter, we passed a billboard that said, "Xiangyin. A famous Qing Dynasty county and home to Zuo Zongtang." In the corner was a picture of a refined and bearded Chinese man who was obviously General Tso. I studied his likeness. It was nice, as they say, to finally put a face to a name.

Outside a restaurant a sign advertised high-quality dog meat, a claim substantiated by a photograph of two doe-eyed puppies. Inside I inquired about the general's chicken. The waitress gave me a confused look. I showed her the picture of the dish on my digital camera. She shook her head. "It doesn't look like chicken," she said. If I wanted chicken, she offered, she could kill a fresh one for less than two American dollars. She gestured toward the back. Whichever chicken you pick, she said. But it would take too long to pluck all the feathers, delaying my hunt for the general's roots; we opted for some vegetables and a pork dish instead.

The restaurant's owner gave us a hand-drawn map. The route led us down a dirt road flanked by rice paddies and to the old home—an abandoned building that had been converted into a school, then abandoned again.

In the rice paddies near the house, I encountered two men from the general's family, Zuo Kuanxun and Zuo Ziwei, Zuo family members some five generations removed from the general. I asked them about General Tso's chicken.

They had never seen the dish. "No one here eats this," said Zuo Kuanxun, a faded sixty-six-year-old farmer. Zuo Ziwei shrugged as well.

There were chickens everywhere. Black ones. Brown ones. Speckled ones. Wandering around the backyards. Tussling with puppies. Climbing up compost piles. Crossing the road. These were clearly the original free-range chickens—not the pathetic, debeaked, declawed, force-fed ones of the American agro-industrial complex. But despite the widespread presence of live poultry, there was no General Tso's chicken to be found.

Zuo Kuanxun invited us into his home, a century-old stone structure with wooden doors, dirt floors, and hand-pumped well water. Except for his telephone, which he'd gotten ten years ago to keep in contact with his children, his home was probably not too different from residences during the general's time. He handed us freshly washed apples. After I'd finished mine, I looked around for a place to put the core.

Toss it on the floor, he said. I hesitated.

"Don't worry, I'll sweep it later."

Onto the dirt floor went the apple core.

I offered him a fortune cookie in return. He examined it. And put on the polite smile and averted eyes of Chinese nonenthusiasm.

No one seemed to know whether the general had had a fondness for chicken. They did note that he probably didn't cook it himself. "He had servants to cook and clean for him," Zuo Ziwei pointed out.

"They must have used his name to do business," Zuo Kuanxun said. It didn't surprise him that Americans know the general's name. "He's famous all over the world!" he said. "He was very talented. A lot of people respected and admired him."

I didn't have the heart to tell him that in the United States we respected him only for his chicken—which in the end may not even be his.

Zuo Kuanxun said he'd once raised chickens but now focuses on pigs—the preferred meat in Chinese cooking. He didn't, however, raise only pigs. When I'd walked in, I'd noticed two energetic brown dogs wandering around with some chickens. Occasionally, they yelped outside as we talked inside. Our conversation wandered onto the topic of his dogs.

"Dog tastes good. It's good for you," he said.

I mumbled something about how in the United States we don't eat dogs because we have sentimental attachments to them as pets. He nodded. "Those dogs are made for pets. They look good. These dogs are raised for eating."

I pictured how Americans would react to General Tso's puppy on their take-out menus.

The general's childhood home, later converted to a school, had long been abandoned. It looked like any other sad building in rural areas across the world, only this one had riling Chinese slogans like "Seek Knowledge!" scrawled in gigantic red writing across the front.

"They want to develop it into a tourist destination, but there is no money," Zuo Kuanxun said, standing at the building's gate.

Over tea the same day, a young official named Jiang Wei told me about the big dreams they had for the general's home, if only they could find some capital. "We don't have the money, but we are hoping to attract tourism and to sell some General Tso–branded goods," he said. "We want to build some industry around him. We want to make it big."

Sitting in an open courtyard in front of the village hall, he gestured expansively. One could relive the General Tso experience. "You could buy the things he liked to eat. You could buy the things he liked to use," he said. "You could sell the liquor he liked to drink." He flicked his cigarette and rattled off other product lines: "Clothes. Hats. His official robes. You could put on a set of his official robes and have your picture taken in them."

Truth be told, there was little else going for this town in China, so its boosters had seized upon the identity of the general as their means to economic salvation.

Suddenly Jiang Wei remembered the reason that I had traveled thousands of miles by plane, boat, bus, car, and foot to the little town of Jietoupu in the first place. His eyes lit up with an idea. "They could come here and eat true authentic General Tso's chicken!"

As we got up to leave, one of the women at the table with us stopped me and asked, "You said you were from the United States?"

"Yes."

"But you look Chinese!" she exclaimed, confused.

My question remained: Why had the general been able to conquer America with his chicken with greater ease and less bloodshed than he had conquered China? My host in Hunan was a classmate from my time at Beijing University. Wang Wei was beautiful in the way that women in classical Chinese paintings are beautiful, with large expressive eyes, flawless skin, and a slim, shapely figure. She had gone to Syracuse University for her master's degree, but then she'd returned to Hunan to marry her high school sweetheart.

When I asked her about the chicken dish, she laughed and burst into a tirade about why General Tso's chicken is the ultimate Chinese-American dish.

"It has broccoli. Americans *looove* broccoli. They add broccoli with everything." She continued: "Americans like chicken. You can go to a supermarket and you buy chicken breast, chicken legs, chicken drumsticks, chicken wings, boneless chicken. All different types of chicken," she said, gesturing to various parts of her body. "They don't do that with pigs, do they?" she challenged. "It's very American. It's all-American: very big pieces of chicken, fried and sweet."

For generations, Chinese immigrants and students have been warned not to be shocked by the Chinese food in American Chinese restaurants. Among those dishes most likely to confuse them is General Tso's chicken. Wei remembered her first impression of the dish when she encountered it in a restaurant in Syracuse: "Is it edible?"

Watch what the workers in American Chinese restaurants eat. In general, it is not what they are serving to the customers. It is, however, more representative of the Chinese diet. For instance, you will often find a soup—and not egg drop, wonton, or and-sour. It will be thin and simple, usually with seafood, pork bones, or melon in it. There will be lots of dishes with single vegetables.

Periodically a fervor erupts over whether or not Chinese food is healthful. The Center for Science in the Public Interest shocked the Chinese-restaurant industry in 1993 when it published a study saying that many Chinese dishes, like kung pao chicken and egg rolls, were high in fat and sodium. But Chinese food, cooked in a Chinese style for Chinese taste buds, is actually relatively healthy: lots of vegetables and seafood and low in sodium, with few deep-fried ingredients. The problem is that most Americans prefer American-style Chinese food to the real thing.

How did General Tso's chicken come to be? It seemed America must have had a hand in it. Chinese food in China is a diverse lot, but once it came to the United States it developed a few central characteristics.

First of all: Chinese restaurants in America tend to shy away from anything that is recognizably animal. Mainstream Americans don't like to be reminded that the food on their plate once lived, breathed, swam, or walked. That means nothing with eyeballs. No appendages or extremities (no tongues, no feet, no claws, no ears). Secondly, opacity. That means nothing transparent or even semitransparent (this eliminates certain kinds of fungus and all jellyfish). There is also a limit to the textures Americans will allow in their mouths: nothing rubbery or oddly gelatinous (no tripe and, again, no jellyfish or sea cucumber). There is also an acceptable color palate. Nothing organic should be too black (no black seaweed or black mushrooms). Nothing made with flour should be too white (steamed white buns have the undone look of the Pillsbury Doughboy; toasty brown is better).

But perhaps most important in American eating is the idea

...mouth should never come out. That is,
...g where you have to chew on something
...inedible part. This means no chicken feet,
...no shrimp with shells. Peanuts come shelled,
...elon is preferred seedless.

...wever, the aftermath of most restaurant meals is a
pile ...shells, and other detritus on the table at every place
setting: the casualties of a personal battle between the diner and
the items on the plate. In particular, much of the debris is due
to the Chinese love of seafood, and the love of that seafood in its
God-created entirety. Chinese buy their fish whole. When she
was in America, my friend Wei bemoaned the difficulty of getting a whole fish. "They cut it up into these clean little pieces,"
she said. "If fish doesn't have bones, it's not tasty." And shrimp?
My friends like to eat their shrimp with the eyes and tails still
on. You can tell if a shrimp was cooked dead or alive by how the
tail splits.

The meat nearest the bone is the most tender and most flavorful. So Chinese people like chicken feet and legs (lots of bones)
and are confounded by Americans' preference for chicken breast
(boneless and bland). Following the law that says something
is worth only as much as someone is willing to pay for it, in
China, the tender feet and legs are the most expensive part of the
chicken; in America, they are almost worthless. This creates arbi-
trage opportunities to buy low and sell high. A Chinese customs
official confided over dinner in Changsha one night that one of
the biggest, most frequent illegal exports from the United States
to China is chicken feet—along with pigs' ears, cows' stomach,
and assorted other animal parts. International rings of organized
smugglers bring the goods into Hong Kong, and then over the
border on slow boats to China. "They wait until the middle of
the night and sneak in," he explained to me. "It goes up during
New Year's, when demand is greater."

Officials have intercepted as many as ten ships a night, each carrying tons of animal products. In two separate incidents in 2006, lumbering ships crashed into shore, strewing thousands of pounds of chicken and pork parts along the sandy beaches and rocky headlands.

Why do the Chinese mine so much of an animal's body? The original Chinese food philosophy is one designed for shortage and storage, as the food historian E. N. Anderson noted in *The Food of China*. Despite the opulent images of the country's emperors, much of China was traditionally poor, so everything on an animal was eaten: ears, feet, tongue, intestines, liver. Since refrigeration did not exist for much of Chinese culinary history, food had to be dried or pickled to make it through the winter. With cooking fuel scarce, stir-frying was a popular technique because it used little oil and consumed energy efficiently. Many of General Tso's family still burn dried branches for their woks, a device that, with its rounded bottom, evenly distributes high heat along its surface. In contrast, the Chinese historically had little use for baking, one of the least energy-efficient ways of cooking. American Chinese food developed under few such constraints. Refrigeration aided a fundamental shift in the American diet. Oil, necessary for deep-frying, was readily available. Refined sugar was easily accessible. Meat, much demanded and made plentiful by our agricultural-industrial complex, has become incredibly cheap by historical standards. Americans like chicken, sweetness, and deep-frying. These three desires converged in General Tso's chicken.

I finally found a promising lead in my hunt for the general's chicken in Changsha: Tang Keyuan, the general manager of the Xinchangfu Restaurant, who had been in the hospitality business for over two decades.

I first showed him a picture of corpulent pieces of General

Tso's chicken laid on a bed of broccoli. He squinted. "Is that oxtail?"

No, it's chicken, I said. It's a dish in America called General Tso's chicken—*Zuo Zong ji*—which is exceptionally famous.

His eyes lit up. "Ah! *Zuo Zongtang tuji!*" he said, using the long form of the translation of "General Tso's chicken." My heart skipped a beat. Finally, I'd found someone in Hunan who knew of the dish!

"But that is not how you make it," he sniffed. "It's totally different. The pieces are too big. You have to cut the pieces of chicken smaller.

"My brother knows how to make this dish," he added.

Where had he learned of it?

He thought. The dish had been introduced in Changsha by a Chef Peng in the 1990s. (The 1990s? I thought. That's more than a decade after the dish had already made the greatest-hits list in America.) Chef Peng had featured the dish when he opened up the Peng Yuan restaurant in Changsha's Great Wall Hotel. But the restaurant hadn't lasted.

Why had it closed down? I inquired.

"It didn't keep up with the market." He paused. "He didn't innovate enough."

Was Chef Peng even still alive?

Four men had helped redefine American cuisine in the early 1970s. Three of them were Chinese culinary greats who worked out of New York City; the fourth was Richard Nixon, whose historic state visit to China in 1972, the first since the Communists had taken over the mainland, sparked an instant frenzy for all things Chinese. Suddenly, Americans learned that there was much more to Chinese food than chop suey and chow mein. A Chinese restaurateur who has owned more than twenty restaurants in Louisiana told me, "Lines formed overnight."

The three China chefs had much in common. As youngsters, they were classically trained in kitchens in mainland China. When the Communists took over the mainland, they fled to Taiwan. After a few decades in Taiwan, they ventured to the United States. In the late 1960s and early 1970s, they began opening restaurants in New York City. Chef Peng opened Peng Yuan on the East Side. Chef T. T. Wang opened Hunam and the different Shun Lees. Wen Dah Tai, also known as Uncle Tai, joined forces with David Keh and opened Uncle Tai's Hunan Yuan on Third Avenue and Sixty-second Street. As they innovated and introduced new dishes, the American media fawned over them. But even though Henry Kissinger loved Peng Yuan, Chef Peng closed it down and moved back to Taiwan in the early 1980s. Owning a restaurant in America was too stressful.

Both Uncle Tai and Chef Wang had passed away. A friend helped me locate the number for Peng Yuan restaurant in Taipei. I called and held my breath. The woman who picked up the phone got the manager, Chuck Peng, Chef Peng's son. Yes, he said in mellifluous English, they served General Tso's chicken there. And yes, his father was still alive, though mostly retired. At that moment I had to taste that chicken.

I flew into Taipei on a Friday morning and made my way to the newest Peng Yuan, in the eastern part of the city—a sleek, modern restaurant on the fifth floor of a newly constructed high-rise. Chuck Peng joked, "If General Tso's chicken had been patented, my father would have prospered." He ordered a small plate of General Tso's chicken for me. A sweet-faced waitress arrived carrying the dish.

There it was! General Tso's chicken! In the flesh! Big chunks of chicken drenched in a rich, caramelized brown sauce, with chili peppers seductively tucked in between the pieces. It even had a sprig of decorative broccoli.

I took a breath. At last, the original General Tso's chicken.

Disappointment soon followed. First, the "broccoli" was not broccoli at all, but some kind of flimsy decorative herb that also happened to have florets. It was like looking behind stage scenery and realizing that the castles and trees were all flat.

I picked up a piece of chicken and examined it. The thick sauce had disguised the fact that the chicken still had the skin on it.

Skin?

I took a bite. The dominant flavor was soy sauce. That was followed by chopped garlic and a kick from spicy chili peppers. The chicken was appropriately chewy, but there was no crispy, fried-batter coating.

Where was the sweetness? The tanginess? Instead, it had a strong salty flavor.

It was good. And it was chicken. It just wasn't General Tso's. Or at least not the General Tso's I had come to know and love.

As we left the restaurant, I glanced at the menu. It listed the dish as "Geojeol Tso's chicken." That may have been the most comforting and familiar part of the meal.

If this was the original General Tso's chicken, where had the sweetness and crispy coating come from?

The answer, perhaps, lay back at home: New York City. Over lunch at Shun Lee, which had survived past the glamorous 1970s Chinese-cuisine era, Michael Tong recalled a little friendly chicken-general rivalry between his partner, Chef Wang, and Chef Peng back when Hunan cuisine was becoming popular.

"I think there was a lot of so-called competition between the chefs," said Michael.

Before Chef Wang opened Hunam in 1972, he and Michael had visited Hong Kong and Taiwan, where they'd been inspired by the General Tso's chicken dish at Chef Peng's restaurant in Taipei. (When Michael said that, I knew I was getting closer: this was two decades before Peng had opened his restaurant in the Great Wall Hotel.) In response, Chef Wang had created his own general's chicken dish, but with an American twist, Michael told me. "Once you are serving the American public, you change the texture," he said. The key, he added, was to crispy-coat things. Chef Wang used that concept on several dishes in that era, including Hunan beef and Lake Tungting shrimp. But ultimately it would be the chicken that would really capture America's popular imagination.

Chef Wang needed a name for his chicken dish. "We all wanted to use the name of a renowned general from Hunan in the Qing Dynasty," said Michael. But one esteemed general was already taken. "The idea is that one guy used Zuo Zongtang. The other wanted to use another general, General Zeng Guofan." The very same General Zeng who had been our General Tso's mentor.

So in this great man's honor, Chef Wang introduced General Ching's chicken—another Hunan chicken dish in tribute to a Qing Dynasty military leader. (How Zeng, also spelled Tseng, became Ching is another one of those mysteries of Chinese-English transliterations.)

Which means that today, according to Michael Tong, the dish we are eating is actually closer to General Ching's chicken.

So what happened to General Ching? Why was he vanquished by his former protégé and his chicken recipe stolen?

General Ching's chicken did conquer some territory beyond Hunam in the late 1970s, with a few scattered appearances on other restaurant menus, but he never seemed to establish a beachhead. Today his name is rarely mentioned. In contrast, General Tso's ubiquity is likely due to his embrace of modern technology: television. All great military men know that in the modern age, war is fought in the media as well on the battlefields.

In 1974, the local ABC news station in New York did a segment on Chef Peng's restaurant. Reporter Bob Lape, the Eyewitness Gourmet, visited Chef Peng in his kitchen and taped the making of General Tso's chicken. After the segment ran, about fifteen hundred people wrote in and asked for the recipe, Mr. Lape remembered. "It was a serenade to the mouth. It's that kind of dish. It's a one-time instant love affair."

Television is perhaps how General Tso's name achieved recognition, but somewhere along the way General Ching's recipe became more popular. The name of one dish got merged with the recipe of another. Had the pupil conquered the master?

I finally met Chef Peng during an afternoon mah-jongg game in his apartment building in central Taipei. He was a tall, patrician man with white hair carefully combed in neat parallel lines. At eighty-eight, he was hard of hearing, so the conversation mostly consisted of me yelling into his ear in Mandarin. He spoke slowly and methodically, the way some elderly people do, as though operating in slow motion.

He recounted that he had created the original dish in perhaps 1955 or 1956, on the island of Taiwan, after the Nationalists had been ousted by the Communists. He had named it after the general because he had wanted to use a symbol of Hunan; the other great Hunan figure, Mao Zedong, was obviously persona non grata.

In carefully enunciated Mandarin, I told him that the dish known as General Tso's chicken was now perhaps the most popular Chinese dish in all of America. In fact, I had also seen his version in Korea, the Philippines, and the Dominican Republic.

His curiosity piqued, Chef Peng asked me if I had tried General Tso's chicken at his restaurant and if the versions in America were similar.

Unsure of how he would react, I hesitated before answering. "The American versions are sweet," I finally said.

"Sweet?" he asked, his eyes growing wide. He waved his hand.

"The dish can't be sweet. This isn't the taste of Hunan cuisine. The taste of Hunan cuisine is not sweet," he said emphatically.

I had brought numerous pictures of General Tso's chicken on my laptop, accumulated over months of travels across the States and beyond. I began to scroll through them, showing the rich range into which General Tso's chicken had evolved.

All of a sudden he pointed his finger at my screen accusingly. I looked. He was indicating the lush bed of green broccoli under the chicken. "This isn't right," he said. He was perplexed and asked, "What is that doing there?" His son and I explained that the single most popular vegetable in American Chinese cuisine is broccoli. He shook his head and said General Tso's chicken should just be served as is. It doesn't need to rest on a bed of broccoli.

He criticized the next picture because the chilies were red instead of black. But that was a minor crime compared to the travesties in some of the other versions he saw. One was clearly made of tasteless cubes of chicken breast, instead of the succulent dark leg meat. He shook his head when he saw the baby corn and carrots in a version from Dover, New Hampshire. He would never use baby corn, he said. He barely recognized the version that uses sesame seeds—one I had tried at a food court in the Minneapolis–St. Paul airport.

"What is that?" he asked when he saw the gooey brown chicken pieces decorated with pale flecks.

I pointed at the sign that read "General Tao's chicken."

He waved his hand again. "That's not right. This isn't authentic."

At the end, he spoke again. "Chinese cuisine took on an American influence in order to make a business out of it," he said. "If you give them real authentic Chinese cuisine, Americans can't accept it." As he left, he told me that this was all *moming-qimiao*. Nonsense.

Then he shuffled away.

CHAPTER 6

The Bean Sprout People Are in the Same Boat We Are

Once teeming with opium dens, brothels, and gambling parlors, Ross Alley, in San Francisco's Chinatown, has been cleansed of its lurid past. Today, the sweet, heavy smell of opium has been replaced by the fragrant scent of vanilla, luring tourists rather than sin seekers. The alley's number one draw: the Golden Gate Fortune Cookie Company, which shares the narrow path with a one-seat barbershop and a florist that sells orange trees before Chinese New Year.

Day after day, two elderly Chinese women fold hot fortune cookie wafers, their fingertips toughened by years of sticky heat. They each sit next to a fortune cookie machine, and the scene is strictly Willy Wonka meets Dickens: spigots squirt out circles of batter, which are then whisked on a conveyor belt into a dark tunnel lit by blue gas flames. The women pick up the toasted wafers emerging from the tunnel and pinch them into the familiar crescent shape as they tuck the fortune neatly inside.

Generations of San Francisco schoolchildren have fond memories of this shop. Whenever I mentioned my fortune cookie research, my friends who grew up in the area often piped up with "Oh, have you been to the fortune cookie factory in that alleyway?"

On my first visit there, one of the women, Vivian, looked at my hands. Without slowing her tempo of stab-fold-tuck, she observed in thick Cantonese-tinged Mandarin, "Those are not a laborer's hands."

I examined my hands, which were holding a green steno notepad and a pen. The only callus I have on either hand is on one middle finger, from where the pen rests as I scribble my notes. "You are lucky, because you speak English," she murmured. "We can't speak English. What can we do but work with our hands?"

I thought of my grandmother, whose hands were stubby and cracked from years of working along the sea, in the fields, and selling dumplings in the night markets in Taiwan. The last time we had seen each other, a decade earlier, she had held my young hands in her thick callused ones. "You have an educated person's hands," she'd said proudly.

A sign sternly informs visitors that they must pay fifty cents before taking a picture; the bucket next to the injunction is filled with the quarters and dollar bills of tourists eager to comply. Despite its quaint appeal, the little shop is an anachronism. In reality, fortune cookies are rarely folded by hand anymore. Sleek industrial machines bake, stuff, and fold the cookies, then wrap them in plastic, with little human intervention. They can churn out 6,000 per hour, compared to 1,000 an hour each for the women in Ross Alley.

The process was revolutionized in the early 1980s when Yong Lee, a Korean-born engineer, invented a fully automated fortune cookie machine at the request of a Boston restaurant owner, then started a business selling contraptions. Later on, Lee unveiled the Fortune III, a compact Rube Goldbergian machine that could churn out 1,500 cookies an hour. This 2,500-pound, six-foot cube of hot steel, fans, conveyor belts, and robotic arms needed only to be fed: five pounds of flour, twenty-five pounds of sugar, a few gallons of oil, a quart or so each of vanilla and water, and one hundred egg whites. The Fortune III was followed by bigger and better machines. Sensing a lucrative market, competitors inevitably followed. Now the largest, fastest fortune cookie machines come from Japan, made by the Kitamura company in Osaka, which markets an extensive line of confectionery devices. The long, sleek yellow Kitamura machines can make 6,000 cookies an hour.

Thirty years ago, a cookie could be sold for the wholesale rate of just under a penny and a half. With automation, and adjusted for inflation, the price of a fortune cookie has fallen more than 75 percent.

As a result, a decade-long shakeout in the fortune cookie industry has squeezed the mom-and-pop cookie manufacturers. Even the company started by the Chinese-American truck driver who turned fortune cookies from a regional oddity into a mainstream product has been driven to the edge.

Edward Louie, an immigrant from rural Guangdong Province, in southeast China, established Lotus Fortune Cookie Company in 1946 with his father and brother. An artist and a tinkerer convinced that he could always build a better mousetrap, Edward earned his place in cookie history with a machine he introduced in 1967. The increased production allowed him to sell the cookies at cheap enough prices to propel their popularity as complimentary desserts in Chinese restaurants.

The machine would slip the pieces of paper into the hot wafers as they were being folded, an improvement on the practices of the day. Up until then, Louie family members would flip and fold the cookies themselves, using a combination of fingers and chopsticks. Grandfather, grandmother, uncles, aunts, and grandchildren all pitched in with the labor-intensive work, napping under the stairwell when they were exhausted. Five-year-old children were taught to fold. A good fortune folder could do 17 cookies a minute, or about 1,000 per hour. The workers put tape on the tips of their fingers to insulate their nerve endings and protect against developing tough calluses.

The cookies became a supermarket-shelf product. The hexagonal Lotus Fortune Cookie boxes informed customers that the cookies, "from the storied courts of the Mandarins," had been "smuggled into San Francisco" and "baked from a still secret imperial Chinese recipe." As Edward admitted at the time, "We make up stories for what they are worth. That's part of the romance." Among his fortune cookie innovations was the risqué fortune, which drew national media attention to Lotus. Confucius, it turned out, could say some very naughty things.

Edward never retired; returning from a visit to China in 1990, he headed straight to work, and died of a heart attack.

When I visited the Lotus Fortune Cookie Factory on Otis Street, a cavernous San Francisco machine shop, sandwiched between a glazier and an industrial rug seller, it was nearly silent. The machines were oiled, but there was no customer demand to power them.

In contrast to the lively bustle of two decades ago, the front office now had but two people: Greg Louie, Edward's son, and a woman who helped out with administrative duties. Greg's cherubic uncle Chang was visiting at the time.

Lotus had almost been closed the day I visited—and shortly after my visit the factory would shut down permanently. But at that point the company still sporadically made custom fortune cookies, which are more profitable than the generic ones. The mass market had moved past Lotus, which was unable to match its bigger competitors' prices.

The company's risqué fortunes still remained one of its most popular lines. But Greg no longer even printed his fortunes himself. Instead, a man named Steven Yang, who also worked out of San Francisco, printed and cut the fortunes for Lotus.

Greg—with his bald head, wire-rimmed glasses, and flat American accent—resembled a wiseass, clean-shaven, updated version of Confucius. During the Vietnam War, he'd been drafted into the army—a hazardous occupation indeed for a Chinese-American. One time another soldier in Greg's company mistook him for a member of the Vietcong and assaulted him. Greg tried to dissuade him, saying, "Relax, guy. I'm American. Easy, easy." When that didn't work, he spoke in language that any American would understand: "Goddammit! Don't shoot, motherfucker!"

Greg watched over an atrophying family business. As I interviewed him, I realized that once he retired, the company that had given birth to the mass-produced fortune cookie might cease to exist.

The culprits? The noodle companies that had become the Wal-Marts of the Chinese-restaurant-supply world. Greg lamented, "If you are just a cookie manufacturer, you are competing with noodle people." He said noodle companies, like Brooklyn's Wonton Food and Los Angeles's Peking Noodle, had moved aggressively into the fortune cookie sector, forcing razor-thin margins on the rest of the players. The noodle companies were using fortune cookies as a loss leader, he argued.

"They started making fortune cookies to add to a product line when they deliver to a restaurant. They sell the cookies at cost. We can't."

Then Greg's uncle piped up: "The bean sprout people are in the same boat we are."

Why Chow Mein Is the Chosen Food of the Chosen People—or, The Kosher Duck Scandal of 1989

If the nation hadn't been in the midst of a kosher duck shortage, Michael Mayer's suspicions wouldn't have been piqued when he walked into the Moshe Dragon Chinese restaurant that fateful August morning. If the crispy, sweet taste of Peking duck hadn't become de rigueur for upscale Jewish house parties in suburban Washington, D.C., there might not have been such an unmet appetite for kosher duck, leading to the kind of temptations that arise when demand outstrips supply. If all this had not been so, the Great Kosher Duck Scandal of 1989 might have been averted and the community's faith in its religious leaders might not have been shaken. Reputations might not have been sullied, careers might not have been derailed, and cover-ups might not have been alleged. Moshe Dragon might even still exist today, hosting bar mitzvahs and catering celebratory Shabbat dinners. But "if" is a word upon which history pivots into hypothesis. What happened happened. In a community filled with long memories and short tempers, the effects still reverberate today.

• • •

Until the spring of 1989, there was one—and only one—farm in the entire country that produced kosher ducks: Moriches Duck Farm, on the East End of Long Island.

In the region's heyday of the 1950s and 1960s, there had been dozens upon dozens of family duck farms on the East End, responsible for some 75 percent of the nation's duck production. Millions of Pekin ducks were shipped westward each year. Housewives made extra pin money by hatching duck eggs in their homes for five cents apiece.

Pekin, a breed of duck, is not to be confused with Peking duck, the delicate Chinese dish that will figure prominently in this saga, though both originated in China. Local lore has it that Pekin ducks first arrived on Long Island around 1873, either when a New York merchant named Ed McGrath hatched a clutch of eggs brought back from China or when James Palmer, a shipping captain, transported two dozen white ducks from China, nine of which survived the journey.

Pekins are the snowy white ducks with orange bills and feet of popular imagination. The most famous Pekin duck is, of course, Donald, followed by his entourage of Daisy, Uncle Scrooge, Huey, Dewey, and Louie. The Pekins became farmers' favorites because they breed like bunnies (up to 150 eggs a year) and fatten up quickly. They are also not the brightest creatures, so they can be mindlessly herded, like sheep—a character trait favored by the agriculture industry.

The East End blossomed as the duck-producing capital because its environment—humid climate, sandy soil, and proximity to water—was ideal for raising Pekins.

But in the 1970s the Long Island duck industry began a precipitous decline. A combination of environmental pressures on duck farmers and tempting real estate deals brought about by eastward suburban expansion made it appealing for duck farmers to sell out and close up shop.

In 1989, a holdout, Moriches Duck Farm, closed down. The specifics are no longer clear, but it seems safe to surmise Moriches was simply following the fate of the dozens of duck farms before it. Suddenly, the nation's kosher duck supply dried up. "There was a short period of time where kosher ducks became almost nonexistent," recalled Tom Jurgielewicz, a third-generation duck farmer whose property once bordered the Moriches farm. It might seem that there would be at least one other kosher duck supplier out there, but truth be told, the audience for kosher duck is rather limited, given the scope of American Jewish cuisine. There was only one duck farm in the United States that processed kosher ducks, and after it closed there were none.

To combat the crisis, a group of rabbis and businessmen identified a poultry producer in South Dakota. South Dakota seemed like a safe business bet, a place with few real estate pressures to drive a farmer to sell out.

The South Dakota poultry producer normally processed geese, which are not a year-round product (think of the last time you had barbecued goose at a Fourth of July picnic), so his facility was idle for much of the year. The Jewish consortium convinced the goose processor that it would be good business to process kosher ducks when he wasn't busy with the holiday season.

It took months for the South Dakota operation to get up to speed; processing kosher ducks is not a simple matter. In the meantime, the only remaining kosher ducks were ones already killed, frozen, and on their way down the supply chain. Prices immediately doubled. Kosher duck prices, like that of light sweet crude oil, are sensitive to the laws of supply and demand. While duck at the local Giant supermarket was $1 a pound, kosher duck was pushing $6 a pound. Of course, most people weren't aware there was a kosher duck shortage. But it was Michael Mayer's job to know. He was the mashgiach, or kosher cop, for Moshe Dragon, the first kosher Chinese restaurant in the Washington, D.C., area. He had been hired by the Rabbinical Council of Greater Washington to oversee Moshe Dragon, which had opened during Rosh Hashanah in September 1988 in Rockville, Maryland, with much aplomb.

Washington, unlike Baltimore, to the north, did not have a deeply rooted Orthodox community. The population was too new and too transient, made up largely of transplants who worked in, influenced, or wrote about government. In the same way that having a hometown professional basketball or baseball team signals that a city like Charlotte or Phoenix has arrived, a kosher Chinese restaurant signified the establishment of the Washington Orthodox Jewish community.

Political, religious, and investment capital went into bringing Moshe Dragon to the Washington area. A charismatic young rabbi sought out two successful area entrepreneurs to provide the backing, then recruited a Chinese-Cambodian immigrant, Lenny Ung, who had experience with a kosher Chinese restaurant in Philadelphia.

The opening night of Moshe Dragon in a Rockville strip mall drew a dense, designer-clad crowd. In the first week alone, the restaurant reportedly brought in at least $30,000 in sales.

Ung, who had the chiseled features of a Hong Kong pop star, was an immediate hit with the customers. He had a charming smile, and he embraced his customers enthusiastically, making everyone feel like a regular (which, in an Orthodox community that kept kosher, nearly everyone was).

As the only nice sit-down kosher restaurant, Moshe Dragon became a magnet for the Orthodox business crowd, then a popular source for catered dinners. "Everyone wanted to have a duck party," Mayer recalled. The obsession was striking. Mayer spent some fifty hours a week, from before the restaurant opened to after it closed, making sure that Moshe Dragon was abiding by the kosher rules. He circulated, inspected the deliveries, and kept an eye on the kitchen. No violations were going to happen on his watch.

The kosher laws, also known as kashruth, are a complex set of dietary rules rooted in religious writings; learned Jews have spent a great deal of time parsing them, with one eye on biology and the other on production. Once upon a time, most cooking was done in the family kitchen or local business, and it was relatively easy to ascertain if the product was reliably kosher. Today, industrialization, transcontinental shipping, and processed food additives have made interpreting and enforcing the dietary rules a full-time job for a phalanx of rabbis. Americans have the FDA and the USDA; the Jewish community has OK (Organized Kashrut) and OU (Orthodox Union). The kashruth regulations get deep into the physiology of creatures or the minutiae of industrial food processing. The nuances can take years of training to master.

The guidance is rooted in the books of Leviticus and Deuteronomy, from the Torah. The most well-known rule forbids the mixing of milk and meat, an interpretation of the injunction that kids—young goats—should not be cooked in their mother's milk. Mammals must have split hooves and chew their cud, which excludes pigs but includes giraffes. Sea creatures must have scales and fins—which means no sharks or catfish (they lack scales), no whales (which are mammals anyway), and no shellfish. While the Torah has a list of forbidden birds, the exact translation of most of these species is no longer known. Scavengers—such as vultures—are considered nonkosher. To play it safe, the rules stick with birds known by tradition to be kosher, including chicken, goose, and duck. (There is a minor controversy about whether turkey is kosher, but most authorities maintain that it is acceptable, much to the relief of those at Thanksgiving dinner tables every year.)

There are also rules regarding how kosher meat can be slaughtered and what it can touch in the kitchen and still remain kosher. Rabbis issue rulings all the time: cream of tartar was deemed kosher by some, while certain kinds of chewing gum, because of their emulsifiers, were not.

Some Jews take kosher rules very very seriously. Mayer was one of them. A redheaded man with soft features, he had spent years studying at a yeshiva in Baltimore and had mastered the rules enough to keep kosher in the harshest of conditions. In the jungles of Vietnam, where he served in the military, he existed on only berries, plants, and occasional care packages of kosher C rations from his mom. He'd told Ung, "If I could keep kosher in Nam, you can keep kosher in this restaurant."

Being a mashgiach is like being a high-pressure security guard, with a watchfulness akin to that exhibited by aviation inspectors at airports today. Only a mashgiach doesn't answer to the Department of Homeland Security; he answers to God.

So Mayer, having kept up with the latest kosher news, was fully aware that there was a kosher duck shortage when he walked into Moshe Dragon at around nine A.M. on August 21, 1989. What he saw baffled him. There, in the Buick-sized commercial oven, hung thirteen smoking ducks. In the freezer sat another seventeen. Where had these ducks come from?

"You couldn't buy it for any kind of money. It just wasn't going to be had," he remembered. "You can't just open the Yellow Pages and say, 'I want to order a hundred pounds of kosher duck.'"

Mayer walked into the office and found three receipts lying on the desk. The letterhead was from Donald Chin, a local Chinese grocer and restaurant supplier, but the orders themselves were written in Chinese. Mayer didn't read Chinese, though he knew where he could find someone who did. He walked a few doors down to the Chinese laundry and asked the man behind the counter what it said.

The man translated for him: Ducks. Ribs. Chicken. Substantial amounts of each.

Mayer went on a mashgiach tear. Using the waiters' receipts, he calculated the amount of duck that had been served over the past few months. He compared it to the purchase receipts of duck from the local kosher supplier, Shaul's and Hersel's. There was a clear duck-accounting discrepancy, not unlike what happened more recently with Enron's books. There was no way these amounts could be reconciled. The last duck shipment had been over a month earlier, on July 19, as both the restaurant's and the supplier's receipts showed. Hundreds of pounds of duck of mysterious provenance had appeared after that date.

With a sick feeling in his stomach, Mayer called one of the oldest and most conservative members of the rabbinical council, a man who had total control over kashruth certification in the Washington area. "We have a problem," Mayer told him.

They immediately impounded the ducks.

Ung, who was in Philadelphia at the time, rushed home to face accusations. The receipts belonged to a cousin of his, he claimed. Somehow they had made their way to his desk.

The rabbical council can act with the ruthlessness of a Delta strike force should a kashruth violation call for it. In October 1989, it raided a bagel bakery at midnight, during the sandwich shift; within twenty-four hours of learning that the owner had been using its kosher kitchen to secretly package ham-on-bagel sandwiches for another vendor, it cut off the business's kashruth certification. But the resolution to the Moshe Dragon crisis would not be that simple. There were too many vested interests at stake. The council shut down the restaurant and began an investigation into Mayer's charges.

Moshe Dragon reopened a week later. During that time, the

kitchen had been koshered and another mashgiach had been hired; Mayer had been placed on "paid vacation."

Soon the local Jewish weekly picked up the scent of a larger story for the restaurant's closure, not fully buying Ung's explanation about "broken air-conditioning." Perhaps a reporter had been tipped off by someone with an agenda, though Mayer denies that it was he. The headline of *Washington Jewish Week*'s first article, which continued over four pages, was a taste of what was to come over the next year: "Chinese Kosher Clash at Moshe Dragon: Food Fraud or Frame-up?"

The tectonic plates within the Jewish community began to grind against each other.

Now, if you are a non-Jewish reader, you might wonder: All this over Chinese food? A Jewish reader may read this and nod in understanding: of course, all this over Chinese food.

Six thousand miles from the Holy Land, five thousand miles from eastern Europe, eight thousand miles from China, Chinese food had become a more significant part of the Jewish-American diet than the eastern European dishes of most Jews' immigrant ancestors. Chinese food had become, arguably, the ethnic cuisine of the American Jew.

For many Jews, Chinese food is a weekly ritual, steeped in family tradition and childhood memories. The average American Reform Jew is more likely to know how to use chopsticks than how to write the Hebrew alphabet. Chinese food on Christmas Day is as much an American Jewish ritual as the Seder on Passover (maybe even more so, once you take into account non-observant Jews). When my friend Orli Bahcall was growing up, her family even had take-out Chinese food for family Shabbat dinner. To this day, she associates Chinese food with the religious rituals of Shabbat.

This close relationship has been the subject of at least two academic publications and hundreds, if not thousands, of stand-up jokes delivered by comedians from Jackie Mason to Jerry Seinfeld. Many share their favorite Jewish-Chinese joke, some variation of "According to the Jewish calendar, the year is 5768. According to the Chinese calendar, it's 4705. That means for 1,063 years, Jews went without Chinese food."

Of course, not all Jewish people have eyed Chinese cuisine with good-natured affinity. In 1928, a Yiddish reporter sounded the alarm at the height of the chop suey madness, saying that Jewish fans of Chinese food were destined to forget their own culinary traditions. The *Der Tog* reporter lightheartedly suggested that perhaps communal-minded American Jews everywhere should raise this protest sign: "Down with chop suey! Long live gefilte fish!"

A number of Jewish entrepreneurs have built their careers and fortunes on their connection with Chinese cuisine. Eddie Scher, a businessman who lives in Felton, California, developed a monstrously popular brand of Asian-themed sauces widely sold in Trader Joe's, Whole Foods, and Dean & DeLuca. He drives around with the company name on his vanity license plate: SOY VAY. Kari-Out, the largest distributor of soy sauce packets in the country, is owned by a Jewish family, the Epsteins of Westchester, New York.

There are even a number of Jewish-owned Chinese restaurants. Perhaps none is as impressive as Chai Peking, a glatt kosher Chinese place in Atlanta, which demonstrates the lengths Jews will go to get their Chinese food. Tucked in a Kroger supermarket in a strip mall, Chai Peking doesn't appear any more sophisticated than a food-court joint, yet it has some of the most fiercely loyal customers in all of Atlanta, maybe even the entire Southeast. It is believed to be the only glatt kosher Chinese restaurant within a radius of almost seven hundred miles—up to Maryland and down to Miami.

Chai Peking has raised takeout and delivery to another level. Takeout often means customers making four-hour round-trip drives through multiple states to pick up huge orders. In 2003 a Nashville man flew his plane to the Atlanta airport to pick up an order for a synagogue fund-raiser back home. Included in his order, twenty-eight gallons of soup, packed in five-gallon buckets. Deliveries are often sent by FedEx, frozen and packed on dry ice to arrive in Texas, Mississippi, or North Carolina the next day for whatever anniversary, birthday party, or other celebration merited the appearance of Chinese food.

At Chai Peking, I ate one of their house specialties: a Chinese hot dog. A beef hot dog is wrapped in pastrami and egg-roll skin, then deep-fried. It had familiar sensations—the crispness of the flaky egg-roll skin, the juicy hot dog, and the cured taste of pastrami—but layered together a new way.

I had found all of this interesting information, but so far my exploration had only deepened, not clarified, the central mystery: Why is chow mein the chosen food of the chosen people?

The academic literature turned up some interesting hypotheses. For one thing, Chinese people and Jews were among the two largest non-Christian immigrant groups in the United States, which meant they didn't share the same days of worship as the rest of the predominantly Protestant and Catholic country. Even today, Christmas is often the busiest day of the year for Chinese Restaurants in New York, Florida, and other Jewish-American urban hubs. At Shun Lee, an upscale restaurant on the Upper West Side of Manhattan, the onslaught of Jewish customers begins at noon and does not stop until eleven P.M., making Christmas twice as busy as the next-busiest day of the year; Singing Bamboo in West Palm Beach expects three times the normal number of customers on Christmas. The Christmas-and-Chinese-food ritual has even been systematized. At the 92nd Street Y in New York, you can come in for an all-you-can-eat Chinese buffet and a movie or two. Jews in the Bay Area have launched ChopShticks, comedy shows at Chinese restaurants during the holidays that have been continuously sold out.

The academics also note that Chinese cooking uses essentially no dairy. Thus it is easy to make kosher, more so than Italian and Mexican food, the other two main ethnic cuisines in the United States.

But there are more subtle reasons for the connection, such as those put forth by two sociologists. Gaye Tuchman and Harry G. Levine interviewed over one hundred people about their experiences with Chinese food and compiled their observations in a paper called "Safe Treyf" ("treyf" is the word for nonkosher food), so named because they found that Chinese restaurants were where many Jews felt safe in breaking the laws of kashruth. The two sociologists posit that Chinese food helped the generation of immigrant Jews feel more American, in part by making them feel more cosmopolitan at a time when they were trying to shed their image as hicks from eastern Europe. Chinese food used to symbolize worldiness. As Tuchman and Levine write: "Of all the peoples whom immigrant Jews and their children met, of all the foods they encountered in America, the Chinese were the most foreign, the most 'un-Jewish.' Yet Jews defined this particular foreignness not as forbidding but as appealing, attractive, and desirable. They viewed Chinese restaurants and food as exotic and cosmopolitan and therefore as good. Indeed, many Jews saw eating in Chinese restaurants as an antidote for Jewish parochialism, for the exclusive and overweening emphasis on the culture of the Jews as it had been."

Another paper focused on a more prosaic explanation: geographic proximity. New York City's Lower East Side, which three-quarters of all Jewish immigrants who arrived between 1880 and 1920 passed through, was only a fifteen-minute walk from

Chinatown, notes Hanna R. Miller in a paper titled "Identity Takeout: How American Jews Made Chinese Food Their Ethnic Cuisine." That proximity encouraged culinary crossover. The Eldridge Street Synagogue, erected by eastern European Jewish immigrants in 1887 as the first permanent synagogue in their new homeland, is now surrounded by Chinese restaurants and specialty stores. It has decided not to fight the inevitable: now it hosts the Kosher Egg Roll Festival.

As Jews moved out of the Lower East Side and to other New York neighborhoods, other cities, and the suburbs, Chinese restaurants followed. There was a ready-made audience with ready-made appreciation for their food. Over time, the two groups helped each other become more American. "Jews!" one Chinese restaurant owner enthusiastically gushed to me. "They're our best customers!"

More subtly, Chinese restaurants emphasized Jews' proximity to the Euro-Christian tradition, rather than its distance. Christian imagery in Chinese restaurants was almost nonexistent, in contrast to Irish or Italian establishments. A friend of mine, Brian Chirls, excitedly alerted me to a passage in Philip Roth's novel *Portnoy's Complaint* in which Portnoy discusses nonkosher Chinese food: "Yes, the only people in the world whom it seems to me the Jews are not afraid of are the Chinese. Because one, the way they speak English makes my father sound like Lord Chesterfield; two, the insides of their heads are just so much fried rice anyway; and three, to them we are not Jews but *white*—and maybe even Anglo Saxon. Imagine! No wonder the waiters can't intimidate us. To them we're just some big-nosed variety of WASP! Boy, do we eat. Suddenly even the pig is no threat."

In search of someone who spoke from the stomach rather than the head, I turned to an expert on Chinese restaurants—a Jewish man named Ed Schoenfeld from Brooklyn, who started as a busboy in a Chinese restaurant and has risen to become one of the country's leading Chinese-restaurant consultants. We met in the dining room of one of his clients, an upscale Chinese restaurant in lower Manhattan called Chinatown Brasserie. "It was part of the secular European Jewish experience," he said. He elaborated at length on different flavor profiles and accessibility. Then he noted: "Jews are concerned with value."

Still unsatisfied, I sought someone who could speak with both Jewish and Chinese authority: the lost Chinese Jews of Kaifeng.

Chinese Jews appeared in the city of Kaifeng about a thousand years ago during the Song Dynasty, a period of rapid innovation in which China gave the world gunpowder, movable type, and the magnetic compass. In 1163, as part of the Jewish diaspora, the community built a synagogue in Kaifeng, once the capital of the Northern Song Dynasty. The Chinese synagogue rose and fell in Kaifeng, destroyed by fire and flood, until the last one was demolished in the 1860s. Without a gravitational center for the community's religious heritage, the Chinese Jews largely blended in with the surrounding Chinese community. But the smattering of Chinese Jews who have remained in Kaifeng draw pilgrims from around the world.

I had received a tip from a professor who had been there months earlier: that an old Jewish woman still lived in the alley that had been the epicenter of Jewish life in Kaifeng, Jiaojing Hutong, or "Teaching Scriptures Alley." I found her home among the narrow passageways and knocked on the screen door of her one-room home. An old Chinese woman cleaning vegetables on the floor looked up and welcomed me in. She was small, with a cheerful, round face and a belly-shaking giggle. As the remaining Jew in the *hutong*, she had grown used to foreign visitors over the years—mostly Jews from America or Israel, but occasionally people from Japan or Hong Kong. During peak holiday seasons, she said, she got up to three or four visits in a single day. "Sometimes there are so many that they don't even fit in here," she added, gesturing at the dark room, where she lived by herself; her husband had died and her five daughters were all married.

She was not a practicing Jew, but she kept on display a few menorahs that had been passed down through her husband's family. Much of the other Jewish paraphernalia, like a Jerusalem plate and an Israeli flag, had been given to her by strangers. She was shrewd enough, however, to capitalize on her popularity. Three or four years earlier she had started selling elaborate red paper carvings that combined Jewish and Chinese themes: the star of David flanked by gently curving lotus flowers; a menorah with the Chinese character for fortune; the word "shalom" with a pair of graceful swallows; flowers with the star of David at their center, sandwiched between "I Love Israel" in English and "China Kaifeng" in Chinese.

She earned all her income from these paper carvings. "I have to make a living. I have to eat," she said. This eighty-one-year-old Chinese woman was a professional Jew.

She invited me to sit down at the table. I explained to her at length the research I was doing about Jews in America. I was hoping that she, being one of the rare Chinese Jews in the world today, would be able to shed light on a question that had vexed academics, bolstered comedy routines, and intrigued Portnoy.

"Why," I asked, "do Jews in America like Chinese food so much?"

With a glint in her eye, she slapped the wooden table.

She knew.

I leaned in. This was the insight for which I had traveled thousands of miles, walked along a highway at midnight, and scoured alleyways.

Her Buddhist koan–like response was profound in its simplicity:

"Because Chinese food tastes good."

• • •

That brings us back to the psychological importance of a kosher Chinese restaurant, and why the community wanted the Moshe Dragon issue to go away.

The newspaper accounts pressured the rabbinical council into launching an intensive, three-month investigation of the restaurant. The rabbis brought in a big-time Washington lawyer to work pro bono; he, in turn, brought in a private investigator who had earned her stripes on a kashruth corruption story a dozen years earlier. Meanwhile, they fired Mayer, though officially the council said that this had nothing to do with the ruckus he had stirred up—something *Washington Jewish Week* reporters approached with skepticism.

Invoices were scrutinized. Translators were hired. Suppliers were interviewed. Accountants were called in.

One particularly heated confrontation between Mayer and investigators ended with Ung collapsing on the floor. He was taken by ambulance to Holy Cross Hospital, where he was diagnosed with a stress-related condition and given sedatives. Moshe Dragon's backers said he'd suffered a nervous breakdown, perhaps an echo of his experience in the Cambodian holocaust. Mayer scoffed: "He saw his whole thing fall apart right in front of him."

Despite the winds of the early evidence, at the end of the investigation the rabbinical council issued a solemn two-page report clearing Ung of any wrongdoing.

The council said it had belatedly discovered that Moshe Dragon had purchased ducks from Shaul's and Hersel's kosher market on August 16—nearly a month after the previously presumed last sale. The council traced the ducks back to a supplier in Philadelphia that had also been a supplier to Ung's restaurant in that city. While these experienced businessmen had somehow created no paper trail for hundreds of pounds of duck, the council found many people who vouched for the duck delivery. "This evidence supports Ung's contention that the ducks sold at Moshe Dragon during the summer of 1989 were purchased from kosher sources," the report stated.

In a world that tracks the provenance of kosher food with the rigor of high-end art dealers, this was the equivalent of accepting a photocopied letter and a pinky swear to vet a Rembrandt. The report hastened to add that the kitchen had been kashered—not that there was any need for kashering, given that there was no violation to begin with—back when the controversy had first started.

The private investigator retained by the council, and later dismissed for murky reasons, issued a statement to *Regardie's*, a local business magazine, after the report came out: "The council's statement supporting Ung flies in the face of facts presented to the council during mid-November," she said.

Many in the community sensed a cover-up and boycotted the restaurant.

"The trust between the restaurant's owner, the general public and the council has been damaged beyond repair," read one indignant letter in *Washington Jewish Week*.

Others were happy to get back to their duck parties with the rabbinical blessings of their leadership.

But the local Jewish newspaper wasn't satisfied. Were they beholden to truth or God? The *Washington Jewish Week* reporters kept probing. The paper ran an editorial entitled "Ung Jury."

The council rabbis called the reporters "despicable" to their faces and cursed them under their breath. The community paper was given tongue-lashings in local synagogues. Hundreds of people canceled their subscriptions. Local businesses muttered about pulling their advertising. The community wanted a "don't ask, don't tell" policy for its only Chinese kosher restaurant. Residents today still hiss at the paper's coverage, accusing the tabloid of sensationalizing the topic. "Did you see the issue where they put the picture of the dead duck on its cover?" one person asked me. There it was: an almost life-size photograph of a glassy-eyed plucked duck, its beak fallen open, splashed across the full front cover below the headline "The Saga Continues."

Ung's troubles multiplied when *Regardie's* magazine sent some moo shu pancakes from Moshe Dragon to be tested and they came back showing traces of whey—a dairy product that helps prolong shelf life but is strictly unkosher. Another cycle of accusation, investigation, and scandal began. *Washington Jewish Week* ran articles with headlines like "Rabbis Face New Questions over Kosher Pancake Flap" and "Maryland Attorney General's Office Reviewing Moshe Dragon Charges."

A group of Reform and Conservative rabbis tried to rescue the situation by issuing a statement saying that they believed the restaurant was kosher "at the present time." This was like attempting to use duct tape to repair a boat that was already sinking. As they were issuing their statement, however, the restaurant's new mashgiach complained of violations and resigned.

The months-long controversy dragged down sales at Moshe Dragon. Ung couldn't deal with it anymore. In mid-1990, he sold the restaurant to a family of Iranian Orthodox Jews who owned a kosher Chinese restaurant in Baltimore. After less than two years of existence, Moshe Dragon was dead.

Ung, his wife, and their four children still live in the Rockville area. His wife is employed at a jewelry store on Georgia Avenue; he works long hours, including time at a grocery store. The Moshe Dragon incident remains a sore point with the family, and mention of it still draws bitter tones. Ung is working hard and too busy to do an interview, his wife explained when I called their home.

After it was sold, Moshe Dragon was reopened under a new name, Royal Dragon. It still operates today two doors down: its owners are Orthodox and Iranian, but its chefs are Chinese. It still lists duck on the menu. The kosher duck shortage of 1989 is long over now. It would be but a single asterisk in the annals of food-commodity history were it not for the scandal.

Nearly fifteen years later, Mayer told me that the scandal made him question his relationship with God. "I come from a very strong Orthodox family," he said. "I had doubts after the incident with the rabbinical council. It really tested my faith really deeply." He still lives in the Silver Spring area, but he maintains a frosty relationship with the rabbinical council and Moshe Dragon's former investors. "They all pretty much shun me," he said. "To them, it was like it was yesterday. They don't let go."

He believes he was scapegoated because of the Jewish love of Chinese food: "I think it got a lot of breaks because it was a Chinese restaurant. People didn't want to see it closed down. This wasn't like one McDonald's out of a thousand. This was the only game in town. And people really wanted to see something like this continue. There was no way to pull that off." He paused, then remarked, "Washington is a city that learns that if you do something bad, put it out right away. But back then obfuscation was the rule of the day."

CHAPTER 8

The *Golden Venture:*
Restaurant Workers to Go

T hose who saw the scene later compared it to the invasion of Normandy, except with scrawny Chinese men scrambling to America's unprotected beachy shores, some dressed only in their underwear.

As a social metaphor, an "invasion" of the United States may be apt—though it was a fragmented, haphazard one, and this group was merely a tiny piece of it. These clandestine immigrants captured the nation's attention only because of the vivid, inescapable television imagery that accompanied them: the frantic sense of desperation as bodies were cast ashore, some conscious, others never to breathe again. Then the details trickled in: 112 days at sea; massive debts incurred; Thailand; Kenya; dark, sardine-like conditions. There were fewer than three hundred passengers on the rickety 150-foot steamer that lodged itself a hundred yards off New York's Rockaway Beach that moonlit June night in 1993. But their sudden, stark appearance meant the public could no longer avert their eyes from the cost of the American dream.

• • •

When the passengers on the boat felt the bump, they thought they had hit land. They scurried up to the deck, a thin, wiry man leading the charge. The crew told the passengers to throw mattresses onto the rocks and to jump, that the water was only chest-high and they could wade ashore. In reality, the sand dipped, the water ran deep, and the passengers were soon in over their heads. Ten of them didn't make it through alive.

An eighteen-year-old boy who would later take on the name Michael listened to his fellow passengers scream as the force of the waves hit them. He couldn't swim, so he remained on board. His idea was to use some of the empty propane gas canisters as flotation devices to reach the store. When the police and the Coast Guard came aboard, he was elated. The immediate fear of death had passed. Word back home in the villages was that U.S. immigration authorities would often lock people up, but they could be bailed out within a matter of days. Then they would be given a court date that they would never appear at.

Michael welcomed the arrival of the government officials as a hopeful ending to a torturous two-year journey that had started when he was sixteen years old, when his father put him on a train heading west. It had cost more than $20,000 in smuggling fees to send the only son, the second of five children, off to the United States.

That journey, which Michael, carrying only a backpack, had started in northern Fujian Province, had taken him into the jungles of Burma, where one of his fellow villagers had died; through a year of semicaptivity in Bangkok; and on a seventeen-thousand-mile boat journey that often seemed fatal.

But the stories that Michael had heard were wrong, at least for them. That night's well-publicized disaster changed the entire equation. It would be four years, not days, before he was free again, and only then because a congressman stepped in front of

President Bill Clinton the evening of the State of the Union address and made a personal plea.

The soft, hazy rays of the early-morning sun illuminated the scene. The name of their boat, written in white block letters, became visible: *Golden Venture.* From the beach the passengers could also see the Statue of Liberty for the first time.

Over the next few days, investigators discovered that the boat had been deliberately crashed into the sandy peninsula. As of early that morning, the man who had instructed the captain to crash was unaware how disastrously his order had been executed. Something had gone wrong, because the captain was unreachable. But it was only hours later, when the man, Weng Yu Hui, walked into a store on East Broadway in Chinatown and saw a short, plain Chinese woman with a blunt haircut watching the early-morning news, that he became aware of the consequences of the crash. The two had known each other across two continents, having grown up in Chinese villages separated by a thirty-minute walk. In the closed tangle of rural villages where everyone is connected to everyone else, the father of Weng's brother-in-law had been the woman's teacher.

Weng had been the main organizer behind the doomed boat trip. But it was the woman, a business partner in the boat, whose name and face would later be splashed across the New York City tabloids, with headlines like "Evil Incarnate." Known as Sister Ping, she was an internationally renowned businesswoman who had helped provide hundreds of thousands of dollars of financing for the boat. Two of the men on the boat, both of whom had boarded in Kenya, had been her clients.

Sister Ping looked at Weng and told him to leave New York City. With such a spectacle blowing up in the media capital of the world in the early months of a new presidential administration, law enforcement agencies would be looking vigorously for them. She was worried about her two clients. Weng told her not to fret: there had been almost three hundred people on the boat; it would be unlikely that any of hers had died. He was wrong. One of her passengers had been among those who drowned.

The most precise estimates today say there were thirteen crew members and 286 illegal immigrants aboard the *Golden Venture*. Some fifteen years later, advocates estimated that about half of those illegal immigrants were still in the United States. Some won asylum. Some were deported but snuck back. Some existed in a legal netherworld. The *Golden Venture* immigrants had fanned out from New York City along the coast and into the heartland: Virginia, Kansas, Ohio, Arkansas, Texas, Arizona. They had one thing in common: Chinese restaurants. About 90 percent of the *Golden Venture* survivors were involved in the Chinese-restaurant business, according to their own estimates. Of the others, a handful were in construction, one was a New York City cabdriver, a few had become artists. But most of those people who washed onto the shore that day worked as cooks, delivery boys, and waiters. A lucky few owned their own restaurants.

The *Golden Venture* was in essence, a delivery of Chinese restaurant workers to the United States that had gone haywire.

For the past two decades, the vast majority of Chinese restaurant workers in the United States have come from a Delaware-sized region in southeastern China surrounding the coastal city of Fuzhou (roughly pronounced foo-JOE).

The average American has no mental picture of Fuzhou, or even its home province of Fujian. The area is not known for its cuisine, like Sichuan or Hunan or Guangdong (formerly Canton). It is not known for its culture or history, like Xi'an, with its terra-cotta warriors, or Beijing, with its Forbidden Palace. It is not known for its dramatic mountainscape, like Guilin, or its modern skyline, like Shanghai. In fact, the most remarkable trait of that area may be that it is the single largest exporter of Chinese restaurant workers in the world today. Of the passengers on the *Golden Venture*, 246 were from Fujian.

The majority of the Fujianese arrived illegally, so precise figures are hard to come by. But based on his surveys of the number of people now missing in the villages and towns around Fuzhou, and estimating conservatively, Professor Zai Liang notes that perhaps 300,000 Fujianese have migrated from China to the United States over the past two decades. If those people all got together and formed their own city (even without the children they've had since), they would form the sixtieth-largest city in the United States—just behind Pittsburgh, Cincinnati, and Toledo. And if you add the children in, the number grows. "That number is also tricky," Zai Liang says. The typical Fujianese immigrant either paid tens of thousands of dollars to be smuggled to the United States or followed a family member who had emigrated. In the early days, in the 1980s, the going rate was about $18,000. By the time I visited China in 2006, it had climbed to upwards of $70,000. The costs needed to bribe officials and forge increasingly sophisticated identity documents in a post-9/11 world had increased sharply.

Put another way: there is a fairly good chance that the Chinese restaurant worker who cooked your roast pork fried rice, or the woman who took your order on the phone, or the deliveryman who showed up at your door paid tens of thousands of dollars for the privilege of doing so.

It is in the region around Fuzhou, in a little fishing village called Houyu, where Michael's journey began in 1991. Houyu, whose name means "Monkey Island," has no monkeys and is not an island. It is located on a piece of land that juts out into a crook of the muddy Min River. It is down the road from another little town, called Xiangyu, or "Elephant Island."

Houyu has a natural population of some 5,000 people. The

village was neatly divided in two: in one half most of the people had the last name Zheng; in the other half, Zhang. Michael's family, with the last name Chen, belonged to neither. Michael's Chinese name was Chen Xuedian, and his given name loosely translates to "learn from the model." It was an indication that his father, a fisherman-farmer, had educational aspirations for his only son. With five children, the family could not afford to buy books for all of them to go to school. Michael always ranked in the top three students in the class, but he got only as far as finishing ninth grade. Then Michael's father decided that his son would head to America. He contacted some smugglers, made arrangements, and put Michael on a train one night. Michael carried a backpack containing two changes of clothes, three types of medicine, $1,000 in American currency, and about the same amount in Chinese cash. The train headed west.

Today Houyu is a village of gnarled banyan trees, languid afternoon naps, and abundant hand-caught fresh seafood. It bursts out of the grassy wetlands in a cacophony of smooth colors and glinting metal—monstrous four-story mansions with bulbous spires, ornate front gates, and tiered balconies. Many of them have stone lions out front, the females with their paws on cubs. This wonderland has been made possible with money from Chinese restaurants in America. This is what General Tso's chicken buys in China.

But what makes Houyu strange is that many of the houses—each built with hundreds of thousands of American dollars—are empty. Except for the sound of construction and an occasional chicken clucking, few sounds of life bounce down the narrow alleys.

The residents of the town do not live there. The village has sent more than three-quarters of its population to the United States, including Michael and one of his sisters. The working-age men are missing. Old men and women, dressed in drab outfits, shuffle down the streets or sit on stoops. Chubby toddlers run about. It is like a village in a nation at war, except the men are not at war. They are working at Chinese restaurants in the United States.

The town has a busy Bank of China office but no middle school. The school shut down a few years earlier, for lack of students. It is death by prosperity. Everyone has either left, is planning to leave, or has too few years left to live to make it worth leaving.

Fujian Province, along with neighboring Guangdong Province, has an epic history of overseas migration. It is so mountainous, the locals quip that it is "eight parts mountain to one part water to one part farmland." With many rocky hills and little arable land, the Fujianese traditionally turned to the ocean for their livelihoods.

The men were sons of the seas—among them was my grandfather, a Fujianese fisherman. When war, uprisings, and famine came—and they came with regularity in China—the Fujianese again turned to the sea, and the land that lay beyond, as an economic refuge. By the thousands, they poured onto ships headed south to "Nanyang," a sweeping, general term that technically means "Southern Ocean" but encompasses much of Southeast Asia. Over the centuries, the Fujianese, or the Hokkien, as they called themselves, transformed the demographics and economics of many nations in that region: Indonesia, Singapore, the Philippines. They became the business elite, invoking admiration and vicious, sometimes deadly backlash. Even today, many of Southeast Asia's richest families are of Chinese ethnicity, with roots in Fujian.

The Fujianese people's love of the ocean and their ensuing reputation as sailors brought them to the United States. They worked on foreign vessels and started jumping ship at New York in the 1960s and early 1970s. These sailors were illegal, but many managed to establish an economic foothold through hard labor. They were the beachhead for the giant waves of Fujianese soon to come. The Fuzhou illegal-immigration network was established with two strokes of a pen, both by Republican presidents. The first was Ronald Reagan's signing of the 1986 Immigration and Control Act, which offered amnesty to any undocumented aliens who could prove, by the November 1988 deadline, that they had been living in the United States on or before January 1, 1982. Some legitimately had; others, for a fee of $500 or so, could appear to have been by buying fake backdated tax receipts and employment records. Thus opened a two-year window for the cash-rich, document-poor Fuzhou immigrants to bring their family members in from China. The second stroke came in the aftermath of the 1989 Tiananmen Square massacre when President George H. W. Bush instructed the State and Justice Departments to give enhanced consideration to individuals who expressed fear based on China's one-child policy. While they were waiting for their asylum applications to go through, they could start earning money in the United States.

These American federal policies, signed almost ten thousand miles away from Houyu, affected the village perhaps more than any other event in its history. Soon, international consortiums of human smugglers, or snakeheads, emerged to take advantage of the demand. Village men started to disappear. Night after night, another dozen or so would simply vanish. No one needed to ask where they had gone.

Among those smugglers who rose in prominence and reputation was Sister Ping, whose family home is located across the muddy river from Houyu—fifteen minutes by ferry or about an hour by land. Even as she became a millionaire many times over, her family kept their house at No. 398 in the compact village of Shengmei, which translates to "Prospering Beauty." Shengmei's narrow alleys are also flanked by empty modern homes now. The village, which takes less than fifteen minutes to walk through, is contained within a larger town called Tingjiang. Of Shengmei's natural population of 800, residents estimate that only 100 today are left. Almost all of those who left owe their passage in some way to Sister Ping. The town is not completely barren, for there has been an influx of a few hundred residents from other parts of the country, like Sichuan. A number of them are there to help tend to the empty, gargantuan homes.

Sister Ping's family home is a modern four-story, white-tiled house with a red-capped pagoda on top and an arched entryway. It is an older home and, by the region's standards, not anything spectacular. American prosecutors said she had sat at "the apex of an international empire" that was "a conglomerate built upon misery and greed." But around her home, the neighbors speak enthusiastically about Sister Ping's deeds. She was the oldest of five children—three girls and two boys. Neighbors remembered Sister Ping and her youngest sister as the talented ones of the bunch, the other three as just average.

Her sharp mind and focus were evident when she was a young girl, neighbors recalled. A natural leader, she was the head of the local Red Guard troop during the Cultural Revolution. She was also very fair-minded and would intervene when bullies picked on other classmates. She was never flashy; even as a young woman she dressed very plainly. She disliked jewelry and makeup.

Sister Ping's imprint is everywhere in the community, from the gaudy temple being constructed a few hundred feet from her home to the shuttered elementary school that her funds built.

Within a few years, so many men were leaving Houyu that those who had been left behind were subject to the subtle glances of neighbors. The expectation was that real men went to the United States and sent what seemed like massive amounts of money back—with only a hint of the difficult conditions needed to earn that money. In order to keep up with the Zhangs, you had to send your sons and husbands abroad.

Michael joined the pipeline of Houyu men heading to America. When he boarded the train that first night, the little Michael knew about the United States had come from evening news programs. Villagers had been smuggling in color televisions from Taiwan for several years, to enjoy the limited local programming. Two years later, he would show up on news programs himself, but only in the United States. The Chinese media ignored the embarrassment of the *Golden Venture*.

The dirt roads have since been replaced by smooth, paved lanes running from the village to Changle, whose rampant growth earned it reclassification as a city in 1995. The brown river and the plush fields are now largely empty. The grass alongside the banks has grown so long that it bends and whispers in the wind. The villagers don't need to work. Those who farm and fish generally do so because otherwise they become bored. In fact, the one lone farmer I found during my time there had originally moved to the United States to be with his son, but he'd returned home out of boredom and frustration. He couldn't drive or speak English. Back in Houyu, he could tend his vegetable garden every morning. It kept him from dying, he told people.

The main economic activity in Houyu today is construction. Almost all the sounds you here are the banging, clanging, and drilling of expansive mansions being built. The construction is done mostly by *waidiren,* out-of-towners. Many of the men are from Shanghai and Sichuan; they come to this area because work is available. It is trickle-down economics, Chinese style.

Some Shanghainese men also come for another reason: to

entertain the lonely housewives in local bars. These men, who have a reputation for being handsome and charming, are called "ducks." In the local Chinese slang, spending time with them is called "eating duck."

In my drive across the United States to visit the Chinese restaurants whose fortune cookies had dispensed the winning Powerball numbers, I encountered a restaurant owner from Houyu, Dong Zheng. Dong owned King's Buffet in Lawrence, Kansas, where Joseph Macek of Paola, Kansas, got his lucky numbers and won $100,000. Dong left Houyu in 1995, when he was fifteen years old, following his father, who had come seven years earlier. Dong attended high school in the States and then studied business at Indiana State University, but he too joined the Chinese-restaurant industry. "I haven't heard of anyone who isn't in the restaurant business; if they are not running a restaurant, they are doing construction for restaurants," he said. All his middle school classmates are in the United States.

His customers are primarily a mix of people from the University of Kansas and Mexican construction workers. He gestured to the workers, who had heaped their plates full of noodles. "They are like us Fuzhounese. They work very hard for money that they send back home."

Most of the local ambitions in Houyu revolve around Chinese restaurants. At the end of one village lane, I happened upon a school that taught restaurant English to young people who were planning to go to the United States. There are many such schools scattered all across the region. This particular class met five days a week in a barren classroom with an electric fan that sometimes did and sometimes didn't work. Were it not for the students' spiked, colored, and elaborately coiffed hair, it could have been a Chinese classroom scene from the 1950s.

The teacher, whose last name was Zheng, was going over the

vocabulary he had written on the blackboard: VEGETABLE, CAWLI-FLOWER, CELERY, ASPARAGUS, BAMBOO SHOOTS, NAPA, ONION, CABBGE (which was later corrected to CABBAGE), ZUCCHINI.

The teacher drew his material from photocopies of a textbook titled *Practical English for Chinese Restaurants*. He drilled the students on vocabulary, first calling out the English and having them give the Chinese translation, then vice versa.

He wrote the names of a number of dishes common in Chinese restaurants on the board. Among them was "French fries." He pointed to the board and warned the students not to pronounce it "French flies."

There is one main nursery school in Houyu, located near the center of the village, and it is full of toddlers. Many of them have been brought back to be raised by their grandparents because their parents are too busy working in America to take care of them.

I picked up one pudgy five-year-old girl with thick pigtails. She felt pleasantly hefty in my arms.

"Where were you born?" I asked her in Mandarin.

"America."

"Where are your parents?"

"America."

"Why are they in America?"

"*Zuogong*," she said. Working.

"Where is America?"

She looked up at me and blinked. "At the airport."

Three days into his train journey, Michael arrived in the southwestern city of Kunming, about three hundred miles from Thailand. At the train station, Michael was approached by a man who had been sent his photo. He was reunited with two other customers, familiar faces from Houyu: a cousin and a tall, friendly neighbor with the last name of Zheng who had lived no more than a three-minute walk from Michael. Unlike Michael, who was young and single, Zheng had left his wife and two young children at home.

From Kunming, Michael and a few other men hid in a truck for a day-long trip to a town called Menghai, near the Burmese border. The men stepped inside a metal cage and were handed plastic bags to use if they needed to relieve themselves. Sacks of rice were then placed over the cage. They drove in the dark. At Menghai, the men put on old clothing so they could blend in with the locals. This had only a limited effect because their skin tone was noticeably paler than that of the people who lived in the area.

After a few days in Menghai, one night they were instructed to walk down a road. A truck would pick them up, they were told. At the meeting place, other Fuzhou men were also waiting. The truck brought them closer to the border, where they were met by a guide who led them to a mountainous and hilly area. There they were told to run up the slopes until they couldn't run anymore.

Some of the men struggled. Since Michael was younger, he was in better shape. "The border is very dangerous," Michael told me. "If someone crosses the border, the guards can open fire."

They climbed for two hours. On the other side, they were met by a group of men wearing military uniforms and carrying machine guns. Michael, scared and homesick, wanted to turn around and go back to Houyu when he saw the men with the guns. But they told him he had no choice: either he moved forward or he died. The sixteen-year-old cried.

The smugglers were all Burmese. They earned between $3,000 and $4,000 for each person who crossed the Burmese border—a considerable sum for a pariah economy under a military dictatorship.

The men from Fuzhou began walking. They kept asking their three Burmese guides how long it would be before they got to their destination. The guides always replied that it would "only be a few more days" or promised that they would get there "tomorrow." They were lying. If Michael and the others had known it would be a month before they would get to Thailand, none of them would have gone.

Burmese weather is strange. During the day it was so hot they had to take off their shirts. It was freezing at night, but they couldn't light a fire because it would give them away. The Burmese jungle was like a primeval forest, like some lost era of the earth's history. Things were moving all the time. When it rained, leeches would mysteriously appear in their shoes. Michael was never sure how that happened. Did the leeches arise from inanimate spores that sprang to life with the addition of water? Did they sneak in through tiny holes in the shoes? Did they wriggle in when he stepped into a particularly large puddle? Periodically the men had to stop to pull the leeches off. Along the way, they passed decaying bodies, people who had died on the way to the West. Some had drowned in a flash flood. Others had died from drinking the water, Michael was told.

One night, during a thunderstorm, Michael and five other men lost track of the people in front of them. It was so dark, Michael couldn't see his fingers two feet in front of his face. Holding hands, the men kept walking until the ground gave way under one of them. They had reached a cliff. They screamed into the night, but their cries drifted into the vastness.

Human smuggling is perhaps second only to narcotics as the largest cross-border illegal trafficking in the world. It has accelerated in recent decades for two reasons. The first is that the income inequality between the world's citizens is now perhaps the highest it has ever been in human history. The second is that transportation and communications technology has vastly improved. Both are consequences of globalization.

The greatest traffic is between the United States and Mexico, the international border that straddles the largest per capita income difference in the world. But at the turn of the millennium, the most expensive journey anywhere is the journey of the Fujianese to the United States. The sums of money needed by Fujianese to come to the United States are staggering by American standards, and even more so by Chinese. A question naturally arises: Where do these immigrants get the money? The short answer is that they borrow it—from family, neighbors, and, occasionally, from loan sharks. That this much money can change hands is surprising to Westerners, who are comfortable with the idea of borrowing from large banks, but not so much from close associates. Perhaps it is worth noting that in Chinese, the word for "lend," *jie,* is the same as the word for "borrow." There is only one word: "lendborrow." The context of the sentence makes the meaning clear: "I lendborrow money to him" or "I lendborrow money from him." The act of lendborrowing is a reciprocal relationship. A person who borrows one day may lend on another.

In the smuggling world, illegal Chinese immigrants are called "PRCs," for the People's Republic of China, the official name of the Communist-led country. In contrast, Taiwan is ROC, for Republic of China, but no one ever talks about ROCs because these days ROCs aren't usually illegal immigrants. If you listen in on law enforcement chatter on the radio in port cities, you will often hear comments like "We got a boat with five PRCs on board."

Illegal Chinese immigration to the United States is hardly new—especially given the long history of the Chinese Exclusion Act. The destruction of public records in the 1906 San Francisco earthquake allowed thousands of Chinese-American men to falsely claim citizenship and thus the right to bring over any "sons" (real or fictional) they had in China. What is new, however, is the rise of organized human smuggling in illegal immigration, a phenomenon that has intrigued criminologists and sociologists.

I visited one of the leading criminologists involved in investigating Chinese smuggling, Professor Ko-lin Chin, at his office at Rutgers University in Newark, New Jersey. In Fuzhou a few years ago, he had been approached in his hotel lobby by men who had tried to recruit him to become a smuggler. He had used the opportunity to interview these snakeheads about what the job would entail. They had been especially excited when they found out Professor Chin still held a passport from Taiwan, which arouses less attention than an American passport in China. Despite the icy diplomatic relations between China and Taiwan, Taiwanese nationals have played a critical role in moving Fujianese across the world. The lure of profit trumps the pride of patriotism. Every single one of the thirty-seven smuggling boats that were intercepted by the United States government from mid-1991 to mid-1994 had some connection to Taiwan: registration, crew, ownership, or home port.

Until recently, most scholarly work had looked at Chinese criminal organizations in terms of the traditional paradigm of hierarchical, corporation-like entities like the Mafia or the drug cartels. An alternative, more entrepreneur-centered view sees criminal enterprises as networks and alliances that expand and contract with the nature of the crime at hand.

Chin, who has interviewed dozens of snakeheads, argues that the Chinese human-smuggling organizations are an amalgam of the two. In many ways, they are organized like networks, with largely horizontal groups of smugglers joining together around specific tasks—moving a particular group of people, for example. But the groups, while somewhat flat, also resemble corporations in that individual smugglers tend to take on very specific roles: investors, recruiters, transporters, debt collectors, guides. The "big snakeheads," who are investors and arrangers, are often overseas Chinese who rarely meet their smuggled human cargo face-to-face. "Little snakeheads" handle all the day-to-day tasks.

Chin maintains that his research turned up little evidence suggesting any significant connection between these smuggling groups and traditional Chinese criminal societies such as triads, tongs, and street gangs. Since smuggling organizations are largely dynamic, the hunt for "godfathers" who run them is largely futile, he has argued. The cells will just organize themselves around other "big snakeheads." In talking to him, I got the sense that human-smuggling organizations are like any other multinational shipping enterprise, with investors, profit margins, international divisions, hubs, and local outsourcing. The only difference is that their product is Chinese restaurant workers.

At the top of the cliff in Burma, Michael and the other five men waited for hours, certain they were going to die. Then the distant light of torches appeared. They were ecstatic. Their guides had found them.

The group was given horses to ride for one stretch of the journey. But they had to move at night, and even the horses had trouble maneuvering in the dark. Once Zheng's horse took a bad step and it tumbled down a hill, almost bringing Zheng with it; in the nick of time he grabbed some nearby bamboo branches. It took the group two hours to go down and retrieve the horse, which, miraculously, had escaped uninjured.

The impetus for traveling only at night was not so much the government as the powerful heroin traffickers in the region. These men would not hesitate to kill anyone who seemed a threat to their poppy crops. Michael and the others had to dodge the searchlights that constantly swept the area.

Weeks into the journey, they arrived at a mountain clearing, joining between two and three hundred people, almost all from around Fuzhou. Michael looked at the faces and recognized many of them as from Houyu. From the clearing, Michael rode a series of trucks to Bangkok, where the various groups of smuggled people then headed in different directions. Some traveled toward Spain. Others, from the region of Fuqing, aimed for Japan.

In Bangkok, the men were handed passports from Singapore, Japan, and Korea. Michael was handed a Korean passport. The smugglers made him practice signing his Korean name until he could do it without hesitation. They taught him enough English so that he could say he was on vacation.

In Bangkok (the only place I've been where my hotel minibar included condoms), I met with Major General Krerkphong Pukprayura at his offices in the Royal Thai Police Headquarters. The general was a coordinator of an international coalition to combat the smuggling and trafficking of people in the Asia-Pacific region called the Bali Process. Bangkok, for a number of reasons, has historically served as a transit hub for illegal migrants—not just from China but from all over Asia to the West, he explained. The city is one of the main aviation hubs for Asia but two of the other primary hubs, Singapore and Hong Kong, are islands and therefore much easier to patrol. In contrast, Thailand shares a massive land border with four countries: Laos, Cambodia, Malaysia, and Burma. It is easy to cross by land into Thailand and then continue on to Bangkok. As a result of the illegal migrants, Bangkok has also become a world capital for forged documents: stolen passports, manufactured passports, and passports in which the photographs have been changed.

The smuggling is helped by the existence of Sino-Thais, Chinese who have become very successful in Thailand over the last few generations, making up the bulk of the business establishment and adopting Thai last names. "In Thailand they have been able to assimilate to the point where they don't consider themselves Chinese. They consider themselves Thai," he said. Some of the younger generations barely speak any Chinese at all.

The Chinese are only part of the illegal flow in and out of Bangkok. Thailand has been drawing people from Iraq, Iran, Afghanistan, India, and Pakistan, all of them on their way elsewhere. The most interesting migrant population in Thailand may be the North Koreans. Many of them crossed the northern border into China and then walked all the way to Bangkok, he said, running his finger down the length of China. I gawked. It was a massive distance—equivalent to walking from Maine to Texas. He had heard the stories thousands of times. "It's human nature," he said. "Everyone wants to better their life."

Michael wasted a month in Bangkok after he broke his foot running from Thai government officials. He lost another month when he was captured by Thai police. It cost his father $6,000 in bribes and fees to get him out.

Bangkok became a bottleneck during the time when Michael and the others were waiting. Thai authorities had cracked down after a flood of PRCs bearing false travel documents had shown up at John F. Kennedy International Airport in New York. It was getting too difficult to move people out by air, so the snakeheads turned their attention to the seas. A consortium of snakeheads, including Sister Ping and Weng, in New York City, were busy arranging the boat that would eventually bring Michael and his group to the United States.

One of the partners in the *Golden Venture,* Guo Liang Qi, was connected to Sister Ping through an odd history. He had robbed her twice. Guo, also known as Ah Kay, was a leader in a street gang called Fuk Ching who had committed multiple murders. He robbed Sister Ping for the first time in 1985, when he followed her daughter to their Brooklyn home. There was less money than he'd expected. A few months later the gang robbed Sister Ping's home again, finding $20,000 stashed in her refrigerator.

Later on, while they were planning a smuggling venture together in September 1991, he apologized for the robberies. She waved it off, telling him on the phone, "That's what happened in the past. We're talking business now." They agreed that for $750,000, Ah Kay would take 130 passengers from a boat off the coast of Massachusetts and bring them to New York City in three U-Haul trucks.

Of the sum owed to him, Ah Kay instructed Sister Ping to wire $300,000 through her banking network so he could invest it in a Panama-registered steamer, the *Tong Sern*, in Singapore. At sea the Panamanian flag was lowered and a Honduran flag was raised. The *Tong Sern* was rechristened *Golden Venture*.

The partners were on a nervous timetable. They were focused on retrieving a group of two hundred or so Chinese, including twenty of Sister Ping's clients, who had been stranded in Kenya when the captain of their boat, the *Najd II*, decided that his share of the smuggling profit was too small and refused to go any farther. He was being paid $500,000 on human cargo he estimated to be worth $7 to $8 million. On the way to pick up their stranded passengers in Mombasa, Kenya, the *Golden Venture* stopped in Thailand to load an additional hundred or so passengers, including Michael's group. Some of the men had worked as sailors in Hong Kong or Shanghai. They told Michael that 750 tons was small for a boat traveling across an ocean and refused to get on.

Michael and others were transported by speedboat out into the dark ocean at night to meet the *Golden Venture*.

To Michael, the steamer looked terrifyingly small bumping around on the waves. He could barely see it in the ocean.

But they really didn't have a choice. Some one hundred people boarded in Thailand. The ship then steamed through the Strait of Malacca and across the Indian Ocean to Kenya.

Human smuggling is not to be confused with human trafficking, where women or young children are moved across borders against their will and sometimes forced to do sex work. Human smuggling is used to describe the willing movement of people. This was emphasized and reemphasized to me when I met a human smuggler in the Dominican Republic, which had been a key staging point for the PRCs to enter the United States.

The meeting was arranged by a friend of a friend, who was also acting as the chauffeur. Naum, as the smuggler wanted to be called, was waiting for us on the street wearing dark sunglasses. We circled around a number of times before picking him up in an SUV. He shook my hand and said in Spanish, "Before we start, I just have one question for you." He paused. "Do you believe in God?"

Were we going to start with an existential evaluation? I hesitated. "Yes," I said. "But I am not Catholic."

He smiled. "Then do you believe God put borders on this earth?"

We rode around in the SUV for an hour and a half, talking through an interpreter. "I don't consider myself a criminal because I'm not doing anything against the natural will of God," Naum said. "I'm just helping people who want a better future. The majority of the people I move are honest workers." There are the good reasons to cross borders. There are the bad reasons to cross borders. The Chinos, or PRCs, are good business because they pay the highest fees of anyone not involved in anything explicitly shady. Naum said he does not move criminals, terrorists, or people from suspicious countries, such as Pakistan and Saudi Arabia. He stays away from Chechens in particular, he said. "They kill children."

The PRCs are a better business proposition. They have less risk of drawing the ire of the U.S. Homeland Security Department. They pay lucrative fees. And there is a steady flow of them. In addition, PRCs almost always pay in full once they reach their destination, he said.

"The trafficking of Chinese is very different from others. Most people we are smuggling are paying their own way," he explained. So when smugglers need money to deal with unexpected problems—to bribe a police official for example—they often have to pressure the clients' family members to come up with the cash. In contrast, with the Chinese smuggling is more centralized. Naum can make a single phone call to a snakehead boss somewhere and the boss will front the money to deal with a problem. It's the same thing with the payments. The smugglers always get paid by the big boss, who in turn will get payments over time from his clients.

Naum had settled in the Dominican Republic, which, due to its proximity to both the United States and Puerto Rico, has often been a popular transit point for illegal immigrants. The most desperate illegal immigrants are shipped over in *yolas*—rickety homemade boats cobbled together from plywood and tree limbs and powered by engines. *Yolas* are seaworthy only in the sense that you can toss them into the high seas. By ferry, the journey from the eastern coast of the Dominican Republic to Puerto Rico takes a few hours. Passengers traveling the Mona Passage by *yola* will get to Puerto Rico in four days if things go smoothly, twelve days if they're less lucky, or never if the boat capsizes in the stiff winds and unrelenting waves, tossing its inhabitants into the ocean.

The highly financed PRCs traveled by boats, but seaworthy ones. Right before we met, Naum had gotten an anxious phone call from a business associate in Peru who was stuck with nineteen Chinos. The previous boat leaving Peru had been intercepted by the U.S. Coast Guard. That smuggling route was now hot, and they were backing way off it. How are we going to move them out? his associate had wanted to know. Naum had spent ninety minutes calling around to other business folks so he could answer that question.

If there is one problem with PRCs, it is that, well, they have a hard time blending in. As one immigration official put it to me, "A PRC sticks out from a mile away." Even the South Asians from India and Pakistan can be passed off as a South American, but, "A PRC is nothing but a PRC."

On the *Golden Venture,* food, water, light, and space were all scarce. The passengers ate rice and vegetables until the vegetables ran out. They were given water to drink, clean, and cook with, but slowly that supply dwindled too, so they started collecting rainwater in plastic bags. There was only one bathroom for the three hundred or so people. Men started relieving themselves off the deck of the boat.

Most passengers killed time by playing poker and Chinese chess; the boredom could be mind-numbing. One passenger played a handheld computer game, punching the buttons long after the batteries wore out.

Then one night the ship's crew warned the passengers that there would be a storm. The boat was rounding the southern tip of Africa, near the Cape of Good Hope. Waves, some fifty feet high, tossed the vessel back and forth. Bodies tumbled like rag dolls within the hull. Michael thought they were surely going to perish. Others agreed and put on their best clothes in preparation. People prayed to any deity they thought would listen: Jesus. Buddha. The Chinese Goddess of Mercy, Guan Yin. The Goddess of the Seas, Mazu. The boat rocked for seven or eight hours. The skies cleared. They had survived.

• • •

Days before the *Golden Venture* approached American shores, the Fuk Ching gang—which had been tasked with moving the passengers from boat to shore—melted into bloody disarray. Intergang warfare erupted, resulting in a number of deaths. Ah Kay was in China. There was no one to bring the passengers off the *Golden Venture*.

When Weng and the others learned of this, they decided on a Plan B: to have the boat land directly on the shore. They considered the piers under the Manhattan Bridge but settled on Rockaway. If the boat lodged in the right time and place, the water would be only a little bit over three feet high, shallow enough for a person to stand in. The boat steamed between Boston and New York, unsure of where it would land. They were so close to land that Michael and the others could see the lights. "We were so excited," he remembered.

Weng instructed the boat's crew to run the ship aground, then tell the passengers to throw down the mattresses and jump down. Weng gave the final instruction to run aground around nine P.M. on June 5, 1993. Within hours, the boat did exactly that.

The Fuzhou region is not the only one in China that has sent an absurdly high concentration of its residents abroad. Before Fuzhou, there was the Taishan region (also known as Toisan), in the southeastern province of Guangdong, where some 80 percent of Chinese-American immigrants before the 1950s had their roots. Many of the first generation of restaurant workers and laundry owners in America came from a four-county area. If Fuzhou is the region that is supported by General Tso's chicken, this is the area that was supported by chop suey.

Today Taishan remains a lush but depressed area about a four-hour bus ride from Hong Kong. The legacy of the sojourners is laced throughout the county, popping up in unexpected places among the verdant rice paddies and dusty roads. But as in the villages around Fuzhou, Taishan's architecture is evidence of the people who journeyed across the ocean. Crumbling century-old Western-style castles are sprinkled throughout the villages—a faint echo through time and space.

The local museum has an extensive exhibit on overseas Chinese, in both Chinese and English, the only display on Chinese emigration I encountered during my travels across China. A life-size diorama shows two Chinese men hopping into a rickety boat as their family members tearfully bid them good-bye from the shore, an angry sea painted in the background. In the lobby, there is a huge map of the world, about thirty feet across, with a red dot in the center of each country that Taishanese have immigrated to. The little red dots freckle the Americas, Africa, Europe, and the Pacific Rim; I stopped counting when I got to fifty.

Back around Fuzhou, news of the *Golden Venture* crash did not reach the villages through traditional news outlets. Instead, word of mouth from New York carried back the rumors about the sunken ship and dead sons and husbands. Michael's mother collapsed into bed and cried for more than three days. It would be a month before they received a letter from Michael saying that he was in prison and he expected to get out.

Based on what they'd heard from earlier illegal immigrants, Michael and the other *Golden Venture* passengers expected to be briefly detained before being released. However, they'd arrived during the Clinton administration's first five months. The high visibility of the boat crash and the ensuing political fallout meant that the administration could not simply treat the *Golden Venture* passengers with the same bureaucratic anonymity it did other illegal immigrants that slipped into their net. Twelve days after the crash, President Clinton announced a shift in immigration policy. "We cannot tolerate those who traffic in human cargo," he said. "Those who attempt to enter the United States illegally should know that they will be intercepted, detained, and returned home." Michael invoked a popular Chinese aphorism to describe the decision. They "killed the chicken to scare the monkey," he said, meaning that Clinton's people intended to make a warning lesson out of them.

Michael and most of the others were sent to the York County Prison in Pennsylvania. To break up the monotony, many of them took up sports, which is how Michael got his English name: because he liked to play basketball, the guards called him Michael, after Michael Jordan.

Meanwhile, the York detainees found fervent advocates in a local coalition of anti-abortion evangelicals, pro bono lawyers, and feminists. The volunteer lawyers took a one-day crash course in immigration law and learned how to help their clients apply for asylum. Neighbors held daily vigils for the *Golden Venture* detainees, helping to keep the goal of their release in the public eye. Every Sunday, a group converged at the prison and sang "God Bless America." Beverly Church, a former nurse and a staunch Republican, began visiting the prison on a regular basis.

Michael, like many others, started to learn English. He used a dictionary and would slowly and painfully translate the numerous articles that the *Golden Venture* passengers were writing. Others improved their conversational skills by talking to the Christians who would regularly come to chat with them, often about Jesus. Over time, many of the detainees got sick, which some of them attributed partially to the prison food: too much meat, fried food, and starch.

Meanwhile, in New York, investigators were accumulating evidence against Sister Ping and her role in the *Golden Venture* fiasco. Ah Kay was arrested in Hong Kong in August 1993. Federal agents executed a search warrant on Sister Ping's restaurant on East Broadway in September 1993 and found a cash-counting machine, a lamination machine, airline-ticket receipts, and passports belonging to various individuals. By December 1994, federal officials had enough to indict Sister Ping and issue a warrant for her arrest.

It was too late. By then Sister Ping had already ceased to exist. She had last used her own passport three months earlier, on September 20, 1994, when she'd departed Hong Kong. After that, her trail effectively disappeared.

At York, the detainees eventually latched on to an unusual activity: creating elaborate paper sculptures. It started when one man taught the others how to make origami pineapples out of recycled paper. Within the tightly confined spaces of the prison, this activity afforded an acceptable creative outlet; production exploded.

The first pieces were rough-hewn and given to attorneys and friendly prison workers as gestures of thanks. But over time, the creations became startlingly sophisticated: a twisting dragon with an outstretched claw and a slithering tongue; a family of snowy-white owls, the adults hovering over two babies; a grinning Buddha lounging like Jabba the Hutt; a lobster with delicately outstretched antennae. One piece, an idyllic foot-and-a-half-high model of the *Golden Venture,* seemed much more pleasant in the artist's rendition than it had ever been in actuality.

The prisoners eventually made over ten thousand sculptures. A number of the most elaborate and gripping, from the dozen or so most skilled artists, were exhibited from Santa Fe to the Smithsonian. Some of the pieces were sold in galleries and at auctions. The money was sent back home or used to pay the detainees' lawyers.

In 1996, the Immigration and Naturalization Service did something unprecedented. It reclassified one of the *Golden Venture* prisoners, Wu Luzhong, as an "alien of extraordinary ability in the arts"—the first time this agency had ever done so with an imprisoned illegal alien. Four more of the prisoners would also be granted the rare artists' visa.

A few members of Congress mounted a private lobbying campaign to get the *Golden Venture* detainees freed. On the third anniversary of their detention, in June 1996, Congressman Bill Goodling, a Republican whose district included the York County Prison, phoned Clinton to plead for the prisoners' release, with limited success. At the State of the Union address in February 1997, Goodling took the opportunity to step into the path of President Clinton as he was making his way out of the House of Representatives chamber. Eight days later, Goodling met with Clinton in the Oval Office. He brought two elaborate pieces of the prisoners' paper sculptures, a pine tree and a "freedom bird."

The president admired them.

A few days after that, Goodling got a call from the president. The prisoners would be freed. This was not a unanimous decision in the administration, Clinton warned.

On February 26, Michael and the others—wearing identical blue sweatshirts, gray pants, and sneakers—stepped out of the York County Jail and onto a prison bus. They were taken to the nearby Codorus Church of the Brethren, which was packed with the local activists and national media.

At the church, they were served their first Chinese meal in nearly four years: General Tso's chicken, a broccoli-shrimp dish, steamed rice, egg rolls, and fortune cookies from the Hunan East restaurant in York. Most of them had never seen such strange Chinese food: General Tso's chicken and the fortune cookies were unrecognizable. But soon enough, for most of them that food would become their lifeblood.

It took more than five years after the arrest warrant was issued for law enforcement to catch up with Sister Ping.

In April 2000, Hong Kong police were waiting for her when she showed up at the Korean Airlines counter. At the time of her arrest Sister Ping was carrying in her purse over $60,000 in American and Hong Kong currency, several Belizean passports with different names, and airline tickets. The American currency was wrapped in newspaper, in packets of $8,000 each. Law enforcement officials found a genuine passport from Belize issued in the name of Lily Zheng; it used Sister Ping's photo and listed her occupation as "housewife." (At the trial American prosecutors would ask, What kind of housewife makes over fifty trips to foreign countries within a three-month time period?)

Sister Ping fought extradition for three years, but in 2003 she took a United Airlines flight back to the United States, arriving in San Francisco on June 20. She was confident she could get out. The trial lasted over a month in the late spring of 2005. On June 22, 2005, Sister Ping became the twenty-third person convicted in conjunction with the *Golden Venture.* A jury found her guilty of conspiracy to smuggle aliens and take hostages, money laundering, and trafficking in ransom proceeds. By that time, most of her co-conspirators had been released, many because they had cooperated with the government in her trial.

The next day, a New York tabloid blared the headline "Snake is Hiss-tory."

At the hearing for her sentencing, Sister Ping made a plea in Chinese. "I would like to explain to the judge I am not the kind of person that they depicted me and charged me with being," she said through a translator. "In the way that I have led my life, I have always gone to kindness and uprightness because since I was young my father had instructed me that one has to be a good human being." She went on for an hour, saying how she had been a victim and that evidence in the trial had been faked. "I love the United States because it is a society of laws," she said.

In the shadow of her sentencing, the boat survivors reunited in New York City at the opening of *Golden Venture,* a documentary by Peter Cohn that showed at the Tribeca Film Festival. Beforehand, the group held a press conference at the Museum of the Chinese in the Americas to highlight the precarious legal situation they were in: they still could be deported.

Craig Trebilcock, a personal-injury lawyer who had become one of their most fervent advocates, compared the *Golden Venture* passengers to the East Germans he saw while stationed with the military in West Germany. "They had risked their lives for freedom," he said. "Their misfortune was arriving at a certain point in our nation's history." There is "no such thing as immigration law," he added. "There is really only immigration politics. It may be wrapped up in law, but it's really politics."

Michael, who had become quite media savvy by that time, also took the podium. Under the bright lights, the television reporters tried to coax the *Golden Venture* passengers into producing a usable sound bite. Michael was one of the few whose English was good enough for the challenge. "This is a lovely country. This is a free country," he said. The cameras rolled.

By the time I met up with Michael at his restaurant, a few weeks after Sister Ping's sentencing, he had been out of York County for nine years. He owned his own 150-seat Chinese restaurant in an upscale suburb of Columbus, Ohio, called Dublin—a town full of families with 4 bedrooms, 3.5 bathrooms, and 2.3 kids.

Michael's restaurant is located in a classy strip mall (if that isn't an oxymoron) that looks like a quaint European town from one vantage point and spills into a sprawling parking lot from another. His restaurant does a brisk business, mostly at lunch; a large professional population works in Dublin. He and his wife have two children. A few years ago, just after their son, Allen, was born, he bought a four-bedroom house in a new development two miles away from the restaurant. Their yard still had the spindly sycamore and weeping willow trees that are common in new developments, but he already was building a new house in another subdivision a few miles away. It had one more bedroom, but more important, it was in a better school district. His son was only three years old, but Michael was thinking ahead. "First off I want them to be well educated for sure, not like us in a restaurant," he said.

Like many from the region, Michael spoke highly of Sister Ping, praising her character. "She is more trustworthy and she is willing to help people," he told me. Of Ah Kay, he said, "His hands are covered with blood." The people around Fuzhou remember Sister Ping for being generous, for giving money to people in need, and for charging less for people who couldn't afford the full smuggling fee. "If a family had four or five children, she would make sure that one of them could go to America," one neighbor told me. Her neighbors related that they would have gladly done some of her prison time, to repay some of their karmic debt to her. "If you do a good deed for someone else, it is a good deed for yourself," one neighbor said.

Michael has picked up some Americanisms. He drinks coffee in the morning as he reads the local paper. He's a big football fan. But he has other habits that are still very Chinese—like clearing his throat and spitting.

Of all the *Golden Venture* survivors, in 2006 Michael was

among the most well off. He bought a three-bedroom apartment in a new development in Fuzhou for his parents to retire in. He acts as a translator when other survivors run into problems. His success is due to a convergence of factors: his youth when he came, his fierce desire to learn English, his entrepreneurial spirit, and—no small matter—his luck.

I asked Michael if, looking back now, it was worth it: the thirty days through the Burmese jungles, the year in semicaptivity in Bangkok, the 112 days on the *Golden Venture,* and the nearly four years in detention. Was what he had now worth all that?

He hesitated.

"If you had told me to do it again, I wouldn't do it again," he said. "You are gambling with your life." He looked up. "It's half and half. For right now, it's worth it. If you think back, it's not worth it to risk your life to cross the Atlantic Ocean."

But it wasn't about him, was it?

No, he said softly. They don't gamble with their lives for their own sakes. They do it for their parents—and their children.

CHAPTER 9

Take-out Takeaways

The white take-out carton is an amazingly elegant product. It is a simple design, yet it connotes so much: Chineseness, harried lifestyles, working mothers, cheap yet filling, late night, transience, eating together without dining together, meal as afterthought. When FedEx started delivering to Beijing, it showed ads with a Chinese take-out carton emblazoned with the purple-and-orange FedEx logo. Continental Airlines followed suit: when it began offering nonstop flights from new York to Beijing, the company made thousands upon thousands of blue-and-white take-out boxes that said "We deliver too." *Avenue Q,* a Tony-winning Broadway musical, used the boxes in its street ads to represent the Upper West Side of Manhattan—the original milieu for delivery. All this captured in a single piece of white industrial cardboard, neatly folded, held by a single wire with no seams and no glue.

Pick up a white carton sometime, and you'll likely see the name Fold-Pak inscribed unobtrusively on the bottom; this is the company that makes some two-thirds of the take-out containers in the country. The industry calls the cartons "food pails"—which seems more Little House on the Prairie than House of Peking.

Tim Roach, a vice president who started his career with Dixie cups, explained why when I visited the company's largest factory, in Hazleton, Pennsylvania: in the early twentieth century, the cartons were used to hold shucked oysters. "Many people still refer to it an oyster pail even though, to our knowledge, it's not used anymore for that," he said. At various points, Tim explained, the carton was used to hold ice cream, deli goods, and even goldfish at carnivals. ("Now they put them in a bag," he said.) Around World War II, the box found a different audience. "Somehow, I don't know how, it worked its way into Chinese restaurants as the take-out container and it became the dominant package for Chinese takeout," he said. "Once it evolved into a container for Chinese food, the company put a generic Chinese design on it. Pagoda was it," he said. They also added "Thank you" in an ersatz Chinese font.

The demand for take-out boxes across the country is considerable, so the factory operates three shifts, twenty-four hours a day, nonstop. During my visit the factory floor was a spinning, whirring, rhythmic hubbub of pneumatic tubes, printing presses, and wire-snapping machines. On the sides of the manufacturing floor were bins of discarded take-out containers from the production line: ones where the wire was misaligned, or the printing was faded, or where the cardboard had failed to separate properly.

I found something depressing about the piles of take-out boxes that had been thrown away. Take-out cartons are meant to be thrown away; but these virginal white boxes, which had never seen garlic sauce or roast pork grease, seemed almost free of original sin. Suddenly I understood why their loss was so unsettling: these boxes were stillborn—purposeless.

Fold-Pak doesn't exist as a separate company anymore. It has a complicated corporate family tree, tangled by buyouts, mergers, bankruptcies, and joint ventures. Today, suffice it to say, Fold-Pak has become a unit within a company called GSD Packaging. The splintered history may explain one puzzling phenomenon: Fold-Pak boxes from the East and West Coasts of the United States are made slightly differently. On the East Coast, the wire always runs the short length of the box; on the West Coast, it runs the long way. In Texas you'll see both. I placed the two different cartons from the two different coasts side by side and felt the same disoriented sense as when someone tells you that water rotates one way around the drain north of the equator and in the opposite direction south of the equator.

The white take-out containers are a fairly mature market item, so aside from the industry itself, there's not a lot of outside opportunities for growth. "It's so identified with Chinese food that delis and other places could use it—it's a great package—but they identify it with Chinese food," Tim explained. So the company adapted, pushing a new upscale product called Bio-Pak. These flatter, wireless versions of the traditional take-out carton, available in neutral, warm colors, are preferred by classier food establishments that don't want the connotation of the white carton. Whole Foods, for example, uses them at the salad bar.

Decades ago, Fold-Pak company executives visited China to see if there was an opportunity there for the take-out boxes but decided against moving into the market. "It really would have been an uphill climb," Tim said.

Why? I asked.

"Because the Chinese take-out phenomenon in the United States doesn't exist in China."

The take-out cartons aren't even sold in Canada, he told me. I was surprised, given Canada's geographical and cultural proximity to the United States. "We're still trying to get into the Canadian market," he said. "They do the foam and the aluminum."

But international buyers spring up in unexpected places. Fold-Pak often gets telephone calls and e-mail messages from distant parts of the world. "We'll get inquiries from different countries in Europe and Africa, wanting to get the product they see in *Seinfeld*," he said. American television shows have a world-wide audience. Viewers see the box as hip and glamorous, he explained. "They'll say, 'We saw this on *Seinfeld* or *Friends*—where do we get it?' "

When Americans look at the box they see something Chinese. When others look at the box, they think of America.

CHAPTER 10

The Oldest Surviving
Fortune Cookies in the World?

Most fortune cookies from the Los Angeles area are now made by Mexican labor, as is a surprising amount of the Chinese food in the area: noodles, wonton wrappers, egg-roll skins—even the handmade dumplings in some of the most famous dumpling houses around Los Angeles. Your waitress up front may be Chinese, but there's a good chance a cook in the back is Chicano.

A large source for Mexican-made Chinese food is one of the largest fortune cookie factories on the West Coast today, Peking Noodle, founded in 1922.

Stephen Tong, a sprightly ninety-year-old man whose family owns Peking Noodle, greeted me in the company's office. He had plump cheeks and wore a newsboy cap, producing the overall effect of a man from Mao-era China. But when he spoke, instead of a barrage of rural Chinese aphorisms, I heard a native southern California accent; he has lived in the area more or less continuously for eighty-six years, since arriving from China in 1921 as a toddler, to join his father. His daughter Beverly hurried in and chided her father to put in his teeth before our interview.

As a child in the 1930s, Stephen had to fold fortune cookies after school. "I burned my fingers to a crisp," he barked. But he did it to earn money for dates.

"In those days, we sold directly to the restaurants. Business was pretty small-scale," he said. Were fortune cookies Chinese or Japanese in origin? I asked him point-blank. "Japanese," he said without hesitation. By his recollection, the first dominant fortune cookie manufacturer in the Los Angeles area was the Hamano family, whose company, Umeya, was one of the earliest mass producers of fortune cookies. By the 1930s, Umeya was distributing fortune cookies to more than 120 Japanese-owned restaurants throughout central and southern California. "A lot of Chinese restaurants were owned by Japanese," Stephen said, noting that there wasn't a lot of demand for sushi back then. "They opened Chinese restaurants as a means to an income."

One day, Stephen was in his car when the radio reported that Japan had attacked Pearl Harbor. He immediately drove home. "When you hear news that your country has been attacked, there is a fear in you that you may not survive this, because the attack was massive, sort of like 9/11," he recalled. His Japanese neighbors were forced to evacuate. "They had to dispose of their businesses and their automobiles. It was frightening. The Japanese had to give up everything," he remembered. Umeya closed down shop and relocated to Denver, where it continued to make Japanese sweets. After the war, Umeya moved back to Los Angeles and started producing fortune cookies again. The company divvied up the national fortune cookie territory with its sister company in New York City, called Twixt, owned by the Okuno family.

But things had changed. Beverly added, "The relationship between the Chinese and Japanese was very different after the war than before the war."

Eighty-five years ago, Peking Noodle splintered off from the Hong Kong Noodle Company, one of the longest continuously running Chinese businesses on the West Coast today—and a candidate for the originator of the fortune cookie. Though much has changed around the Hong Kong Noodle Company, little about the factory itself has. It is still located in the same flat-roofed building in the same nook of a street where it was founded in 1913. It still makes noodles, wonton skins, egg-roll wrappers. The biggest change may be its Mexican employees.

Merlin Lowe, whose father bought the company from David Jung's family, met me outside the building and led me inside, where he sat down at a desk that had been in the building for four generations. As company lore had it, fortune cookies were invented by David Jung as an appetizer, not a dessert, Merlin explained. There used to be a restaurant around the corner attached to the Hong Kong Noodle Company, and it had some very impatient customers. "When they used to wait, they would get—I wouldn't say 'violent,' that's a strong word," he told me. "They would get restless because they had to wait such a long time."

David Jung's son George Cheng had long claimed that his father had gotten the idea of fortune cookies from an ancient game played among the upper classes in China. Individuals would be given pen, paper, and a twisted cake that contained a scrap of paper with a subject written on it. Using the pen, the paper, and the subject, the writers were expected to compose a narrative of wisdom.

Hong Kong Noodle Company stopped making cookies around 2000. For Merlin, the decision was emotional and traumatic. "That really hurt. Not only is it part of my childhood, it's part of the history of Hong Kong Noodle Company," he said. But the finances demanded it—the competition from the larger companies, the same as that faced by Lotus, in San Francisco, was vicious. "We were losing money," he said. "If we were breaking even on it, I would have kept it going."

As we were talking, Merlin's father looked in the office door, said nothing, and moved past. Merlin explained that his father didn't like to talk about the fortune cookie or make a big deal about Hong Kong Noodle's role in its origins; it's a Chinese approach not to talk about things. Merlin, on the other hand, thought it was good to share their history.

Back then, the residents of the surrounding neighborhood, a mix of Chinese, Japanese, blacks, whites, and Latinos, easily intermingled. "Around this neighborhood, Chinese and Japanese were all friends," he said. Ideas were freely shared. "David Jung had a Japanese friend that helped him make the first fortune cookie machine," Merlin told me.

I asked him about a widespread story that had been printed in the *New York Times* and used in the 1983 trial: that David Jung had invented the cookie to cheer up downtrodden men on the streets of Los Angeles and that a minister had written the messages inside. Merlin didn't buy it. "If it were true then I would have heard it from my dad, but since we are Chinese, things like that wouldn't be 'bragged' about," he explained. "So, yes, the cookies could have been made for that purpose, but I have a hard time believing it." (That widely shared story, it turns out, has a sketchy provenance. Some digging in library archives turned up paperwork that traced it back to a library researcher in the San Joaquin Valley who was a friend of the Jung family.)

As we were sitting there, Merlin fished among the debris on the ancient desk and pulled out a brightly colored tin can whose yellow, green, and red label read "Hong Kong Brand Tea Cakes."

Beside the name was a drawing of two fortune cookies lying side by side.

"Tea cakes?" I asked. Why were the cookies called tea cakes?

Merlin shrugged. "In my experience, they were just called tea cakes," he told me. He also showed me a baker's hat imprinted with the words "Fortune tea cakes." "Tea cake" and "fortune tea cake" were common names for the cookie early on, before it became known as "fortune cooky" and ultimately, with a modern spelling, "fortune cookie." During World War II, "Chinese fortune tea cakes" were brought under the control of the Office of Price Administration. They were freed in August 1946.

Merlin guesstimated that the tin can must be at least sixty years old, because the company had stopped using such cans by the 1950s. Based on the style of the art, which was something I associated with children's books from the 1930s, I would have guessed so too.

The next thing out of his mouth astounded me.

"It's never been opened," he said.

I inspected the top of the can and saw that, indeed, it was still sealed. I held it up to my ear and shook. There was the rustle of crunchy confectionery against metal. While the cookies had not all disintegrated to powder, they were definitely not entirely whole anymore. I looked in amazement at this tin of sixty-year-old fortune cookies that had sat in this office all this time. They may very well be the oldest surviving fortune cookies on the planet.

Later in the conversation, I moved my arm and accidentally knocked over the tin can. Horrified, I envisioned the final cookie fragments disintegrating from the jolt. I began effusively apologizing to Merlin.

"It's okay." He shrugged. "I wouldn't want to open it now anyway."

• • •

Less than a mile from the Hong Kong Noodle Company was yet another artifact attesting to the fortune cookie's origin. This one came from the oldest surviving store in Little Tokyo, a small Japanese sweetshop called Fugetsu-do. The shop, originally started by a Japanese immigrant named Seiichi Kito in 1903, had been passed down through three generations. At one time, the store had displayed black iron molds in the window, ones that had supposedly been used to make the original fortune cookies.

I walked inside Fugetsu-do and was confronted with glass cases containing a whole array of treats: colorful rice taffy called *mochi,* steamed red bean cakes called *manju,* and round and curved Japanese crackers of various shapes called *senbei.*

Brian Kito, the founder's grandson, still made the Japanese sweets by hand in the back rooms of the shop, where a light dusting of flour stuck to everything that passed through (including me). Fugetsu-do's clientele had a strong geriatric bent. Old Japanese-American men shuffled in on canes; old Japanese-American women with wispy gray hair and liver spots approached the counter. This was a candy store filled with the elderly rather than children. To broaden the appeal of the traditional Japanese desserts, the store had started making rice cakes in grape, orange, and lemon flavors, hoping to attract the generation that had grown up with Blow Pops and Sour Patch Kids. It even sold a version of strawberry-flavored *mochi* filled with crunchy peanut butter instead of red bean paste, which made it seem like an eccentric cousin of the peanut butter and jelly sandwich.

When he was growing up in Los Angeles, Brian was skeptical about his father's stories about his grandfather's role in the fortune cookie creation. After all, everyone knew that fortune cookies were Chinese. Then, as a teenager, he watched an episode of *Ripley's Believe It or Not* that said the fortune cookie was actually invented by the Japanese in Los Angeles. Once he had seen it on television, he thought his father might actually be telling the truth.

Brian brought me to Fugetsu-do's warehouse, located a few blocks away in downtown Los Angeles. He gestured to a disassembled fortune cookie machine in the center. Fugetsu-do had bought it from a Japanese bakery when it went bankrupt a few decades ago. What was left was crumpled mechanics: a large wheel, gas pipes, and various gears. Rummaging in the dark crevice beneath the wheel, Brian pulled out a set of black iron molds—similar to the ones that Sally Osaki must have exhibited at the trial. Two round black discs were connected to handles that separated them, like a pair of pliers. I eyed them. Could these be the original fortune cookie molds?

A lot of things had been lost during the war, Brian said. The family had stored their confectionery equipment in a warehouse before they were interned. But at the end of the war they could not get their belongings out, because either someone had stolen the equipment or the landlord had demanded several years of back rent. It took them years to reestablish their store.

A few blocks down from Fugetsu-do lived Gary Ono, the amateur historian of the family that owned the Benkyodo store in San Francisco, one of the claimants to the invention of the fortune cookie.

Gary dug around and pulled out his set of black grills, similar to the ones at Fugetsu-do, called *kata*. They were heavy. I looked at the inside of the discs and saw the letters "HM" etched there.

"Makoto Hagiwara," Gary said, referring to the man who'd originally overseen the Japanese Tea Garden.

The mirror image of "HM"—the way the letters would read on a cookie—was "MH," Makoto Hagiwara's initials. Gary said that a few years back he had found them, rusting, on the floor of a room used to store Benkyodo equipment behind a family garage.

A Japanese researcher had come to San Francisco a while ago, asking probing questions about fortune cookies. Her research showed that fortune cookies were Japanese, based on something called *tsujiura senbei,* which she had traced to shrines outside Kyoto.

This was the first I had heard of such a researcher. Gary pulled out a binder and showed me her paper, which, unfortunately for both of us, was written in Japanese. I could at least read a little bit of the Japanese characters, because they were based on Chinese written language. The Chinese word *jianbing* ("grilled biscuit") appeared often—I assumed that was *senbei* in Japanese, a term that could be used to describe a cookie or cracker, often served with tea.

Gary couldn't read any of the writing. His first language was English and, like many third-generation Japanese-Americans, he had never developed strong Japanese reading and writing skills. But there was something that neither of us needed language ability to translate. On one page of the paper was a Meiji-era wood-block print of a man in a kimono, his hair swept up in a bun. He was working in a Japanese shop and manipulating what appeared to be about a dozen fortune cookie grills over a fire—similar to the *kata* grills that belonged to Gary and Brian. But it was the date that grabbed my attention. Amid the Japanese cutline was a single year, 1878—decades earlier than any of the claims of other would-be fortune cookie inventors in the United States. My quest to understand the phenomenon of Chinese fortune cookies in America had suddenly pointed me to Japan.

CHAPTER 11

The Mystery of the
Missing Chinese Deliveryman

Crime reporters in New York City quickly become versed in the vocabulary of death. A "DOA" is a dead body. A "floater" is a body found in the water. A "jumper" is a person on the verge of committing suicide, usually from a building, a bridge, or in the subway. A "likely" is someone likely to die. A "not likely" is someone injured but likely to survive. A police rundown of a multiple shooting might go: "We have two DOAs, one likely, and one not likely."

Each of the cramped newspaper offices in the headquarters of the New York Police Department has an old-school beige telephone. The public relations office of the police department makes calls—referred to as hotline calls—when, late in the day, it has something pressing to announce to the media en masse. When nothing is pressing, the police simply send out summaries of the crimes.

One slow Saturday April afternoon, I was working when the beige phone, the hotline phone, rang. We all picked up.

"We have a missing person," said the police sergeant on the other end.

A police hotline call about a missing person is unusual. People go missing all the time in New York, especially teenagers. With a burgeoning population of Alzheimer's patients, the city is finding itself with an increasing number of people who simply wander off, misled by their own dementia. (In one recent case, an elderly man passed through immigration at John F. Kennedy Airport but disappeared before he got to the curb.) Others run away because of debt, or bad marriages. Usually the police simply send out a sheet with an attached photo, asking for the public's help in locating the person. For the police to do a late-afternoon hotline call meant that the investigators thought this was a bad situation. Then we found out why.

It was a Chinese deliveryman.

The sergeant gave a quick rundown of what the investigators knew: a Chinese deliveryman had gone missing Friday night in the Bronx while making a delivery to a big apartment building. He had left for the Tracey Towers apartment complex, a few blocks from the restaurant, with an order of large curried shrimp with onion and a small shrimp fried rice. He never came back. His worried restaurant coworkers went to look for him and found his bike still locked up outside the building. They called the police.

The investigators started treating the case seriously when they realized that he had none of the debts or conflicts that generally explain why people disappear. By the time the sergeant called the reporters, the search had been going for some eighteen hours.

The police subsequently sent out a sheet, written in the department's standard terse, capitalized style, with the missing man's name misspelled:

ON APRIL 1, 2005 AT 2200 HRS, THE FOLLOW-
ING PERSON WAS REPORTED MISSING BY A FAMILY
MEMBER:

MISSING: MING KUNG CHEN M/A/35
4211 THROGS NECK EXPRESSWAY
BRONX NY

MISSING WAS LAST SEEN V/O WEST MOSHOLU
PKWY AT 2030 HRS WHILE HE WAS WORKING AS A
FOOD DELIVERY PERSON. ANYONE WITH INFOR-
MATION ON HIS WHEREABOUTS IS ASKED TO CALL
POLICE AT 800 577-TIPS. ALL CALLS WILL BE KEPT
CONFIDENTIAL. NO PHOTO AVAIL AT THIS TIME.

I called a young freelance reporter, Rachel Metz, and sent her
up to the take-out Chinese restaurant in the Bronx. It turns out
that Rachel, who is Jewish, has a longtime family connection to
Chinese restaurants; her grandfather owned and operated one in
Syracuse for years. Rachel called me back with some information
from the restaurant. Chen had paid $60,000 to emigrate from
Fujian Province two years earlier, where he had left behind his
wife and their twelve-year-old son. After adding further details
from Rachel's reporting, I tapped out a brief story. Things didn't
look good for Mr. Chen.

Chinese deliverymen are one of the most vulnerable species
in the urban ecosystem. Homicide is a leading cause of on-the-
job deaths; the motive is nearly always robbery. Five New York
City Chinese deliverymen were killed between 1998 and 2003
alone, simply for free food and a handful of cash. None of their
killers was even old enough to drink. Three teenagers, a girl and
two boys, were sentenced for the 2002 murder of Jian Lin-Chun,

a Chinese deliveryman in the Bronx. The girl had called in an order to Happy House Chinese restaurant. The two boys pulled a gun on the deliveryman when he showed up and shot him when he pulled out a knife to defend himself. He had twelve dollars in his pocket. The girl took no share of the cash; all she wanted was the Chinese food: thirteen dollars' worth of General Tso's chicken, chicken and broccoli, chicken wings, and fries. Two years earlier, in Queens, a forty-four-year-old Chinese deliveryman, Jin-Sheng Liu, was brutally murdered; five teenagers beat him to death with a brick to get sixty dollars' worth of Chinese food. After they killed him, they went back to one home and ate the Chinese food. But perhaps the most callous of all was the 2004 murder of an eighteen-year-old student named Huang Chen, who was helping out at his parents' restaurant in Queens. His older sister Yvonne had told him he needed to do well in school or he would also be forced to work in the Chinese-restaurant business. His killers, who were sixteen years old at the time, later told police that they wanted money to buy Air Jordan sneakers. Though he pleaded for his life, they stabbed him with their knives; to prevent his body from being recognized, they beat his head in with a hammer and a baseball bat. Then they wrapped his body in a piece of plastic and dumped it in a pond three miles away. When police found the teens, they still had the blood-soaked dollar bills on them; they'd aroused suspicion when one of the killers had asked a friend if dead bodies float.

The violence doesn't always grab headlines. There is a constant hum of low-level assaults. During a stop in Hutchinson, Minnesota, on my Powerball restaurant tour, I met Ting Young Zheng, the owner of King's Wok, a huge buffet restaurant where one of the winners had gotten his lucky numbers. "When I hear of New York, my head still hurts," said Ting, who had been robbed three times as a New York City deliveryman, once at gunpoint. "Sometimes you get through half the route and you are robbed," he said, shaking his head. In 1992 he was kidnapped and held for ransom. As a deliveryman, he was beaten so severely that his bones still ache when the weather changes.

The NYPD carried out a massive search for Ming Kuang Chen. Helicopters conducting aerial searches hovered overhead. Dogs trained to smell cadavers spread out over an area encompassing Van Cortlandt Park and Woodlawn Cemetery. Divers were sent to the bottom of the Jerome Park Reservoir in case the body, like Huang Chen's, had been submerged in water. And over one hundred police officers and detectives fanned out to search the 871 apartments in the two high-rise towers.

On Sunday, the police sent out another update.

*****UPDATE 4-3-05 LC*****

ATTACHED IS A PHOTO OF THE MISSING ASIAN MALE MING KUNG CHEN. THE MISSING WAS LAST SEEN ON FRIDAY 4/01/05 AT APPROX. 2030 HRS AT 40 WEST MOSHOLU PARKWAY SOUTH. MR. CHEN IS DESCRIBED AS A M/A/35, 5'8'', THIN BUILD, BLACK HAIR, LAST SEEN WEARING A GREY BASEBALL CAP, WAIST LENGTH BLUE JACKET WITH STRIPES ON THE SLEEVES, BLUE JEANS, BLACK SHOES. THE BICY-CLE THE MISSING USED TO MAKE DELIVERIES WAS FOUND CHAINED TO A FIXED OBJECT OUTSIDE THE LOCATION. THE INVESTIGATION IS ONGOING.

Officially it was still a missing-persons report. Off the record, investigators were saying he was probably dead. "It's only a mat-ter of time before they are going to find a body," one officer con-fided to me on the phone.

It is unusually difficult to hide a corpse in New York City.

Nearly everything is paved, so you can't bury it. Only a fraction of people have cars, so the odds are slim that a killer can toss a body in a trunk and drive far away. Ordinary people are about during all hours, so it's hard to lug a large, bulky package around without attracting attention. And there aren't that many woods to go dumping bodies in. Murderers aren't, in general, the sharpest pencils in the box. Nor are they necessarily forward thinkers. With such a high-density population, the bodies are almost always discovered, sometimes in unpredictable locations—wrapped in carpets, in suitcases, in giant Rubbermaid winter storage boxes.

Death is only the lowest point in what is almost universally the miserable existence of a Chinese restaurant worker. As many told me, "What choice do we have when we don't speak English?" They are treated like farm animals or machines. Their purpose is simply to feed Americans: frying, delivering, waiting tables, stirring, bussing, chopping. They may be fathers, daughters, cousins, uncles, brothers. But when in front of most Americans, they simply become an anonymous, all-purpose Chinese restaurant worker. They work twelve-hour days and six-day weeks. The abuse is not limited to violence at the hands of Americans; in fact, the average Chinese restaurant worker's misery is actually caused by restaurant owners. Some owners treat their workers respectfully. Others try to get away with as much as they can. In a world inhabited by illegal immigrants afraid of authorities, what they can get away with is a lot: underpaying, overworking, sexual harassment. In recent years, workers have been fighting back with a number of lawsuits spearheaded by advocacy groups.

Restaurant workers live a nomadic existence, bouncing from state to state, restaurant to restaurant, region to region. A chef who's cooking in Connecticut today could be stir-frying in Louisiana next week. The woman who answers the take-out phone today in North Carolina could be in Ohio in a few months. Every week they arrive in Chinatown from all corners of the United States.

The largest and most efficient distribution hub for these restaurant workers lies some seventeen miles south of where Mr. Chen disappeared—under the Manhattan Bridge in New York City's Chinatown. While other urban centers like Boston, Chicago, Houston, and Atlanta have employment agencies, New York still remains the dominant source of Chinese restaurant workers, particularly east of the Rockies.

Unlike a McDonald's or a Burger King, which can find employees from its local population, many Chinese restaurants operate in small cities and out-of-the-way towns where there simply isn't a local Chinese population to draw from. The solution: they import workers from other areas. At the beginning of every week, a steady stream of phone calls from restaurants needing workers flows into the agencies under the Manhattan Bridge. To match them, Chinese workers begin streaming into the Chinatown employment agencies: young men with spiky hair barely out of their teens, smooth-skinned girls who still giggle about their crushes, and stocky older men who left their families behind in China years ago. They are deliverymen, cooks, waitresses, kitchen helpers. They work in restaurants, they say, because they have no choice.

As the deep rumble of the subway passes overhead, the job seekers walk in and out, through the dozens of dusty single-room employment agencies, focusing on the whiteboards and walls of Post-it notes that list the hundreds, if not thousands, of Chinese-restaurant job openings that pass through the area each week. Three numbers identify a job to a restaurant worker: the monthly salary, the area code where the restaurant is located, and the number of hours by bus from New York City. To these Chinese restaurant workers, who can barely read

English, the United States is not a series of towns or states. It is a collection of area codes, almost all of which have dozens upon dozens of Chinese restaurants looking for help. Rent and cost of living are not usually considered when relocating. The restaurant owners feed their workers, and it is standard to provide dorm-style housing.

A job could be summed up thus: $2,400, 440 near Cleveland, 10 hours.

The interviews, done by phone, are practical and blunt. These are jobs, not careers. Instead of "What do you see yourself doing in five years?" it's "Can you leave tonight?"

If the parties agree, the job seeker then pays the agency, and the agency tells him where to catch the bus that night. A network of Chinese bus companies has sprung up to shuttle these restaurant workers between Chinatown and the rest of the country. A typical bus advertisement: "Minnesota (612, 651, 952, 763) $150, Wisconsin (920, 715, 608, 414) $120." The destinations are written by people familiar with American geography but unfamiliar with American spelling: Detrot, Harford, Frankfort, Ann Arbol, Louisuille, Evansiue, Coumbus, Beltimore, Willmington, Teledo.

These Chinese-restaurant buses are not entirely unfamiliar to the American mainstream. The budget "Chinatown buses" that shuttle between New York and Boston and New York and Washington originally started out as routes for Chinese restaurant workers, before college students and the Lonely Planet crowd caught on. The buses exploded in popularity in the late 1990s, and the competition sparked violence between rival bus companies.

I have bussed through Indiana, Ohio, Chicago, Wisconsin, Minnesota, Tennessee, South Carolina, North Carolina, Georgia, and Virginia. Seen from the window of a Chinese-restaurant bus, America looks entirely different: a large web of highways connecting little towns, modest cities, and sprawling suburbs, all of which have Chinese restaurants or will have Chinese restaurants. In one overnight trip, I woke up from my position curled on the bus seat and gazed out into the early-morning light streaming through the smoggy haze. We had stopped at a gas station in Toledo, a transfer point. Half the people got off the bus and were shuttled off in waiting vans. They were being taken to other Ohio cities—Cleveland, Columbus, Cincinnati—and from there to smaller suburbs. Like a river splitting into streams.

The police found their suspect.

A neighbor reported hearing screams from apartment 34A. Police rapped on the door. No one home. The emergency services unit kicked down the door, leaving boot marks on the paint. They overturned the furniture. They ransacked the living room, kitchen, and bedrooms. Drawers, cabinets, freezer—everything was searched.

They found nothing. Then the apartment's inhabitant, Troy Smith, a twenty-one-year-old aspiring rapper, returned. He was shocked to find officers with flak jackets and automatic weapons standing in his apartment.

They noticed a suspicious red stain on his gray T-shirt.

What is that? The detectives asked him.

Barbecue sauce, he replied. It was three days old and from a Chinese restaurant.

Right.

Unfortunately for Troy, he had a five-year-old outstanding warrant; he'd failed to show up for a disorderly conduct summons when he was a teenager. That provided the opening the police needed.

They handcuffed him.

His mother, who had been alerted at work by a phone call from a detective, returned home and was horrified to find her son in handcuffs. In front of gaping neighbors, the police dragged Troy and two friends of his to the police car and drove them to the precinct. They grilled him for hours.

"Where is the Chinese man and what did you do with him?" the detectives growled at Troy.

Troy insisted that he had no idea what they were talking about.

Then you won't mind if we take your shirt in for testing, they said.

Go ahead, he told them. He signed a release for his gray T-shirt. It said, "I'm Troy Smith. You can have my shirt for testing."

Meanwhile one of his friends, a stout man with a goatee, was being questioned in another room.

Don't go down with your friend with the so-called barbecue sauce on his shirt, the detectives cajoled.

Troy's friend insisted he had no idea what had happened to the Chinese deliveryman.

The test came back from the lab.

It was barbecue sauce.

Troy's friend told me, after his release, "Every black man who orders Chinese food is under suspicion." Not only is there DWB, there's also OWB—Ordering While Black.

Within the dreariness of the Chinese restaurant worker's life, there is one day that is different from all the others. For many it is the happiest and most romantic day of the year, full of reunions and laughter and joy. It is not Valentine's Day, with its plump cupids, or New Year's Eve, with its furtive midnight kisses, or even Christmas, with its fresh mistletoe and family dinners.

For Chinese restaurant workers, romantic bliss culminates on Thanksgiving.

More weddings take place in Chinatown on that one single

day than any other for one simple reason: it's the only day that the nation's Chinese restaurant workers can consistently get off. "Americans don't eat Chinese food on Thanksgiving. They eat turkey," said Hong Yi Yuan, the owner of the Wedding Garden bridal shop and one of the main beneficiaries of the Thanksgiving boom.

On the fourth Thursday of each November, you can spot a steady stream of white gowns rustling down the streets of Chinatown, daintily shuffling past the herb shops, acupuncturists' offices, and open seafood markets hawking live crabs and mussels. The brides have glitter in their hair and fake lashes on their eyelids. If you look carefully, you can see that some women are wearing jeans underneath their dresses to keep warm in the chilly weather. Each year, tens of thousands of people, almost all Chinese restaurant workers or former workers, flood into Chinatown on Thanksgiving for hundreds of weddings. Banquet halls are booked more than a year in advance, instead of just a month or two, as is standard for the rest of the year. The marital marathon of multiple simultaneous seatings starts before noon and stretches well into the night.

The chances that Mr. Chen would be found alive seemed more and more remote. I left town for two days. Tuesday morning, as I was stepping off the plane in La Guardia Airport, my phone rang. It was my editor.

"They found him," he announced.

I was confused. Found who? I asked.

"The Chinese deliveryman. They found him in the elevator."

"Alive?"

"Yes, alive."

He had been stuck for three days in an elevator in the building where he'd made his delivery.

My editor commanded: Get to the hospital.

*****UPDATE 04-05-05 0745 HOURS KC*****

AT APPROXIMATELY 0605 HOURS THE ABOVE LISTED MISSING WAS LOCATED IN AN ELEVATOR 40 WEST MOSHOLU PARKWAY IN THE CONFINES OF THE 52 PRECINCT. HE WAS REMOVED TO MONTEFIORE HOSPITAL IN STABLE CONDITION.

Almost eighty-one hours after he had disappeared, Mr. Chen had reappeared, safe and sound—in the very building where he was last seen.

Crime reporters in New York City are a roving pack, a human spotlight that every day lands on another corner of the city. One of the nice things about this is that various reporters in the polyglot swarm will usually take turns translating, depending on the victim. There is the Russian reporter from the *Daily News,* the Dominican-American from *Newsday,* and me, the Mandarin speaker. So that night, we tracked Chen back to the restaurant owner's house in the Bronx, near where Chen himself lived. He recounted his story in Mandarin.

He said he had stepped into the elevator on the thirty-seventh floor on Friday night after making his delivery; the tip, from a retired police officer, had been modest. A man and a woman got into the elevator with him, but then got off at the thirty-fifth floor. As the elevator started moving again, it lurched and then plunged. He felt his body floating off the elevator floor and grabbed the handrail to anchor himself. As he fell to what he thought was certain death, the elevator suddenly slowed, decelerating until it stopped between the third and fourth floors. The car had dropped more than thirty stories.

He banged on the door and screamed, but no one heard him. The elevator, an express, was in a part of its shaft that had no doors between the first floor and the twentieth. He positioned himself in front of the camera. He pressed the emergency button and talked to the security guard. But he didn't speak English. All he could say was "No good! No good!"

Nevertheless, the security guards and the police insisted that they had not known of any of his efforts to contact the outside world.

Three days later, the fire department got a call about a stuck express elevator in the building. There seemed to be a drunk man in it, the security guard said. Using a key, the fireman guided the elevator from its perch to the bottom floor.

The men pried open the door.

There Chen stood, dehydrated but alert.

Improbable as it seems, despite all the dogs, divers, and detectives, no one had ever checked the express elevator. Even though there was a working video camera pointed in the elevator, no one had noticed Chen on the screen.

He had been invisible.

After his brush with the media spotlight, Ming Kuang Chen disappeared. He was afraid the immigration services would come after him, so he found work through the employment agencies in Chinatown. There would be no more delivering for him. He took a kitchen job in another town.

Few stories that start with a Chinese deliveryman as the subject end happily. Several months later another deliveryman, Fa Hua Chen, was shot in the face after making a nine-dollar delivery to a Bronx apartment building and was admitted to the hospital in critical condition. A few days later Chen died from the massive brain injury caused by the bullet. At the time of his death, his daughter, who was studying at the University of Leicester in England, had not seen him in a decade. His wife, who was back in Fujian, China, had not seen him for years either. Bureaucratic red tape threatened to prevent them from attending his funeral in the United States. But John Liu, a Chinese-American New York City Council member from Queens who jumps into all discussions concerning Asian-Americans, lobbied hard to get expedited visas for them.

After the funeral, the mother and daughter went to see the Bronx apartment where the shooting had taken place. They stood there for several minutes. The wife put her hand over the bullet hole in the glass.

Among those at the funeral was Ming Kuang Chen. He slipped in and out of the city quietly. After all, he was only a bus ride away.

CHAPTER 12

The Soy Sauce Trade Dispute

I f visitors from another planet landed in the United States, they would be intrigued by the little transparent packets of brown-black liquid that accumulate in the crevices of households and workplaces across the country. Our visitor would notice that Americans treat the packets with a certain level of carelessness, tossing them aside. Then again, it could be surmised that the packages are precious, because of the way people hoard them for years upon years.

Because Americans are reluctant to throw them away, these visitors might think, the packets must be serving some greater purpose. Perhaps they are stored in preparation for the day when there is a great shortage of the brown-black liquid—in the same way that crude oil will one day run dry. Or perhaps our guest would come to a different conclusion: given that the packets appear in a broad range of households—old, young, black, white, urban, suburban, interior, coastal—the guest might hypothesize that the packets contain an antidote should the nation ever come under a massive biochemical attack.

The vast majority of those clear packets in the United States actually come from a single source: a low-slung soy sauce factory in a quasi-industrial town in New Jersey called Totowa, located about half an hour outside New York City. The factory is owned by a company called Kari-Out, which supplies the things that Chinese restaurants give away: soy sauce packets, fortune cookies, trapezoidal white cartons, wooden chopsticks. I had been led to Kari-Out on the trail of the lucky Powerball numbers.

You have probably never noticed Kari-Out, and you probably aren't familiar with its logo, a ditzy, wide-eyed panda. After all, there's not really much point in a company spending a lot on consumer brand marketing when its entire business model is built on things that are distributed for free. Kari-Out, which is owned by a Jewish family, rose to its prominence in the Chinese-restaurant business from a humble start in soy sauce. Today the factory operates seven days a week, three shifts a day, churning out millions of packets a year.

Look at the label on a bottle of soy sauce from an Asian company, and you'll probably find that the chief ingredients listed are water, soybeans, wheat, and salt. But look at the ingredients on Kari-Out soy sauce—or almost any other American company's soy sauce—and you'll generally find that the most common ingredients are water, hydrolyzed vegetable protein, caramel coloring, and corn syrup.

You may wonder, Where's the soy? Exactly, Asian manufacturers say.

They claim that American soy sauce is not real soy sauce. Soy sauce, the Asians say, should be brewed from soybeans. It's like the difference between vanilla and vanilla extract made from vanilla beans, or real mayonnaise versus the mysterious coagulated substance called Miracle Whip.

Asian "natural-brewed" soy sauce is made by a process not unlike that used with vodka or sake. It requires fermenting a mix of wheat, soybeans, and a particular mold for weeks or even months, then refining, pressing, and pasteurizing it. In contrast, the crudest type of American soy sauce is basically salted water mixed with a flavor enhancer distilled from vegetable proteins. (That flavor enhancer is related to the little flavor packets that come with ramen noodles.) The food coloring and corn syrup give the liquid a vaguely soy sauce–like appearance.

At Kikkoman, the world's largest producer of soy sauce, the managing director of soy sauce operations in Japan, Hiroshi Takamatsu, explained to me what was wrong: "Soy sauce is soy. It comes from soybeans. So the first thing is you have to use soybeans." The Asian companies charge that American processed soy sauce is a Frankensauce chemical counterfeit created by modern science.

Because they believe that it isn't a natural-brewed soy sauce, in 1998 they began a global campaign to prevent it from being classified as such.

The forum for international food-definition battles is the Codex Alimentarius Commission, one of those international regulatory organizations whose actions are barely noticed by the outside world. Yet the bureaucratic jujitsu performed there exercises great influence over many industries and countries. Created in 1962 by two U.N. organizations, Codex sets the international standards for foodstuffs around the world. For instance, international regulations have limited the term "champagne" to sparkling wine from a particular region in the north of France, and "Parmigiano-Reggiano cheese" to a particular region and production method in Italy. These labels are important in cases of exporting and importing as the global food-supply chains become more far-reaching. Codex makes the de facto rules for the World

Trade Organization's trade-dispute court. It is where hummus is defined as hummus, mineral water as mineral water, and cottage cheese as cottage cheese. The agenda for a Codex meeting often reads like a shopping list from Dean & DeLuca: whole dates, dried figs, table olives, shredded coconut.

In Japan, I paid a visit to Natsuko Kumasawa, a food advocate from Tokyo who was involved in pushing the soy sauce labeling campaign. The problem with Codex, Natsuko-san explained as she poured me green tea in her stylish living room, was that it was dominated by foods from European and North American countries. "We feel sort of isolated. Many Asian countries felt we need some standards for Asian food. We thought of some Asian foods and we thought of soy sauce," she said. After all, what could be more quintessentially Asian than soy sauce?

The dark seasoning's history stretches back over several millennia. By legend it began to spread internationally when a Japanese Zen Buddhist monk discovered it during his studies in China. He brought a version back to his native country in the thirteenth century, where he adapted it. In various forms soy sauce spread widely through East and Southeast Asia. Today, it's a staple used in Korea, Malaysia, Indonesia, and Thailand, albeit with local varieties. Western cuisine was introduced to soy sauce primarily through Dutch explorers in the seventeenth century.

The Japanese were not alone in trying to codify their Asian culinary products at Codex. Around the same time, the Koreans applied for a standard for kimchee, their famed spicy pickled cabbage. The dish is such an essential part of the country's cultural identity that Korean supermarkets in United States sell $600 kimchee refrigerators, not unlike the private wine fridges for chardonnay connoisseurs. Kimchee has a fairly narrow audience around the world. Only a smattering of countries took a vigorous interest in the kimchee standard that was proposed in

1996. After some minor tussling that beat back a Japanese attempt to get pickled *kimuchi*, as it is called in Japan, included in the standard, Codex passed a kimchee regulation in 2001.

Soy sauce, however, was of a different order of magnitude. It may have been created in China, but by the turn of the second millennium A.D. it had made its way not only across Asia but around the world as one of civilization's most popular condiments. In Japan it is known as *shoyu*. In Peru it is called *sillao*. In China it is *jiangyou*. Malaysia and Indonesia use a version of sweetened soy sauce called *kecap manis;* that term is often credited as the precursor to "ketchup." (The Asian varieties are tomatoless, however. Culinary historians surmise that the tomato was added when the condiment hopped over to Europe.)

In a way, Asian soy sauce manufacturers had pushed the very mainstreaming that was now causing their problems. Since Kikkoman's earliest days in the United States, it had made grainy black-and-white television commercials urging housewives to use Kikkoman when cooking steaks, pot roasts, chicken, or hamburgers. Executives back then realized that Asians in America were going to buy soy sauce anyway; growth would have to come from convincing mainstream American cooks that soy sauce should be part of their culinary arsenal. Today, an entire department in Kikkoman's American headquarters in San Francisco is devoted to developing recipes for women's magazines, labels, and press releases. Kikkoman recommends adding the product to spaghetti sauce, barbecue sauce, salad dressings, and salmon marinade. The only significant resistance the public relations people ever encountered occurred after they suggested incorporating soy sauce in Thanksgiving recipes.

For the Codex regulations, the Japanese were hoping to adapt a standards system long used in Japan. It would divide soy sauce into long-term brewed, short-term brewed, nonbrewed, and mixed. Natsuko explained that they first tried to build consensus among the Asian countries, so that they would arrive as a united front. The Japanese didn't have nonbrewed soy sauce, but they added the category to accommodate the other Asian nations' concerns. "It's an Asian food," she said. "First we thought no countries except Asian ones will be interested in it."

They were wrong. As politicians would delicately put it, by this point, the soy sauce industry had a lot of stakeholders.

You wouldn't think that American soy sauce manufacturers would care about labels used in exporting soy sauce. But they do. For example, La Choy, the largest American bottled soy sauce manufacturer, exports its soy sauce to fifty-six countries around the world. The top five markets are Jamaica, Haiti, Greece, St. Martin, and Belize.

"They didn't think that this kind of confusion would come up," Natsuko told me. "Because many countries in Europe and North America are interested, we decided to move it to the Processed Foods and Vegetables Committee at the International Association of Consumer Food Organizations." That's where things got more and more hairy, Natsuko said: "The discussion, it became too heated."

What makes Chinese food taste so good?

Part of the answer lies in soy sauce. Brewed soy sauce naturally has what is known as the "fifth flavor." After the easily identified ones—sweet, bitter, salty, and sour—comes "umami," which means "savory" in Japanese. It's hard to describe umami; it is a hearty or meaty taste. It's the low note on a three-note chord. Or, to use another metaphor from music, umami is the subwoofer of taste. It's what gives Parmesan cheese, ripe tomatoes, and mushrooms their hearty flavor. Umami was first identified by Kikunae Ikeda of Tokyo Imperial University, who found it while probing the strong taste in seaweed broth in 1908. That flavor, which came from glutamates, was isolated as a salt and patented in 1909 by the Ajinomoto corporation as the chemical monosodium glutamate, more familiar to Americans as MSG. Today Ajinomoto is the world's largest MSG producer, controlling about one-third of the global market.

MSG's reputation has since become tainted. Fear of it began in 1968, when the concept of "Chinese restaurant syndrome" was introduced in the *New England Journal of Medicine* in a chatty piece by Dr. Ho Man Kwok. "I have experienced a strange syndrome whenever I have eaten out in a Chinese restaurant, especially one that served northern Chinese food," he wrote. "The syndrome, which usually begins 15 to 20 minutes after I have eaten the first dish, lasts for about two hours, without hangover effect. The most prominent symptoms are numbness at the back of the neck, gradually radiating to both arms and the back, general weakness and palpitations."

Finally, in 1992 the FDA asked the Federation of American Societies for Experimental Biology, an independent body of scientists, to review the available scientific data on adverse reactions to MSG. The report identified two groups of people who might develop "MSG symptom complex." One group was made up of people who couldn't tolerate large doses of MSG, generally more than three grams. The second group included people with severe, poorly controlled asthma who experienced temporary worsening of their asthmatic symptoms after consuming MSG. But for most people, MSG was safe at normal levels, the report concluded. Scientific studies following the test have not been able to fully support the report's conclusions.

Despite the fact that the nonbrewed soy sauce category would include the processed American version, the American delegation began a protest. Suddenly, the International Hydrolyzed Protein Council appeared on the horizon. The United States

Department of Agriculture, the lead American agency at Codex, argued against any labeling at all.

Natsuko and the other Asian representatives were dumbfounded. "The International Hydrolyzed Protein Council and the American government thought the distinction was not necessary," she said.

Martin J. Hahn, a Washington lobbyist for the International Hydrolyzed Protein Council, explained the situation to me quite reasonably: "We were trying to make certain that the Codex standards would allow and maintain some degree of flexibility." The products had been manufactured and sold as soy sauce in the United States and in other parts of the world for decades without complaints. Why shake up the system now? Washington lobbyists have a way of sounding incredibly reasonable while simultaneously making new regulations seem unreasonable. He added, "Let's maintain some flexibility. Let's recognize that in different countries, it is common to use hydrolyzed proteins and call it soy sauce."

The Japanese delegation was confused by hydrolyzed vegetable protein, which they had never heard of in the context of soy sauce. They asked for a sample and were confused when they saw it was just a white powder. As Natsuko explained, "We didn't think it [was] a food."

America has simplified—or corrupted, depending on your perspective—and mass-processed many refined foods from around the world: beer (ask Germans what they think of American beer); chocolate (the Swiss grimace when they bite into a waxy Hershey's chocolate bar); cheese (whoever branded the processed orange substance with "American" should be boiled in it). But it was quite another matter for Americans to apply their industrial standards to a product that was so distinctively Asian.

"That's black water with salt," Natsuko said about the sauce in a packet. Real soy sauce is actually reddish-brown. It becomes more brown and less red the more contact it has with oxygen. Soy sauce traditionalists point out that the brewed product has a different chemical profile than the nonbrewed stuff. The brewing process also generates alcohol and aroma-contributing esters that contribute a refined tartness to a good soy sauce.

Hydrolyzed vegetable protein is actually a chemical and industrial relation to MSG, only without the stigma of that acronym. (The connections run deep. When I mentioned to the International Hydrolyzed Protein Council representative that I was looking for a contact for the MSG industry group, he told me it was he.) To create hydrolyzed vegetable protein, a combination of corn, wheat, and soybean meal is boiled in hydrochloric acid for the better part of a day, to isolate the amino acids. American food companies explain that this is simply a sped-up version of what happens during the natural fermentation process. This acid stew is then neutralized with sodium carbonate or sodium hydroxide. When it is filtered, the result is hydrolyzed vegetable protein.

To be fair, at one point Japan also made so-called chemical soy sauce, but that was after World War II, when many supplies, including soybeans, were scarce. Other countries have also depended on the shortcut process now and then. But as Asian economies have grown, food manufacturers have shied away from such additives. That has left the United States as the largest such soy sauce producer in the world. The largest American bottle brand is La Choy, founded in 1922 by two men, neither of whom had Chinese roots. Wally Smith, a Detroit businessman, and Ilhan New, who was born in Korea, met as students at the University of Michigan and joined forces to form a business that would sell the bean sprouts that had become so popular in chop suey. By the late 1930s La Choy was distributing a broad array of Chinese food products, including kumquats, water chestnuts, bamboo shoots, brown sauce, chow mein noodles—and soy sauce. La Choy has since been acquired by the gigantic food conglomerate ConAgra.

But as for the little packets, that market is dominated by Kari-Out. The company was founded in the late 1960s by Howard Epstein, a lanky Bronx-born businessman who had a passion for what he called "small-unit packaging." At different points in his career, he experimented with packaging dry soup mixes, frozen ice pops, hotel toiletries, and chemicals before discovering the joy of soy sauce in 1968. His timing was fortuitous: Chinese takeout started its explosion shortly after President Nixon returned from China and Americans fell in love with pandas. Kari-Out was right behind, pushing packaged soy sauce on a national scale with its newly designed panda logo. Chinese restaurants were among the first to adapt to working women and two-career families by pioneering takeout and delivery. Patronage at "Oriental take-out" restaurants jumped during the 1980s, growing 131 percent between 1982 and 1987 alone, according to a survey by the National Restaurant Association. During that same period, fast-food restaurants grew only 26 percent. Today, about 60 percent of Chinese restaurants in the country are takeouts.

Chinese takeout's biggest rivals for speed and convenience have historically been pizza and fast food. But Chinese food has one advantage: the significant presence of vegetables makes parents feel a bit less guilty about ordering in for dinner. Once upon a time, the whole point of eating restaurant food was going out—dining out was a luxury. Somewhere along the line, however, with more singles and more working mothers, home cooking from scratch instead became the luxury—though judging by the number of richly photographed cookbooks and the popularity of the Food Network, you wouldn't guess how little we actually do of it.

The packets were such a success that by 1972 Howard had added duck sauce and hot mustard to his Kari-Out lineup. He handed the company down to his three sons, who helped grow the business into the largest Chinese-restaurant supplier in the country. Perhaps no single family is as intimately acquainted with the ins and outs of American Chinese takeout as the Epsteins. The sons talk about industry minutiae with the joy that comes from a family-run business. They can discuss the subtleties of the Chinese take-out container. They know fortune cookie shelf life. They converse knowledgeably about the shades of fried rice favored in different parts of the country, and the food coloring that is needed to create those shades. Fried rice tends to be brown in Boston, yellower in New York, and darker in Miami.

A visit to Kari-Out's soy sauce factory naturally produced no soybeans. But their product is still soy sauce, Paul Epstein explained, pointing out that it's actually more sanitary. The natural version involves mold, he said, shaking his head.

Indeed, I encountered both a lot of small organisms and a lot of soy when I visited Kikkoman's main soy sauce factory in the United States. It is even located in the middle of soy and corn fields in Walworth, Wisconsin—a site the company chose in 1970 for its confluence of access to water, soybeans, transportation, and labor. "Microorganisms working every day," said Masaaki Hirose, a senior vice president, with a smile as he gave me a tour. The Kikkoman soy factory looks a lot like a petrochemical factory—massive tanks, running pipes, and glaring fluorescent lights—only with the musky aroma of soy sauce permeating the air. A display case hangs on the wall in the manufacturing area. It has three jars: one each of soy, wheat, and salt. "These are the three main ingredients of soy sauce," said Mr. Hirose. "Unlike chemical soy sauce." Next to the display was a large flowchart of how the soy sauce is made, with boxes featuring the *koji* culture, the *shikomi* fermentation, and soy cakes, a by-product that is turned into cattle feed.

We walked into a room filled with rows of large tanks that reached to the ceiling. This was the fermentation room, where the soy sauce changed color. "Sugar gives color to soy sauce," Kuniki Hatayama, the general manager, said. "They discovered more than three hundred flavors in the soy sauce," he told me. "It's naturally occurring." He ticked some of them off: vanilla, coffee, fruit flavors. He noted that it is possible to extract vanilla flavoring from soy sauce, adding, "These flavors are different than chemical soy sauce."

When air is pushed in from underneath the fermenting *moromi* sludge, it looks like bubbling lava. The *moromi* paste is then layered in a zigzag formation between pieces of cloth, where it spends three days having the soy sauce pressed out of it. During that time, a stack of *moromi* that starts out at more than thirty feet high is compressed down to about six feet.

What is left after the soy sauce is extracted is soy cake, which looks like a cross between wood chips and beef jerky. "Is this edible?" I asked, picking up a few of the brown flakes in my fingers.

"Edible, yes, but it doesn't taste so good," Hatayama said.

I put some into my mouth. It tasted like salty cardboard.

Kikkoman personnel served as unofficial advisers to the Japanese government during the great soy sauce debate. At the Kikkoman headquarters in Tokyo, Hiroshi Takamatsu explained what was wrong with the American chemical soy sauce world.

"For me it's not soy sauce, for the Japanese it's not soy sauce. Because if you look at the ingredients, it's not soy," he said. He didn't understand what had happened when soy sauce first went overseas. "These places have no history of soy sauce. Real soy sauce, the fundamental soy sauce, came from China and Japan. Then people have started adding things, changing things.

"There is a breakdown," he said sadly.

The discussions dragged on. In October 2004, the Codex Processed Fruits and Vegetables Committee decided to move the soy sauce discussion to the Cereals, Pulses, and Legumes committee—a bureaucratic punt.

In 2005, Mr. Takamatsu explained, the Japanese government looked at the resistance the Americans were putting up. They looked at the ever-expanding definition of soy sauce and realized it would take a long time to sort out all the competing standards. "It would take decades," he said. At this point, they decided it was better to wait. They quietly withdrew their proposal, biding their time until Americans understood the subtleties of soy sauce. The Americans lobby and its allies had triumphed. There was no need for whole soybeans to make soy sauce.

Natsuko said there was an odd, comforting irony in having the definition of soy sauce wrestled away from them: "We should be proud of it in one way: soy sauce became an international food."

To be fair, Americans are also pushing the envelope on the soy sauce front. Kari-Out introduced its own significant innovation in 2005: gluten-free soy sauce for people who suffer from celiac disease, a digestive condition. And it's not as though the American companies haven't considered the virtues of naturally brewed soy sauce. In 2004, when ConAgra was thinking of reinvigorating the La Choy brand, it conducted a series of blind taste tests across the country, according to Shannon Bridges, the brand manager.

The results of the soy sauce taste tests were somewhat surprising, she told me during my visit to ConAgra offices in Naperville, Illinois. Despite Kikkoman's significant inroads into the United States, half of the consumers liked La Choy, and half liked the naturally brewed soy sauce. Further research led the team to come to a conclusion: "When you think about preferences, it's really what people grew up on and what they know and love," she said. Since lots of people had grown up with La Choy in the household, there was a built-in consumer demand and comfort level. Shannon herself had grown up with La Choy products in her home.

La Choy's soy sauce formula stayed the same.

When told of La Choy's taste test, Kuniki Hatayama, of Kikkoman's Wisconsin factory, nodded sagely. "Taste is a funny thing," he said. "If you grow up with it you tend to like it."

CHAPTER 13

Waizhou, U.S.A.

By the time John and Jenny heard about the modest Chinese restaurant for sale in Georgia, it had already been through the hands of at least four different owners. The restaurant had first opened as Wong's Kitchen, though Mr. Wong had long since moved to Temecula, California, where he now worked as a high school physics and chemistry teacher. Still, its various owners had changed little but the restaurant name in eight years. The staff played the same tape of Chinese zither music as customers ate on the same Chinese zodiac place mats, which lay atop the same seven dark wooden tables. Before diners left, their waiters brought them fortune cookies, which were still stored in a big box under the cash register.

You can learn a lot about a community by reading its advertisements and seeing which goods and services are for sale. Chinese newspapers, like their English counterparts, have classified ads for real estate, used cars, and jobs. Unlike their English counterparts, they have an additional section devoted entirely to the buying and selling of Chinese restaurants. Sometimes the ads will cover half a page, sometimes a full page. But they are always there.

Much as there is a natural churn in the housing market—job relocations, empty nesters, divorces—there is a natural churn for Chinese restaurants. It is considered easier to buy a restaurant than to start one. Construction permits, credit card merchant accounts, and health department inspections mean you need to know English to open a Chinese restaurant. You don't necessarily need to know English to run one. Some entrepreneurs move around the country opening Chinese restaurants and then selling them.

Newspaper readers accustomed to the sterile language of American commerce find the ads astoundingly personal. Owners try to explain why, if the restaurant is so desirable, they are selling it: "Had a fight with my partner, so must sell the restaurant." Or:

"New wife. New kid. Must move."

"It's too lonely in this town for a single person, but it would be good for a family to run."

"Old. Retiring. Must sell."

"Death in family. No money down."

And unlike cars or houses, the buying and selling of Chinese restaurants is a nationwide market. Even in the New York City edition of the *World Journal,* the largest Chinese-language newspaper in the United States, the restaurants listed for sale are as far-flung as Arizona, Ohio, and Florida.

Chinese restaurants are like hermit-crab shells: the owners come and go; the restaurants, like the shells, are passed along—largely indifferent to the identity of their occupants. Oftentimes when they are sold, there is no remodeling or "Grand Opening" sign announcing a change in ownership. One day, the customers look up to see a different girl behind the cash register and a different cook banging on the wok. A few years later, the faces may change again.

John and Jenny hadn't read about the seven-table restaurant through a newspaper ad. They'd learned of it by word of mouth, the other way that restaurants are commonly bought and sold. In the country-sized village of the Fuzhounese community, someone always knows of someone who was just working at a restaurant and heard about another restaurant being put up for sale. The two were divided on whether to buy the restaurant, because like many couples they differed on the trade-off between money and lifestyle. Jenny had come to America to make money. She had been the first of the pair to leave China, at a time when village women heading overseas was still rare. Focused and excitable, Jenny spoke in a sharp, shrill voice that pierced the air even when I moved the cell phone away from my ear. With her slight frame and her hair always up in a ponytail and bangs, she resembled a high school student. You had to look closely to see the slight lines around her mouth, the hints that she was in her mid-thirties and a mother of three.

In contrast, John had pale skin, large limpid eyes, and a soft delicateness that was unusual in people from rural China. He considered himself a learned man and always spoke in flowery language punctuated with Chinese idioms characteristic of the well-read. John was not out to get rich. He wanted a comfortable life. His immigration to America had produced the opposite effect. In China, he had been a local government accountant; he'd held a predictable, low-stress, relatively well-paying job in an economy where money was tracked by an incessant shuffling of pieces of paper—and the occasional and emphatic red stamp. To this day, Chinese accountants still often use the abacus to calculate transactions.

John hated New York City. He was tired of traveling hours by bus to work in Chinese restaurants every week. He hated the mind-numbing, leg-numbing hours waiting on ungrateful, scornful customers. He'd had it with the crowds, the clutter, the smells. He was sick of their five-person family living in a single room and eating meals cooked in a makeshift kitchen in the bathroom. Life in America was not supposed to be this hard.

If they were successful in Georgia, he reasoned, they could buy a bigger restaurant and move away. If not, they could comfortably spend the rest of their lives there. With expansive mountains, trees, and clean lakes, Georgia was more like their village in China than New York ever would be.

Looking at the two, I guessed immediately who had been the aggressor in their courtship. Jenny had been a seamstress, and had taken a liking to her handsome, scholarly neighbor. She had converted to Christianity and joined John in the clandestine Baptist church services that were held in private homes, away from the watchful eye of the local government. During services the worshippers always harbored the background fear of being caught. When someone knocked, they scurried.

Now Jenny wanted to make money. A tiny restaurant in a tiny town was not going to lead to financial prosperity.

But the two did agree on at least one thing: the restaurant would be a chance to bring the entire family together. Their three children—all of whom had been raised in different households—and the parents would be in one home at last. And they could live as a family.

I believed that too, up until the moment I got the phone call telling me about the first arrest. The price of the seven-table restaurant, set in a mountain town, had been listed at $60,000. In reality, the price was the stability of their family.

Jenny still clearly remembers the night she left behind her oldest daughter, Jolene, in the village outside Fuzhou. Jolene remembers it too. "I cried for three days," she told me. Even though she was only six years old at the time, she knew instinctively that her mother was not coming back. She chased her to the doorway and watched her mother being chauffeured away in a put-putting motor cart. It was the beginning of Jenny's $30,000, illegal journey to New York City. For years after, Jolene communicated with her mother through her drawings. From the time she could pick up a pencil, it was clear that Jolene had been blessed with the hands and grace of an artist. She mailed her mother sketches of the Beijing opera that her grandparents took her to see. She liked to copy Japanese anime characters, with big, luminous eyes like those Jolene herself had inherited from her dad. The drawings always came folded inside handwritten letters from Jenny's father. Jenny taped Jolene's drawings to the wall above her bed so she could look at them as she fell asleep.

A few years later, Jolene also lost her father to America, but his journey was not as smooth as Jenny's. His was a boat trip that took him past the Dominican Republic. The United States Coast Guard scooped up him and the other passengers as they were trying to get to shore under the cover of night. For John, that ended up being a blessing. With the help of an immigration lawyer he applied for religious asylum. He had, after all, been raised Baptist. In the post–Tiananmen Square atmosphere of the early 1990s, the United States was generous in Chinese asylum cases. The Immigration and Naturalization Service tested his knowledge of the Bible: Who was Jesus Christ? What is the Holy Spirit? Who were the twelve disciples? He passed and was given asylum.

As his wife, Jenny was also granted asylum. (In September 2000, the federal government handcuffed their immigration lawyer, Robert Borgas, and charged him with colluding with Chinese snakeheads to help more than six thousand Chinese illegal immigrants get papers so that they could stay in New York. The government estimated that Mr. Borgas had earned $13.5 million in fees. Selling the American dream can be a very lucrative business.)

Jolene's parents did eventually send something back from New York: a baby sister who'd been born in Beekman Downtown Hospital, in Manhattan. They had given her an English name, Nancy; her Chinese name, Nanxi, had been chosen to match.

Her parents were too busy working in restaurants and garment factories, too busy to raise her. Nancy was taken care of by the other set of grandparents in China. Even though the two girls were sisters, they were hardly brought up as such.

The bonds of a Fuzhounese family are expansive yet fragile. At times they seem incredibly elastic, stretching across the oceans, and deep, as relatives can always be summoned from far corners to help out at a restaurant or with the kids. The same way that Eskimos have a multitude of words for snow, the Chinese have a multitude of ways to describe family relationships. In English, there is the single word "cousin," but in Mandarin Chinese, there are eight words. There are at least four words for "aunt" and five words for "uncle"; the fifth word indicates whether your uncle is older or younger than your father. Siblings, cousins, great-uncles, in-laws—in the end they are all *qinqi*: relatives. Many of John and Jenny's relatives came to their aid when they were trying to get their children back. Some moved to Georgia, to help at the restaurant. There are few broken families among the Fuzhounese, few divorces or single mothers or foster children.

Yet I was discomforted by Fuzhounese parents' willingness to send their children back as babies to be raised by other relatives. Once Nancy found a picture of her nanny, the woman who had raised her in China from the time she was a baby living with her grandparents until she left for the United States when she was old enough for school. She brought it to Jenny, who took it away from her. Nancy cried.

Only one child had stayed in New York with Jenny and John: the youngest, a boy named Jeffrey. Everyone called him Momo, for "nohair" in Fuzhounese, because he had been born with a big, round head that never seemed to fit his body. Among the Chinese, sexism is such an entrenched part of the culture that there is a common idiom for it: *Zhongnan qingnu*. Translated literally, it means to "emphasize boys and discount girls."

I first met Jolene in the spring of 2002, about five months before the family bought the restaurant. A photographer and I had been exploring a New York apartment building inhabited by Chinese restaurant workers because he wanted to do a photo essay; I acted as his translator. We stumbled upon a group of children playing with a Hacky Sack on the eighth floor. That is what children who don't have playgrounds or backyards do: they play in hallways and lobbies, under fluorescent lights and against the backdrop of peeling paint.

Jolene had arrived in the United States just a few months earlier. It had taken that many years for her immigration visa to be approved. In the meantime she had been treated like a princess by her grandparents, who doted on her and allowed her to get by without doing many chores around the house. Like many teenage girls, Jolene was shy, lonely, and awkward. Unlike many teenage girls, she had just been thrown into a foreign country where she barely spoke the language and did not understand the social hierarchy. The family lived on the ninth floor of the building in a one-room apartment with a bathroom and without a real kitchen; but it rented for less than $550 a month, an unbelievable bargain by Manhattan standards. For a fourteen-year-old girl, however, the problem with living in a single room is that there are no doors to slam when you fight with your mother.

Nancy had arrived three months after Jolene, brought in the arms of her grandmother. The grandparents stayed in the apartment for a three-month visit, but they were eager to return to China. Despite the rivers of money that were sent back home to build new houses and pay for new appliances, the quality of life in New York City was miserable, the grandparents thought; let their children slave away at the restaurants and in the garment factories if they wanted to. I liked Jolene and the somber way she held herself. I liked the confidence in her drawings, which was sometimes absent in the girl herself. So I offered to teach her English. That's when she told me she liked the English name Jolene.

Although Jenny had lived in the United States for over a decade, she'd been unable to help Jolene improve her English. When I met Jenny, I was surprised that someone could maneuver so adeptly in American society without speaking the language. And I don't mean she spoke broken English—she didn't speak English at all; nor could she read it. She and others like her paid various Fuzhounese individuals to fill out forms for them: $200 for visa applications, $70 to renew refugee status, $30 to help with FEMA applications after September 11, and so on. Back then, I never saw John. He was always off somewhere, working at a Chinese restaurant.

One day Jenny surprised me by saying they were going to buy a small restaurant in Hiawassee, Georgia, that cost $60,000.

Chinese restaurants are like gas, in that they expand to fill a vacuum. They have an enviable ability to take root in any community—urban or rural, cosmopolitan or isolated. If an environment can support life, then, like bacteria, a Chinese restaurant will find it.

A century and a quarter ago, the Cantonese spread eastward from San Francisco, carried by railroad, over dirt roads, and on foot. Today, the Fuzhounese spread westward from New York City, carried by interstate highways and airplanes.

Before telephones and automobiles, they were guided by word of mouth—rumors about which towns were virgin territory for Chinese restaurants. At the turn of the twentieth century, a Chinese man walked into a Chinese-goods store in the Twin Cities and mentioned that there was money to be made in Des Moines for a restaurant that had good food, good prices, and good cleanliness. A man named Lee Din took his suggestion, traveled south, and opened the first chop suey restaurant in Des Moines. King Ying Low, Lee Din's restaurant, celebrated its centennial in 2007, having passed through numerous owners. Outside, a large sign still draws customers with the words CHOP SUEY.

Today, restaurateurs have become shrewder, and more technical in their approach. Every year, *Chinese Restaurant News* and its editor, Betty Xie, publish an inch-thick booklet listing the top places to open a Chinese restaurant. By cross-referencing zip codes, census data, and their own database of existing Chinese restaurants, the magazine's staff generates a long list of markets with the greatest growth potential. The booklet notes the ratio between the local population and the number of Chinese restaurants. It also cites income growth as one of the best predictors for demand. Its recommendations range from very broad (best states) to general (promising towns) to pinpoint (specific zip codes). In 2003, *Chinese Restaurant News* generated a list of three thousand zip codes that didn't have Chinese restaurants, including 23024 (Bumpass, Virginia), 38852 (Iuka, Mississippi), and 99022 (Medical Lake, Washington).

In 2001, if you were looking for a good small city, the top choice was Rochester, Minnesota, which, the magazine noted, was home to the Mayo Clinic and IBM facilities. As for the top states, it suggested that readers consider Indiana, ranked third, pointing out that there had been a lot of manufacturing growth there, specifically in Kokomo, where both GM and Daimler-Chrysler had opened factories.

Today, the driving force of restaurant growth is the Fuzhounese. They were behind a striking number of the Powerball restaurants I visited across the country—more than half. In Boise, a Chinese restaurant manager named Peter wryly explained to me, "First they learned East Broadway and they became familiar with the rest of New York City. Then they kept on going: New York State, New Jersey. Then we went to Tennessee, Missouri, Montana, Idaho." Peter was the manager of No. 1 China Buffet in Ontario, Oregon, just over the Idaho border, where a woman named Jackie Mangum had gotten a fortune cookie with a number that won $100,000 in the Powerball drawing. Peter, who himself was Fuzhounese, had an epic perspective on the saga of his people and Chinese restaurants. "It's the reverse of the Chinese movement after the gold rush," he said. "We are going from the East Coast to the West Coast. After that, what are we going to do?"

In the meantime, the patterns of Chinese migration have crossed in the middle of the country. The Cantonese who came a generation or two ago are now retiring and selling their restaurants to the Fuzhounese, who are eager to take their turn at a wok-fueled American dream.

The Fuzhounese have been converting many of these restaurants into all-you-can-eat buffets or building their own places from scratch. The all-you-can-eat Chinese buffet is an interesting phenomenon in the South and the Midwest, an economic product of the shifts of capital and labor skills. The food costs for a buffet are significantly higher, but the labor costs are lower. In particular, buffets place a low demand on workers in one important way: you don't need as much English to serve a buffet. There are few waiters and waitresses, and they essentially only have to ask you what you want to drink. ("Diet Coke?") Meanwhile, Americans don't have to fumble through the names of Chinese dishes. They can simply take what looks good.

Driving across the United States in my Powerball quest, I came across a Chinese restaurant called Golden Dragon in Spearfish, South Dakota, not too far from Mount Rushmore. The red vinyl booth and ornate dragons screamed a *Happy Days*–era Cantonese restaurant, but inside the owners were a Fujianese family with three children, the youngest of whom was a five-year-old named Nina. (A Chinese girl in America with a Spanish name?) They'd bought the restaurant from its Cantonese owner, Martin Yeung, who had moved to Denver, proudly leaving behind the business card for his son, who worked for a senator on Capitol Hill. For the new family, South Dakota was nothing like their Fujianese hometown, Changle, which was near the ocean. Michelle, the mother, said, "When I first got here, I felt like I was in Mongolia. There is a lot of grass. They eat a lot of meat. There is a lot of sky. There is lots of livestock." Before I left, I asked her husband if they had ever visited Mount Rushmore, the monument to four revered American presidents. They hadn't. He shrugged, saying, "It doesn't have much meaning to us. It's just rock."

The little restaurant in Hiawassee was also started by a Cantonese family, the Wongs; they had settled in northern Georgia for some undetermined reason and needed a family business. It then sold to another Cantonese owner, a Taiwanese owner, and a Fujianese owner before John and Jenny learned of it.

At that point, Jenny wasn't even sure of the name of the restaurant. (It was then called China Grill.) But she knew the name of the town: Hiawassee. She wasn't able to spell Hiawassee, and she wouldn't be able to find it on a map, but she knew it was about fifteen hours by bus from New York City, from Chinatown, from East Broadway—the origin of all things Fujianese in America.

For the Fujianese, there are only two places in America. There is New York City; then there is everywhere else. Places are not called Indiana or Virginia or Georgia. Instead they are collectively known as *waizhou*—Mandarin Chinese for "out of state." *Waizhou* is more than a geographic description. It is the white space left over where there is no New York, no China-town, no East Broadway. Even upstate New York, including the state's capital, Albany, can be considered *waizhou* to the Fujianese. *Waizhou* is where fathers and sons go for weeks and months at a time to sweat twelve-hour days in Chinese res-taurants. *Waizhou* is crisscrossed by interstate bus routes and dotted with little towns, all of which either already have or could use a Chinese restaurant. *Waizhou* schools are better, and the paper towels there are cheaper. The bus system is the Fuzhounese connection to *waizhou*. If the Fujianese had a Saul Steinberg *New Yorker* cover to denote their vision of the world, it would show East Broadway, then the rest of New York City, followed by *waizhou*.

Hiawassee, to Jenny, was as *waizhou* as you could get: a small Georgia town, population 850, nestled in the foothills of the Ap-palachian Mountains. Located far away from the lush soil that once gave rise to plantations, Hiawassee was a white province of Georgia. It was in an area where the Ku Klux Klan gave out busi-ness cards with their Web site URL embossed on it.

Yet there was little, if any, overt racism—just the subtle op-pressiveness of shared experience. The current owner wanted to sell the restaurant because he and his two employees were going crazy with no one to talk to but each other. The Wongs, too, had left because they'd found the town too small.

By the time I heard about the restaurant, John had gone down to Hiawassee to evaluate it. He found it on the town's one main road, in a strip mall sandwiched between a Dairy Queen and a Subway shop that advertised "Senior discount every day." The town is located some two hours of twisting, mountainous road from anywhere: Atlanta, Chattanooga, Asheville. Lush green mountains and crystalline lakes surround it. CNN rated it one of the best towns to retire in. Later on, the beautiful place became full of sad memories, the root of a family's nightmare.

Hiawassee is a place where residents keep police radio scanners on at home to stay abreast of the news more quickly than they can by reading the weekly newspaper. If someone needs an ambulance one night, the next day everyone asks around about their condition.

Chinese restaurants are so plentiful and so common, they're priced and sold almost like commodities. One rule of thumb is that a single restaurant should sell for three times its monthly revenue. So if a Chinese restaurant brings in $30,000 a month, or an average of $1,000 a day, it should sell for roughly $90,000.

Knowing this, Chinese-restaurant owners will sometimes try to artificially inflate their monthly sales figures—or to sell in times when they are busiest. And as so much business is done in cash, it's sometimes hard for the buyer to discern what the true figures are. Due diligence includes asking the suppliers how much the restaurant orders each week or month, though restaurants preparing for a sale will often beef up their orders. So shrewd buyers watch something that is hard to fake: the number of bags of garbage that are produced.

A restaurant sale is not like a home sale, where one family empties the house before the other family moves in. The transition is gradual. The buyer arrives, checks out the restaurant, and works for a few weeks to learn the ropes before deciding whether to buy. It's like two families sharing the house before one family decides to make a bid. Then, if the sale is made, one family moves in as the other leaves.

John liked Hiawassee. The landscape reminded him of the mountainous vistas of home. On the phone, he told Jolene that she could go fishing in the nearby lake. They could scoop small live crabs right out of the water.

Since moving to New York, she hadn't seen any natural bodies of water—no oceans, no ponds, no lakes. (Glimpses of the gray urbanized East River didn't count.) Only buildings and streets and subways. Jenny hated the idea of living in the middle of nowhere, but she relented. Hiawassee seemed safer than a big city, where stories of men being beaten or killed while delivering food were common among the Chinese immigrants. A relative of Jenny's had been shot and killed in a restaurant holdup a few years ago in Philadelphia. Hiawassee wouldn't present those problems. Small towns come with different problems.

So in September 2002, they bought the restaurant for $60,000, borrowing money from friends and family. They paid cash, as is usual for many of these restaurant transactions, which tend to be handled discreetly. John also bought a bumbling blue Cutlass Ciera for $1,300. Then he learned to drive.

I watched the family make the journey by Greyhound in pieces. Jenny's older brother moved down to work as the restaurant's cook. Nancy and Jolene were brought down to Hiawassee in October by an aunt.

It would be a long time before they saw their mother and brother. Jenny kept dragging her feet. She was reluctant to leave New York. She wanted to catch a thief who had burglarized her home. In August, they had been robbed of a lockbox that contained $10,000 in cash, the family jewelry, and many legal papers—including birth certificates, passports, and work visas. Jenny was convinced that the culprit was a Malaysian Chinese woman with a big mole on her face to whom she had once lent money.

Jolene had been home alone at the time. She received a telephone call saying there was someone who wanted to meet her downstairs. She went down, saw no one, and came back up. When she returned to the apartment, it was too late. Someone had broken in and dragged out the safe. When Jenny found out she yelled at Jolene for being stupid. Jolene was frozen with guilt. Jenny became obsessed with catching the woman. She had an artist draw the woman's picture, complete with the mole; then she made flyers offering a reward and hung them on lampposts all around Chinatown. Occasionally she would drag me to the police precinct, where I would act as her translator.

Meanwhile, John was in Hiawassee running the business and trying to raise two daughters who rarely talked to him because they barely knew him. John urged Jenny to hurry up and get down to Hiawassee. He had no idea how to raise children. The children agreed.

Packing to leave a city after a decade, to move eight hundred miles away, is hard. Leaving via Greyhound gives one extra pause. Life has to be collapsed into bags that do not exceed seventy pounds—carefully and cleverly, so that it can be expanded at the other end. Jenny stuffed their belongings into the durable red, white, and blue plaid plastic bags that feel like rice sacks. They are made in China but are the universal symbol of the transience of the developing world: you see them tied with cord to the tops of buses, looking dusty and frayed. In went the rice cooker, clothes, a washboard, frying pans, oranges, even a VCR. Jenny went to Chinatown to stock up on supplies, returning home with orange and red shopping bags teeming with pickled radishes, dried mushrooms, shredded pork, and soy milk. She considered the fourteen video cassettes of a popular Chinese serial drama. The tapes were bulky, but Jolene had complained about boredom in the mountains. Jenny put them in the bag. She took them out. She put them back in.

When the Lincoln Tunnel spit the bus into New Jersey, Jenny held her son, Momo, and looked back at the fading Manhattan skyline. She had paid $30,000 to snakeheads to move to New York. Now she had paid $59 to Greyhound to leave. What was supposed to be a fifteen-hour bus ride stretched into twenty-four when she missed a connection in Danville, Virginia. She arrived in Atlanta after midnight, at the start of Thanksgiving Day.

In Atlanta, an accented voice rang out in the bus terminal. "Hello! Hello!" It was John. He grabbed Momo and swung the boy around. Jenny stood by, watched, and smiled tightly.

Arriving that late meant that Jenny wasn't able to appreciate the sweeping landscape surrounding Hiawassee. But she could see the points of light scattered across the night sky.

Stars. It had been a long time since she had seen stars. New York's luminescence was so competitive, it had long drowned out the constellations.

The 1984 blue Ciera crept down the two-lane road and turned left into a plain strip mall. It was nearly three A.M. by the time Jenny saw the restaurant for the first time. At one end of the strip mall was an extinguished neon sign that read CHINA GRILL in chop suey–style writing.

She opened the glass door and stepped into the darkness. The lights came on. She was struck by how much red there was: red carpet, red chairs.

As of that moment, Jenny had never seen a fortune cookie, never eaten General Tso's chicken, and never heard of crab Rangoon. Those things would soon become a central part of her livelihood.

They continued down the road to the three-bedroom apartment John had rented. He turned on the second bedroom's light and shook his daughters, who were sleeping on a mattress on the floor. Jolene woke up and immediately hugged her brother. She hadn't seen him in two months. "He smells," she said.

"He vomited and peed on himself on the bus," Jenny explained.

The mother looked at her still-sleeping younger daughter.

"She's gotten chubbier," she observed. Nancy's uncle had been feeding her snacks from the restaurant. It was the most she had been doted upon since moving to America.

Jolene dragged the bags in from the car. She eagerly seized the videotapes; they would break the monotony of days split between school and work at the restaurant. For the first time in their lives, all the pieces of the family puzzle were together. Only in Hiawassee was the family finally fully assembled: a mother who had immigrated illegally to work in garment factories, a father who'd been often forced to live apart from his wife to find work as a waiter outside New York City, a teenage daughter raised from the age of six by her maternal grandparents, an American-born preschool daughter who'd been sent back to her paternal grandparents in China, and a toddler who had always lived by his mother's side.

It was a family of strangers, but now, in Hiawassee, all they had was one another, and the restaurant.

That was supposed to be the end of the story, a happy ending. Later on, it would become hard to untangle the strands of responsibility for the complications that followed. It is tempting to run one's finger down a chronology and try to pick out the decision that could have changed everything afterward. Did the fault lie with Jolene, for kicking her mother in the stomach and then laying the blame for the injuries—either inadvertently or purposely—on her father? Or did it lie within an overzealous child welfare agency stymied by language and cultural barriers? Or with the anonymous neighbors who reported Momo and Nancy playing in the parking lot, unsupervised, while their parents worked in the restaurant? Or with John and Jenny, whose marriage had become somewhat tenuous? It was watching a car wreck in slow motion. You could not pull your eyes away even though you expected it to end horribly.

• • •

The restaurant was a struggle. Business was slow now that the summer tourist season was over. There is only so much demand for Chinese food in a town of 850. John and Jenny had bought the restaurant during a peak season. Perhaps the sellers had exaggerated its revenues, or perhaps the customers grew less loyal once they realized the food had changed.

It was hard running a Chinese restaurant. Jenny had been a skilled seamstress, but she had never worked in a restaurant. John had worked as a waiter, but now he was also a chef. Jolene joked that everything he cooked tasted the same.

The couple had a binder with them, an instruction book on how to run a Chinese restaurant. It came with recipes like General Tso's chicken, and it taught them how to roll the napkins around the silverware. But still they called relatives to ask questions about proportions and ingredients.

They worked continuously until eleven P.M. every night, then staggered home and collapsed into bed. Even when there were no customers in the restaurant, there was an unrelenting succession of tasks. They had to roll the egg rolls, fold the crab Rangoon triangles, coat and prefry the meat for General Tso's chicken, devein the shrimp, simmer the brightly red sweet-and-sour sauce, chop the broccoli, prepare the fried rice. They didn't have a babysitter, so they kept Nancy and Momo at the restaurant. Jolene would come to help out after school.

Jenny's sister, who came down to Hiawassee to help out, told me, "In New York, you can still work if you don't speak English. Here, you can't do anything." She also noted, "You are worthless if you can't drive." But some of the neighbors were really kind, including Jane, a retired New York City schoolteacher with an adopted daughter from China, who lived down the road from them.

• • •

A family-run Chinese restaurant is a seven-days-a-week enterprise. I came across many restaurant owners who had not taken a single day off for decades. But it was Jenny's pregnancy in 2003 that made me realize the hard calculus of being the owner of a Chinese restaurant. She thought about having an abortion, which was what she had done with previous pregnancies when she was too busy working in New York City. Abortion in China does not involve the moral dilemma it does in the United States. The culture is not Christian, so life is not considered to begin at conception. Sometimes an individual life doesn't even begin at birth. In certain parts of China, babies weren't named until well after they were born—thirty days, one hundred days, or a year. It's easier to deal with an infant's death if the baby didn't have a name.

Jenny calculated the amount of time needed to get an abortion in Chinatown. She didn't trust the doctors in Georgia; nor were abortions readily available in the rural South. It would take her four weeks to travel there, recover, and get back to Hiawassee to work at the restaurant. If she actually gave birth, she would be out of work for only two weeks. She decided to carry the baby to term.

The last names of the settlers who built Hiawassee, 150 years ago, are now thick in the town telephone book, having multiplied over many generations. There is a thin, invisible barrier separating insiders and outsiders—even for those who speak English and are from other places in the South.

Jolene made few friends among her high school classmates. After all, many had known each other since they were toddlers, and many shared the same last names. Occasionally they regarded her with mild curiosity, since she was from two places that were exotic to them: China and New York City. On Jolene's first day of school, a boy asked her if she'd been in New York on September 11. She couldn't understand the question. So the boy went up to the board and drew two buildings and a plane, a universal hieroglyphic for the ages. She nodded. Yes, she had been in the city.

Math class was the easiest for Jolene, but civics class, required by Georgia so that students would learn the rights and responsibilities of citizens, was the most difficult. There were so many words and concepts she didn't understand, like "Congress," "citizen," and "Constitution." Her civics teacher started with the basics. On the Internet, he found the list of one hundred questions and answers from the United States citizenship test. It was the same list of questions that my parents had studied before they took the citizenship exam, after almost thirty years of living in the United States. For months before the test, my mom kept the three verses of "The Star-Spangled Banner" stuck to the refrigerator door. Though I was in my mid-twenties, until then I hadn't even been aware there were three verses to the song.

Jolene hated living in Hiawassee. She loathed putting on the little black waitress vest and working in the restaurant, but her parents insisted because her English was better than theirs. Working at the restaurant became a never-ending set of chores. Among Jolene's most dreaded tasks was deveining shrimp. If she was not careful, their sharp tails would prick her fingertips, causing them to bleed. It was like Cinderella, only with a deep fryer and a walk-in refrigerator.

In Powerball restaurant after Powerball restaurant, I found dutiful children helping out their parents—dealing with an English-speaking vendor, learning to handle a wok so the father could take a rest; taking orders by phone and at the tables. At the modest thirty-seat China Buffet in Caledonia, Minnesota (the "wild turkey capital" of the state), a ten-year-old boy with gold hoop earrings and dimples named Andy cleared plates, worked the cash register, and watched his baby brother in the corner. "We could open a big store, but it's hard if you don't speak English," Andy's father explained to me in Mandarin. "In ten years, when the boys are older, we can open a larger restaurant. They can speak English for us." Until then? They found other ways to survive. After our conversation ended, he asked me to make a call to an English-speaking vendor to get a new dishwasher installed.

At Lucky Garden in Dover, New Hampshire, teenagers Tony and Jenny had been helping out for as long as they could remember. The two spent more time in the restaurant than in their own living room; they even did their homework there. "It's like home here," said the daughter, who was still helping out although she was now in college. The family loved cars. Their father had bought them each a BMW when they turned sixteen. If you didn't know the family, you would be tempted to call those cars the accoutrements of spoiled teenagers; if you knew how hard they worked, you wouldn't. Helping out, in Chinese restaurant families, is simply part of the deal of being part of the family. But no one had explained the deal to Jolene. She would fall asleep in class after working nights in the restaurant. Her grades slipped, and she struggled to balance schoolwork and late nights at the restaurant. She resented having been dragged down to Georgia, forced to be the outsider. "They think you're strange because of the way you look," she said. "I'd rather go back to my own culture so people don't think of the way you look."

To break the monotony, she painted. She painted pictures of cranes and of the mountains and the lake in Hiawassee. The paintings were placed casually around the restaurant. A customer offered to buy one.

Instead of other girls, she found company among older women, Jehovah's Witnesses. One woman bought her a Chinese Bible, and an alarm clock so she could wake up in the morning. On one visit, I was surprised when she informed me, matter-of-factly, that "God is named Jehovah."

Whenever I visited Hiawassee, she wanted me to take her to Atlanta—or anywhere, as long as she could get away from the restaurant. For her first shopping trip, we drove to Atlanta for Chinese groceries. The winding roads were a shock to her system. Jolene vomited three times. Of course Atlanta, unlike many older cities, doesn't have a Chinatown. We headed to Atlanta's Buford Highway, the immigrant landing strip of the South, a giant multicultural jukebox filled with Mexican taquerias and Vietnamese pho houses. When we pulled into the strip mall with the Chinese Ranch 99 supermarket, I shook her awake. Jolene emerged groggily from her motion-sickness-induced nap. Where was Chinatown? she asked. "Chinatown is straight. It has streets," she insisted. She squinted at the U-shaped strip mall and sniffed, "It's not round like this."

On our way back that night, we merged from Atlanta's Interstate 285 perimeter highway into the fourteen lanes of I-85. Jolene gazed out at the two rivers of densely packed car lights—one red, one white—that flowed to and from the horizon.

She was entranced. "They look like ants moving up a mountain," she marveled. In her year and a half in America, she had known only the concrete of New York City and the mountains of Hiawassee, nothing in between. "It's so beautiful," she said, staring at the traffic-clogged highway full of thousands of cars, Atlantans hurrying to get back to their homes in subdevelopments and cul-de-sacs. "It's prettier than New York."

The first overt signs of trouble came the February after they moved to Hiawassee. One night, Jenny phoned me, hysterical. The police had taken the children away, she said.

We found out that someone had reported that Momo and Nancy had been playing, without supervision, in the parking lot. After three days, Jenny and John got the two younger children back and promised not to leave them alone. But Jolene chose to stay with a foster mom for three more months. She had managed to escape working at the restaurant.

It was the next phone call, one that came a year later, the night that John was arrested for the first time, that the big problems began. That night, the police took all three children away and arrested John on a curious charge of domestic abuse. The officers pointed to the burn scars from cooking oil on the parents' arms and said that was evidence that the couple had a history of fighting. Someone had also reported that Jenny had a sprained finger.

In fact, the aggressor had not been John. The two who'd been fighting had been Jolene and Jenny, everyone said. That day, as always, they'd fought over Jolene's working in the restaurant. Jenny argued that it was the obligation of the daughter to help out, since her family had raised her. The fighting grew violent. At some point, Jenny fell and Jolene kicked her three times in the stomach. Jenny injured her finger in the process and had to be taken to the hospital. But that sprained finger raised people's suspicions.

So the night after the police came, Jenny found herself alone. She walked back and forth between the restaurant and her apartment in the dark, too scared to go home by herself. Finally she knocked at the door of Jane's house, down the road, and slept in her spare bedroom that night, alone.

In jail, John became friends with his cellmate, a twenty-two-year-old drug addict who worked at the local Burger King. Later he told me, "When I was in jail for two days, it was really relaxing." He was away from the restaurant and his wife.

This time, on the second offense, the children were not given back. Once a family is caught in the bull's-eye of the legal system, nothing is simple anymore. The complaints the agency had compiled about the children were small but numerous. Any one of them would have seemed patently ridiculous as a reason to take children away from their parents. But together, they gathered momentum. Momo had shown up at school dressed in girl's clothing; Jenny told me he'd insisted on wearing one of Nancy's shirts. The children were often late to school; the parents sometimes drove them in from Atlanta in the morning after a weekend away. Then there was the issue with the children's teeth. Were they getting proper dental care? Jenny and John told me that in China, you take the children to the dentist only when there is a problem.

John and Jenny's lives become consumed by something they called *Difeh*. *Difeh* had taken control of their lives much more than the authoritarian regime in China ever had. *Difeh* could trigger police cars to come and take away their children. *Difeh* controlled when and where they were allowed to visit the kids. *Difeh* could ask the most private questions about their lives, including their sleeping arrangements and how often they hugged their children. *Difeh* could order them to see a psychiatrist. "Isn't this a violation of my human rights?" John once asked me in frustration.

Difeh was DFACS, or Georgia's Department of Family and Children Services—an overwhelmed bureaucracy in which government employees were trying to make bad situations a little bit better. On a visit to the office, I heard one worker say softly, apologetically, to Jenny, "We don't have the people or the resources to get everything right."

The Chinese restaurant seemed empty without the sound of children's laughter to break up the rhythmic swish and clang of cooking. The yellow school bus no longer came after three o'clock. Instead, every weekday between three and four P.M., John and Jenny brought home-cooked Chinese food to the DFACS office, located in a modest strip mall next to a "God Bless America" sign, in hopes that the food would be passed to the children. They worried that the kids would not be used to the American food. It was a sad ritual. Sometimes, if no one answered the door, they would just hang the plastic bag on the office's doorknob.

Jenny's weight dropped to eighty-six pounds, a massive loss given her original, already slight 110-pound frame. She began wearing multiple pairs of underwear, including men's boxers, in order to keep up her once-tight jeans. John became haggard-looking.

Business at the restaurant trailed off, in part because the parents had to close it so many days of the week in order to go to counseling and deal with the agency.

As will happen in a small town, rumors clouded the restaurant. At the courthouse, I overheard a group of lawyers talking about the family. One remarked that the Chinese-restaurant case was going on. Another replied, "Oh, I can't eat there anymore—that's the DV case." DV? Domestic violence.

Trying to get the children back was a tangled process involving translators, lawyers, caseworkers, and psychiatric evaluations. It turned out that John and Jenny needed separate lawyers, in part because of the domestic abuse charge. Neither of their lawyers spoke Chinese.

Newspapers are always filled with accounts of how child welfare agencies ignored the warning signs and failed to protect the life of some fragile kid who ended up dead. It's less common to hear about the flip side, when the government intervention makes things worse. Outside observers agreed that the family had its share of problems: parents who had barely been parents and were overwhelmed with running a restaurant, a rebellious teenager who loathed the rural Appalachian town where she had few friends, a Chinese culture that favored sons over daughters. Tempers often flared. Yes, the family had its problems, acknowledged friends and neighbors. But enough so that the children should be taken away for months? One of the neighbors later observed, "You know, it's like the lion looks for the easy mark, the ones that can't defend themselves." Jenny, pregnant during the ordeal, miscarried; the stress of running the restaurant, combined with other health issues, had proved too much for her constitution. When the doctors removed the fetus, they told her it had been a boy.

The courts wanted the parents to attend counseling classes, but that meant they would have to drive to Atlanta and back. They would have to close the restaurant for the whole day. Grudgingly, they agreed to attend a limited number of sessions.

In the agency's eyes, Jenny's mental stability was in doubt. She would sob hysterically during meetings. From her perspective, she was becoming unstable because the agency had kept her children away from her for months upon months. But Jenny was also infuriated with the sheer unfairness of it all, and she resisted as retaliation. When they were due at a counseling session and the car happened to break down and they missed it, she was gleeful.

Over time, everyone gradually realized that it was not only Jenny who was resisting but Jolene. It was taking so long to get the children back in part because Jolene didn't want to go home. In her own way, she was using the family court system to punish her mother by keeping the other two children away. Finally, during a weekend family visitation, John took Jolene outside. "It's my fault," he said. The restaurant had been all his idea, he explained. Come back and we'll sell the restaurant, he told her. He pleaded with her.

Jolene was confused. She didn't know what to think. "I don't think I can ever work this out with my mother," she cried. She picked up Nancy and held her.

Jenny placed an $88 ad in the Atlanta edition of the *World*

Journal. A Chinese couple from Birmingham responded. They appeared suddenly one day to help out at the restaurant. It was the first step in the transition.

The situation seemed to be slowly improving. Then one day at work, I got a call from Jane, the neighbor. John and Jenny had been arrested. They had violated court rules by driving near their children's foster home. Because they had sold their restaurant, they were considered a flight risk. Their bail was set exorbitantly high. This time, John and Jenny couldn't afford to bail themselves out, and neither could their neighbors.

Guardian angels come in strange forms. Jim Crawford was a land developer with a salt-and-pepper beard who rode a Harley-Davidson and had found religion late in life. He'd skipped college because he was too focused on making money when he was a young man. But slowly, as he had more time (and more money), he had come to find God. He was never sure if he should call himself Christian or just religious.

He had first seen John and Jenny at McConnell Baptist Church, where they went to pray for the return of their children. From the back of the room, their dark hair stood out against the silvery heads lining the pews. Jim had heard the whispers about their family problems. One day, he rode his Harley to the restaurant. "I'm here to see if I can help you," he told John, who was behind the counter.

What made him step in when so many people didn't or couldn't help? He shrugged. He couldn't explain it. It was an odd thing for him to do, he admitted. He had never been particularly charitable, but there was something about the sadness of this story that drew him in. John and Jenny started visiting him regularly. Sometimes Jim would come home from work and find them there, waiting in their car.

It was weeks into this routine when Jim rode his motorcycle to the restaurant and asked the woman behind the cash register where John and Jenny were. She hesitated. Then she picked up a little computerized dictionary, punched a couple of keys, and held it up so he could read the screen.

"Jail."

Jim was shocked. He headed over to the county jail—a stark, boxy building on the outskirts of town. John and Jenny looked forlorn in their orange jumpsuits. He bailed them out, posting a bond with his property as collateral.

Jim helped John make an impassioned plea in stilted English in front of the church congregation, telling their story with a speech he had laboriously written out in English. Soon church members deluged the judge and the child welfare agency on behalf of the family. There were letters, and Jim personally lobbied the district attorney. Slowly, DFACS's grip on the children loosened. Afternoon-long visits became overnight visits and then weekend visits. In late October, seven months after they were taken away, the kids were returned home. When I met them again at their apartment, Momo and Nancy barely spoke Chinese anymore. At their welcome-back party at the restaurant, a neighbor brought a cake she had bought. The children's names wouldn't all fit, so instead she'd had the supermarket clerk write, "Welcome back, y'all."

With the family whole again and the restaurant sold, the family had to decide where to move next. Jenny's cousin had a restaurant in Augusta, Georgia. John's sister had a takeout on Long Island, east of New York City. With no sense of permanence and only a car's worth of belongings, the family could head anywhere the car could take them. The kids would go to school in whatever neighborhood they ended up in.

Jenny briefly spoke about the possibility of running another restaurant, but Jolene reminded her parents that they'd promised there wouldn't be any more Chinese restaurants. "It's like a big hole. A lot of people jump into it and can't get out anymore," she said angrily. "First generation does it and second generation does it again and third generation. They do it because they think they don't have a choice." Never again, she told herself. She wanted to apply to an arts program at the Brooklyn Museum of Art.

That night the family packed up the car. They returned books to the library and bade cursory farewells to their neighbors. After this two-year-long, tumultuous, failed experiment in owning a restaurant, they decided to head back to New York.

"Let's go! Let's go!" John said, ushering everyone into the car. With the engine roaring, they left in the middle of the night, the car's headlights cutting through the fog. The car sped off, as though to escape the demons that had plagued the family. If they drove fast enough, perhaps the demons would be left behind in Hiawassee.

They stopped only once during the night, so that John could nap in the parking lot of a convenience store in Virginia. The clerk there wore a cap with a Confederate flag on it.

The next time they stopped was to eat at a McDonald's in Hagerstown, Maryland. Jenny peeled the golden crust off her McNuggets and fed it to Momo. "Wherever there are people, there is McDonald's and a Chinese restaurant," she observed.

When the Empire State Building appeared on the horizon, the entire family cheered. They were home. They were uncertain about where they would go once they got to the city. First they tried to find Jenny's brother in Chinatown. He wasn't home, so they headed out to Long Island to find John's sister at her family takeout, which had a red Christian cross taped to the wall near the cash register.

I haven't seen them since they made that drive home. John

found a job at a restaurant in Princeton, New Jersey. He hinted once that they were separated—though given how often Fuzhounese husbands work apart from their wives, I wasn't sure if there was much of a lifestyle difference. Jenny told me she'd seen the thief, the Malaysian woman with the big mole, on the street and had attacked her. She also told me they had bought a house in Philadelphia. The Fuzhounese were moving to Philadelphia in droves—it was close enough to New York, only two hours away, but had cheaper real estate.

They changed their cell phone numbers. Jane, their neighbor from Hiawassee, called me once to ask if I had heard from them. I hadn't. Neither had she.

I suppose it's a good thing that the frantic phone calls stopped. This is a family where no news can be interpreted as good news. As the months, then years, passed by, I wondered about them, imagining that they had found their happy ending somewhere.

CHAPTER 14

The Greatest Chinese Restaurant in the World

C hinese food is served on all seven continents, even Antarctica, where Monday is usually Chinese-food night at McMurdo Station, the main American scientific outpost on the icy continent. It is arguably the most pervasive cuisine on the planet—and beyond: NASA offers its astronauts thermostabilized sweet-and-sour pork and hot-and-sour soup. In order to understand Chinese food in America, you have to understand Chinese food around the world.

My editor came up with a suggestion about how I might do so. "You should find the best restaurant in the world," he told me in his office one day.

I was dumbfounded. I resisted, with a litany of excuses. It was not the best use of my time. I was not a restaurant critic. The world was impossibly vast. How does one define "best" anyway? Could there even be one such restaurant for the entire world? It was insane. Plus, it would cost a fortune. He shrugged all my objections off and told me I would figure it out in time. "It will be great," he assured me as he escorted me to the elevator. "Trust me."

After several weeks of denial, I called up a map of the world on my computer. Could I really pick a single Chinese restaurant? How was I to judge?

Finding good restaurants around the world, it turns out, is not dissimilar to finding great local restaurants: I used word-of-mouth recommendations and restaurant reviews. Only I was compiling my list across borders, on a global scale.

I needed to set some criteria. First, as the idea was to see how Chinese food had been adapted around the world, I would focus my searches on Chinese restaurants outside China and areas that China thinks of as China—so that excluded China, Hong Kong, and Taiwan. Second, the restaurant had to identify itself as Chinese. Nothing too "Pan-Asian," nothing "fusiony." Third, I decided to go with the criteria of "greatest" instead of "best." "Best" made me nervous. Somehow I felt like I could handle "greatest"—lots of things could make a restaurant great, which made that designation seem less subjective than "best."

Looking at the world map, I devised five categories of places that were most likely to breed great Chinese restaurants:

1) Areas where there was significant middle-class Chinese immigration. This meant, essentially, cities where there was a strong demand for quality authentic Chinese food by people who could pay for it. The list of such cities was manageable. In the United States: New York City, the Bay Area, Los Angeles. In Canada: Vancouver and Toronto. In Britain: London. In Australia: Sydney and Melbourne.

2) Industrialized Asian economies where China has historically had a great cultural influence—with enough affluence and demand for great Chinese restaurants. This boiled down to Japan, Korea, and Singapore.

3) Other great culinary nations: Italy and France. What happened to Chinese cuisine when it had to compete with the great cuisines of the world on their own territory?
4) Places in the world where there was just a lot of money sloshing around: Dubai.
5) Assorted developing countries picked for their distinctive cuisine, prominent Chinese population, or both: Peru, India, Brazil, Mauritius, and Jamaica.

I counted: fifteen countries, six continents, twelve months, one writer.

My method was not perfect, but it cast a pretty effective net. When I mentioned my quest to people, I would often get responses along these lines:

"Well, what if it's a hole-in-the-wall in Africa?"

"It's not going to be."

"How do you know?"

"I just know."

Or: "Ohmigod! I went to this fantastic Chinese restaurant in Montreal. I don't remember its name, but I can ask my friend who took me there. You have to go down this alley and then down this dingy staircase. There are, like, only four tables under these horrible fluorescent lights, but the food is absolutely incredible."

What was it about Chinese restaurants that made people share these stories of dives? If I announced I was searching for the greatest French restaurant in the world, would people say, "What if it's a hole-in-the-wall in Samoa that has these ratty plastic tables?"

Another mystery the quest would solve: Do Chinese restaurants around the world give out fortune cookies? If not, what do they serve for dessert?

LOS ANGELES, UNITED STATES

San Francisco and New York may have been the original breeding grounds for Chinese restaurants in the United States, but Los Angeles has shot up there in the last half century. I called a knowledgeable Chinese-American friend in Los Angeles to ask for recommendations.

"Well, what kind of Chinese food are you looking for?" he asked.

"You mean like Cantonese or Sichuan?" I replied.

No. No. No. "There are three types of Chinese restaurants," he asserted. "There is Chinese food for Chinese people, Chinese food for other people, and what I call 'postmodern Chinese.'"

Can't a Chinese restaurant be for both Chinese people and others? I opened up a Los Angeles *Zagat* and rattled off the top-ranked Chinese restaurants.

Chinese people don't go to those, he said dismissively. You can't have a great Chinese restaurant unless Chinese people go.

So I headed out to where Chinese people went to eat: the San Gabriel Valley, full of gargantuan strip malls with neon lights and noodle shops and bubble tea and long lines. In towns like Alhambra, San Gabriel, and Monterey Park, we found authentic restaurants that could have been in Hong Kong, Taiwan, or China: teeming with Chinese people and (sometimes) a couple of non-Chinese adventurous diners. The restaurants had great food: seafood at New Concept, dim sum at Triumphal Palace, soup dumplings at Din Tai Fung. By the end of my visit, I'd figured out patterns to help me define what "Chinese restaurants for Chinese people" meant.

The minimum criteria:

• Chopsticks at the table
• Menus with Chinese writing
• Waiters who understand and speak Chinese

Bonus points for:

- Specialties listed on the wall in Chinese
- Fish tanks with live creatures that might end up on your plate before the end of your meal

Minus points for:

- Chinese zodiac place mats
- Chop suey listed anywhere on the menu
- Charging for rice or tea

Would the greatest Chinese restaurant be a Chinese restaurant for Chinese people? Or it would be for "others"? Could it possibly be for both?

LIMA, PERU

What do Chinese restaurants have to do with slavery?

A lot, in the New World, it turns out.

In many countries—Cuba, Jamaica, Peru—Chinese contract workers arrived in the nineteenth century to fill the gaping demand for agricultural labor left by the abolition of slavery. Eventually, many of them transitioned to opening up Chinese restaurants, perhaps with no greater fervency than in Peru, home to the largest population of Chinese and the largest number of Chinese restaurants in Latin America today. With that in mind, I headed to Lima.

Almost everywhere in the world, Chinese restaurants are called "Chinese restaurants" in the local language. In Peru, Chinese restaurants are so common they have their own vocabulary word—*chifas*, which is derived from the Chinese *chifan*, meaning "to eat food." In Lima, *chifas* have the density of Starbucks cafés in American business districts. Chinese food has become so pervasive in the Peruvian diet that even ordinary restaurants serve *sopa wantan* (wonton soup) and *arroz chaufa* (fried rice).

Most *chifas* in Peru are low-end mom-and-pop shops, casual places where someone can grab a quick lunch. But the *chifa* of all *chifas* in Peru is Restaurant Royale. You can rub shoulders with Peru's television personalities and politicians (before some are charged with corruption). The entrance is grand (curved stone stairs, waterfall, and stone lions). The menu is grand (abalone, pigeon, and shark's fins). The imperial-style menu can hold its own against the high-end restaurants of Hong Kong, where the owners and chef hail from. The spiral-bound menu has photographs and descriptions in both English and Spanish to guide diners through the dizzying array of selections, and, like any high-end Cantonese restaurant, Restaurant Royale showcases its seafood dishes. The seafood and fancy ingredients appealed to the Chinese clientele, but looking over at the other tables, I saw that most people had ordered the Peruvian standards: fried rice, sweet-and-sour pork, and wontons—just extremely high-priced versions of those common dishes.

Yet after finishing dessert—*tres leches* and a creamy cake topped with yellow gooseberry—I felt as if something was missing. Royale was clearly the fanciest, most famous Chinese restaurant in Peru (and perhaps all of Latin America). It was a special experience for the Peruvians because there was nothing else like it in the country. But it didn't resonate with me because it was spectacular in the way that many restaurants around the world are spectacular: good food, obsequious service, opulent atmosphere. Across the board, I wasn't sure what made any of these fancy, special restaurants different from one another.

The greatest Chinese restaurant in the world, I felt, had to offer some kind of twist that would hold up on the global stage.

Maybe greatness wasn't only about the dining experience itself. Perhaps there were intangible psychological factors.

PARIS, FRANCE

The most fashionable place to eat in Paris is located on a side street around the corner from the Théâtre du Palais-Royal. Limousines regularly clog the narrow block, spewing out A-list celebrities in painfully stylish outfits. The shaded windows and a velvet curtain give way to the red, chintzy splendor of a Chinese restaurant that could be in any European country, but is actually like none other in the world.

Davé Cheung's eponymous restaurant, Davé, boasts a clientele list that would launch the career of any aspiring publicist. Leonardo DiCaprio and his buddy Tobey Maguire have been coming here for years; so too have the fashion establishment: Kate Moss, Anna Wintour, and Marc Jacobs are all regulars. Where people sit in Davé's restaurant can take on the portentous symbolism of a fashion show—or a high school cafeteria.

Given that the trendy haunts in New York and Los Angeles rise and fall like Nielsen ratings, the enduring popularity of this modest Chinese restaurant over two decades is something of an enigma. People certainly don't come to Davé because of the food, which is predictable at best, or the decor, which is neither tasteful enough to be classy nor modern enough to be hip. Then again, models aren't the most discerning foodies: they want tofu and bok choy. Paris may be a capital of both fashion and cuisine, but the culinary center of the fashion world is not particularly known for its fine cooking.

Nonetheless, the nicotine-yellowed Polaroids on the restaurant walls prove to be a compelling archive of late-twentieth-century celebrity and the power of Davé's appeal. There is Madonna, with bleached hair and heavy black eyeliner, when she went through her military-bustier *Vogue* phase. There is the cast of *Sex and the City*. There is Janet Jackson before the infamous Super Bowl wardrobe malfunction. There is John Malkovich before *Being John Malkovich*. There is John Malkovich after *Being John Malkovich*. The photographs span the years. Hairstyles inflate and deflate. Neckties narrow and widen. But what all of the pictures have in common is the presence of a single, thick-eyebrowed face: the restaurant owner, Davé Cheung. In some of the pictures he has shoulder-length dark hair and smooth white skin. In others, his hair has turned salt-and-pepper gray and his jawline has softened. Davé is the kind of restaurant owner who doesn't give out menus. Instead, he always takes the orders himself, asking his clients a standard set of questions: "How hungry are you?" and "Is there anything you don't eat?" Then he decides what he will serve his regular and celebrity clients. The bills, averaging 40 euros per person, arrive tastefully at the end.

Davé and I fell into a conversation partly in English and partly in Mandarin, with his occasional use of a French exclamation. Davé's family is originally from the northern port city of Tianjin, near Beijing. They moved to Paris in 1967 because his mother had a friend here. Chinese immigrants have two paths, he told me wryly. Either they labor or they study. His parents belonged to the first group.

Davé's story of success started at his parents' restaurant when a British *Vogue* art director named Barney Wan brought his colleague Grace Coddington, a creative director, to lunch there. Fast-forward to 1982, when Davé opened up his own restaurant only five minutes from the Jardin des Tuileries, where Fashion Week events were being held. The restaurant was appealing because it was geographically convenient, because it was accessible Chinese fare, and because Davé spoke English; the American and British fashion crowd was weary of slogging through Parisian French. Separately, the Hollywood set found its way to Davé. The music industry inevitably followed, mostly because celebrityness is all about "crossing over," Davé told me.

Davé has known many of his customers for years, before they were bold-faced names. He pointed to a picture of a very young, very wispy Leonardo DiCaprio at a birthday party. It was after he made *Romeo and Juliet,* but before *Titanic,* Davé told me. He added that Sofia Coppola had been coming there since she was only thirteen years old. There was also a picture of Kate Moss when she was just starting out. "Nobody wanted her then. She was too short," he commented.

Davé is a workaholic, always at his restaurant. During the midafternoon lull he sits at a restaurant table and plays solitaire, waiting for the phone to ring with reservation requests. He is always the one to pick up the phone and coo. His clients like the consistency of his presence, he confided. For these customers, Davé is the same. His food is the same. The cloisonné table lamps, white plates, and silverware are the same as when he first opened in 1982. For his customers, there is something reassuring about a restaurant that stays constant. "They don't want change," he said. "I don't know. I think sometimes society is moving so fast. Maybe it's good to have something not change."

Davé is like the neighborhood Chinese joint you went to when you were a kid. He remembers you. He knows what you like. He dotes on you. Only his neighborhood happens to be defined as the world of celebrity, with a geographical range that spans the globe.

SINGAPORE

Singaporeans are obsessed with eating. The island is small, and vices are banned, so food has become entertainment. As one

Singaporean food blogger explained to me over dinner, "It's the most fun we can have without getting fined."

"Or arrested," her friend added.

Two centuries ago, the 250-square mile island of Singapore was inhabited by fewer than a thousand natives; then the British arrived and, noting its useful location between India and China, declared it a colonial port. Their demand for labor coincided with a deluge in Southeast Asia of impoverished Chinese immigrants fleeing famine and war. The Chinese settled chiefly in Singapore, where today three out of four of the 4.5 million residents are ethnically Chinese. As Samantha, another food blogger, explained to me, Singapore is "the only majority Chinese country that is not, by someone's interpretation, part of China." So Singapore is a country full of people who identify with various facets of Chinese culture, but not the nation-state of China. As my cabdriver put it, "Chinese is a culture. Singaporean is an identity."

As a result, Singapore, with its affluent, food-obsessed population, has become a center of gravity for modern Chinese cuisine. The city-state has long been famed for its street food—so much so that its local food guide, Makansutra, focuses on hawkers' stands instead of high-end restaurants. Less acknowledged is how Singapore has become a thriving hot spot for high-end, creative Chinese restaurants. There was Xiyan, a "private kitchen" in the Hong Kong tradition where reservations had to be made in groups; Majestic, which paired a trendy, casual decor with a menu of impressive sophistication; Club Chinois and My Humble House, both of which featured original food and elaborate presentation. These were much better than the Chinese restaurants in America. These were even better than the Chinese restaurants in China.

One of Singapore's visionaries of modern Chinese cuisine is Andrew Tijoe, who has made it his mission to update Chinese cuisine on the global stage through his company, the Tung Lok group. Andrew is ethnically Chinese but was raised in Indonesia, where his father was a banker, until his family fled to Singapore because of rising anti-Chinese sentiment in Indonesia. We met over lunch at one of his newest restaurants, My Humble House, where he explained that he'd launched his restaurants because Chinese cuisine needed an overhaul, much as French and Italian cuisine had experienced decades earlier. "Chinese always, always say that Chinese food is the best. Just because you can find Chinese restaurants in any place in the world, that doesn't make you the best," he told me. "Traditional Chinese cuisine, while it tastes good, it does not look good," he said. "I was trying to change people's perceptions—particularly the Westerners or those non-Chinese—of Chinese cuisine. Chinese cuisine can also be trendy."

My Humble House had the most beautiful menu I had ever seen anywhere—a long booklet that mixed elegant, artistic calligraphy and exotic, poetic names for unfamiliar Chinese dishes. Those dishes were less unfamiliar than the names would suggest, he told me: "The so-called modern Chinese cuisine actually draws its influence from traditional Chinese [recipes]. We have selected many, many signature Chinese dishes which have been around the past fifty or one hundred years and then modified it, making the taste more global or giving it [a] global look." But combining Chinese cuisine with other international influences was often done wrong, he said. "If it is not merged perfectly, it's confusion, not fusion."

Change was happening faster outside of China than inside, where the argument that dishes had endured unchanged for so long was used as proof of their perfection. In contrast, he noted, "Singaporeans and Malaysians are more open-minded when it comes to re-creating Chinese cuisine because they have no burden, no cultural burden." They were the ones reimagining the cuisine in top Chinese restaurants all over the world—from Dubai to London.

LONDON, ENGLAND

I hadn't expected that the top-ranked Chinese restaurant in the world, inclusive of China, was in London—but that is where *Restaurant* magazine puts it: Hakkasan, run by Alan Yau and Singapore chef Tong Chee Hwee.

London has emerged as a global restaurant hot spot in recent years, despite the country's unfortunate history of bangers and mash and spotted dick—a reputation it has yet to fully shed. In 2004, French president Jacques Chirac, bitter because London had won the right to host the 2012 Olympics, snidely lashed out at Britain's cuisine. "The only thing they've ever done for European agriculture is mad cow," he said. "We can't trust people who have such bad food. After Finland, it's the country with the worst food."

One of the legacies of the age of empire was the extensive culinary exchange that rode on the backs of military conquest. Like water, cuisine moves from higher levels to lesser ones. So the cuisine of the colonies trickled back to the European powers. Indian flavors merged with British preferences, fusing into the red saucy chicken tikka masala, which the foreign secretary famously declared Great Britain's "national dish." Indonesian cuisine flowed to the Netherlands. France, notably, could hold its own in a two-way exchange. It absorbed influences from Vietnam while in turn giving back rich coffees and baguette sandwiches.

Despite the withering sneers of the neighboring French, London, with its influx of international immigrants and influences, has become home to a number of the world's most recognized restaurants. Hong Kong–born Alan Yau threw Chinese food into the upscale London restaurant mix when he opened Hakkasan in 2001 to fawning reviews and a coveted Michelin star. Three years later, Yau followed up with Yauatcha, a nouvelle dim sum parlor.

Alan Yau made it possible to once again say "sexy" and "Chinese restaurant" in the same sentence without snorting. Once upon a time, Chinese food in England could still be considered exotic and chic. Men impressed their dates with their sophistication by taking them out to Chinese restaurants. Upper-class housewives threw afternoon mah-jongg parties and pored over outlandish recipes calling for black sauce made with beans and sesame oil. But this image slowly eroded as Chinese restaurants became a victim of their own success. Immigrants flooded the dining scene with casual restaurants, selling British-Chinese dishes like crispy shredded beef (which has a whole lot of crisp, a lot of shred, and not a whole lot of beef). Chinese food became commonplace, chintzy, and cheap.

Hakkasan rejected that. Its sprawling underground lair surrounded us with sleekness and beauty. The restaurant's decor was dramatic. The hostesses were striking. Our waiter, a black man born in Paris, could have been a model. Instead of red lanterns and golden dragons, Hakkasan was packed with London yuppies looking glamorous in the dim lighting. I saw few Chinese faces. My friend whispered, "Chinese people wouldn't pay this much for Chinese food." It was true.

The Hakkasan and Yauatcha menus, written in both Chinese and English, listed classic Chinese dishes cast with some surprising twists (ostrich dumplings, stir-fried venison, Chilean sea bass dumplings, mango spring rolls). While the food was indeed impeccable and well executed, what gave Hakkasan its fame was the scene. Anyone could feel hip there, just through osmosis. Even I felt transformed. You are where you eat.

Generations ago, Chinese restaurants sold sophistication along with their food. Today, Hakkasan has reinvigorated that transaction, trading a night of its enchantment for the price of appetizer, entrée, dessert, and drinks.

TOKYO, JAPAN

The Japanese revere good food. They obsess over it. Their prime-time television schedule is full of food-related shows. The hunt for the best bowl of soba noodles. Celebrities eating dumplings and commenting on them. It is as though *American Idol, Survivor, The Amazing Race,* and all our other popular reality shows were replaced by programs from the Food Network. After all, this is the country that gave us the cult hit *Iron Chef,* where contestants faced off with famous Japanese chefs trained in French, Chinese, and Italian cuisine.

In Tokyo, the Chinese Iron Chef, Chen Kenichi, bounded into the room to meet me. Animated and expressive, with round cheeks and a white chef's hat, he was like a cartoon character with a slapstick sense of humor.

Japan is the only country in which the top Chinese chefs are not necessarily themselves Chinese, he told me. Chen said he is considered an anomaly because he's a famous Chinese chef who is in fact part Chinese. After World War II, many Chinese immigrants came to Japan to work, including his father, who is famous for introducing *mapodofu*—spicy bean curd with ground pork—to the Japanese public in 1953. Every country has a Chinese dish that grabs its attention. In Japan, *mapodofu* (known as ma po tofu in the United States) became wildly popular; housewives still make it for their families today.

In America, Chinese cuisine and culture are considered exotic, he told me, but they're not exotic from a Japanese perspective. Because Chinese cuisine is respected there, it is easier for

Japanese chefs to push the boundaries of Chinese cuisine yet still find a receptive audience. Among the top Chinese chefs was Yuji Wakiya, whose French influence makes him the nouvelle rebel of Chinese cuisine. His eponymous restaurant in Tokyo, Wakiya, is unobtrusively tucked into a quiet alley in Akasaka, an upscale neighborhood known for its *ryotei*, discreet high-end restaurants favored by Japanese power brokers for their private negotiations.

Japan was a host to a panoply of top-caliber Chinese restaurants—including a number in the port city of Yokohama, which showed me it was possible for a Chinatown to be both clean and expensive. But one place in Tokyo caught my eye: Reikasai, a three-table restaurant in Tokyo with set menus that ranged up to $400 per person. It was pricey and exclusive, characteristics often valued for their own sakes. It also had a long history: the original Li Family restaurant had been opened in Beijing by a family whose ancestor, Li Zijia, had served as the minister of household affairs for the powerful empress dowager Cixi, the Queen Victoria of nineteenth-century China. After the empress died and the Qing Dynasty was overthrown, Li kept the recipes from the kitchen and passed them down as part of his family home cooking. They would have probably faded away into the past, like so much of China's historical legacy, if not for a national cooking competition during the thirty-fifth-anniversary celebration of the founding of the People's Republic of China, in 1984. Li Zijia's great-granddaughter Li Li won the competition, and reporters descended on her, asking whether she would open a restaurant.

The family thought about it, knocked down a wall in their home, and put a single ten-person table in one room. Over time, the restaurant grew larger but stayed within the Beijing alleys. In Tokyo, all of this had been transformed. The recipes were the same. The chef was still a family member, Li Ai Ying, who had been a doctor in China. But the dining experience had been repackaged: private rooms, jade chopstick holders, dishes presented one at a time with a flourish. The unusual appetizers included a napa cabbage heart marinated in a mustard-and-white-wine sauce, which I had never seen before anywhere. There was also a foie gras–like dish made with green beans and pork. The rice, which came from Niigata, was velvety in the mouth.

The dishes themselves were very good, but what had catapulted them onto the world stage was the story behind them. Without the exclusive decor, the food we ate could have been really good home cooking with some very expensive ingredients—abalone, shark's fins, and bird's nests imported from Thailand.

Nevertheless, we enjoyed the show. Restaurants have always profited from a combination of food and theater. Reikasai placed its bets on theater.

AUSTRALIA

To the average American, the phrase "Australian cuisine" might bring to mind images of Outback Steakhouse; this is unfortunate. Because of the influx of immigrants, bringing influences from around the globe, Australia has developed a sophisticated culinary scene and is home to two of the top Chinese restaurants in the world. The first is Billy Kwong, a home-style restaurant with a rare distinction: it is one of ten restaurants around the world that *New York Times* gourmand R. W. Apple considered worth getting on a plane for. The other is Flower Drum, in Melbourne, which had been one of *Restaurant* magazine's top fifty restaurants in the world for four years in a row.

Located in a slightly bohemian neighborhood in Sydney, Billy Kwong is an establishment of modest size with an outsized reputation. Kylie Kwong, a fourth-generation Chinese-Australian, opened the restaurant in 2000 with her partner, Bill Granger (the merger of their names produced Billy Kwong; there is no Mr. Billy Kwong). While the Chinese language was not maintained through the generations of Kylie's Australian family, the cuisine was. She has also developed an ecofriendly, holistic approach to food, in part from a newly discovered Buddhist outlook on life.

Kylie's mission is to attack the reputation that Chinese food has gained throughout much of the West for being oily and unhealthy. Her menus and cookbooks are sprinkled with terms like "fair trade," "free-range," and "sustainable," and ingredients like line-caught fish and biodynamic eggs.

The dishes I tried were recognizably Chinese food, but with a fresh, inspiring sheen cast over them. The sweet corn soup was made with fresh corn kernels instead of creamed corn. Her sweet-and-sour sauce uses fresh tomatoes instead of bottled ketchup. She prefers the French technique of reducing to the Chinese technique of adding thickeners such as corn starch. She uses no MSG.

"I started to realize how important we could be, how we could make a difference to people's perception of Chinese food," she said. Through the combined platform of the restaurant, her television show, and her cookbooks, her message has rippled throughout Australia. She is greeted with exclamations of "I've never had Chinese food like this!" and "I thought Chinese food was MSG" and "I felt so healthy when I got out of here."

The term "modern Chinese" is often bandied about by reviewers when describing her food. But Kylie's "modern Chinese" is not "modern" in terms of fusion. The evolution occurred not through recipes but through the underlying ingredients. "A lot of young chefs do their thing wrong. They get hung on reinventing the wheel, creating all these amazing dishes without context and structure," she said. Kylie emphasizes another approach: "Forget about that. Let's try to focus on the classics as well, and do them better than everyone." Kylie spoke wisely. Perhaps the gourmand's desire for novelty and stimulation was a Sisyphean quest. Anything that was new eventually would become passé. Instead we may better find fulfillment by returning to the tried-and-true.

In an era of celebrity chefs and multimillion-dollar designers, Flower Drum has achieved international status without the aid of any brand names. It is located in a city, Melbourne, that is (relatively speaking) off the gustatory path. It does not have a chef with his own television show or cookbook line. Its interior design, while elegant, is not particularly dramatic. It has never relied on an innovative gimmick or a media-savvy spin—like $350 chef's choice menus or an imperial historical pedigree. What Flower Drum does offer: superb service and classic Chinese dishes made with high-quality ingredients. The elegant simplicity of the dishes lets the lush ingredients shine through, like a beautiful woman who knows she looks her best in a white summer dress. Each bite—gigantic scallops, Wagyu beef—is to be savored and remembered.

But was that it? Flower Drum's fame, give its global latitude, was puzzling. I asked its founder, Gilbert Lau, point-blank: "Why is Flower Drum famous?"

It took more than twenty years to build the restaurant's reputation, he explained. Flower Drum opened in 1975. But it wasn't until the mid-1990s that it received international recognition. Since then it has appeared on *Restaurant* magazine's list of the top fifty restaurants in the world four times. Ultimately what lifted Flower Drum was the power of word of mouth. "People like to talk about restaurants," Gilbert said. "It's one of the most popular conversation topics." At a certain point, the word of mouth and the ensuing accolades build: people are attracted to the reputation itself. Customers would come in clutching the

Restaurant magazine list, or a guidebook, or the 2003 *New York Times* travel article by R. W. Apple proclaiming that Flower Drum might be one of the best Chinese restaurants anywhere. "People like restaurants they have heard a lot about," he said wryly. "The harder it is to get in, the more they want to go."

His observations have a certain astuteness. People like to talk about their experiences: travel, concerts, books, films. Of those, restaurants provide something that everyone can relate to, that can be enjoyed over and over, and that is relatively affordable. Restaurant dining, however, is an ephemeral experience. Once you have eaten the meal, it is gone. All you have left is the memory. But memories become stories, and stories, in turn, derive value from being shared. So perhaps what we seek in great restaurants is not only the immediate succession of sensations at the dinner table but also the tale that can be told afterward.

SAN FRANCISCO, UNITED STATES

In the San Francisco area, there are multiple Chinatowns, multiple generations of Chinese history, and a myriad of assessments about what the best Chinese restaurants are. The lists went on and on—from friends, online reviews on Yelp.com, restaurant critics' top ten lists. I was urged to try Tommy Toy's, the haute Chinese cuisine with a French flair; R&G Lounge, a family favorite in Chinatown; and Yank Sing, the classic upscale dim sum restaurant in the Financial District. There were also popular restaurants in Cupertino, Millbrae, and Daly City.

At Shanghai 1930, a combined jazz club and Chinese restaurant located in San Francisco's Financial District, I waited patiently behind an older, sturdy-looking woman with blunt-cut gray hair.

"Good evening, madam, how are you today?" the hostess asked pleasantly.

"Terrible!" she barked in a nasal voice.

The hostess and I looked up in surprise.

"I asked my hotel to recommend a Chinese restaurant where *Chinese* people eat." She pointed to the dimly lit dining area, which was full of yuppies, very few of whom looked Chinese. "Where are the *Chinese* people?"

The hostess stammered and the maître d', who looked European, swept into the conversation. "What seems to be the problem, madam?"

"Why *would* my hotel recommend this restaurant?" she demanded.

"Well, because it's the best Chinese restaurant in the city," he said with a forced upbeat laugh. (To its credit, Shanghai 1930 certainly was regarded as one of the best Chinese restaurants in the city; indeed, the food was very good, though on the pricier side.)

But there was no dissuading the woman. "What do *you* know? You're French!"

She had one further comment: "I'll be needing a taxi." With that, she swept out.

Another highly regarded restaurant on the list was Jai Yun, reportedly where Chinatown chefs preferred to dine. When I called to make a reservation for me and my friend Bernard Chang, I was told, "We only do a seven o'clock seating."

The menu at the cramped Chinatown establishment was bizarrely simple: there were no dishes listed. On one side was a list of prices: set menus for $45, $65, and so on, up to $120. Cash only. The chef simply decided what he would cook. The other side of the menu contained an apology from the chef for not speaking English but asked for feedback nonetheless.

"This is a hole-in-the-wall with non-hole-in-the-wall prices," Bernie said, looking at the menu. He had researched Jai Yun on the Internet and had found it drawing passionate opinions on both sides. "This is either going to be brilliant or it's one of the most successful hoaxes I've ever witnessed."

I shushed him. You have to have faith, I told him.

The waitress began the parade of dishes: tiny plates filled with various textures and colors. Pickled. Shredded. Chilled. Reds. Beiges. Various degrees of translucence. Lotus root. Jellyfish. Tofu. The dishes were good, but nothing we hadn't seen before in the United States or China. Bernie rolled his eyes. "I could take you down the street to a Shanghainese place and buy you similar dishes for twenty dollars a person," he said. But we were both impressed with a selection made of thin slices of abalone cushioned on a delicate, fluffy cloud of warm egg whites. "You know what this is," he said, gesturing at the tiny restaurant where most of the crowd was not Chinese. "It's for people who were always afraid of ordering the Chinese specials on the wall. Or don't have someone who is Chinese who can order it for them." This way, he said, they don't have to deal with odd-sounding ingredients like bamboo pith or lotus root or jellyfish. The dishes just arrive at the table. Jai Yun's diners have outsourced the decision making. They don't have to know what something is before they eat it.

The Chinese food was very Chinese, even if the crowd was not. "They like it here because they feel like they are keeping it real," Bernie observed. The Chinese dining experience is all about the dive, he said. From the very early days of Chinese restaurants in San Francisco and New York, young bohemians would go "slumming" in Chinatown as an adventure. (In the days before airplanes, it was the equivalent of backpacking through Southeast Asia.)

Perhaps he's right. In my experience, people talking about Chinese restaurants are more likely to brag about the dive than about opulent establishments like Restaurant Royale in Peru. It's part of the authentic Chinese experience.

DUBAI, UNITED ARAB EMIRATES

Dubai is like Las Vegas, only with scant overt sin: a glittering manufactured metropolis installed amid placid desert hills. Instead of gambling, skin, and alcohol-infused festivities to drive the local economy, Dubai has made an epic embrace of free trade, turning its modest oil revenues into a world-class infrastructure in less than a half century.

What nature doesn't give Dubai, the government creates. The city-state's attempts to defy climate and geography are legendary. In 1976, the sheikh decided to construct the largest man-made harbor in the world, Jebel Ali. In another project, man-made islands are being strung together in archipelago configurations of palm trees and a map of the world. Dubai even has its own ski slope: a winter wonderland inside the Mall of the Emirates, complete with ski lifts, frosted pine trees, and plastic penguins. With its ambition and money, Dubai can will an alternate reality into existence.

Middle Eastern historians may scoff at Dubai because the tiny, family-ruled kingdom is short on the tumultuous legacy that infuses much of the region. But from a culinary perspective, Dubai is fascinating precisely because it is short on history. With a population of over 1 million that is over 85 percent foreign, some of the most difficult cuisine to find is whatever would be considered "local emirate food." It is a city of European McKinsey consultants, American investors, Filipina waitresses, Pakistani laborers, Somalian hotel clerks, and Korean flight attendants. Cuisines from all over the world converge helter-skelter in great street food, and in high-end restaurants with chefs drawn from every corner of the globe.

The Chinese in Dubai are businessmen, manufacturers, and traders. They do not work in restaurants. There is no Chinatown in Dubai. Instead, there is a sprawling dragon-shaped building called Dragon Mart, a collaboration between the Chinese and

Dubai governments. In this wholesale market for Chinese goods, the "spine" of the dragon approaches a mile in length, and Chinese companies sell anything and everything there: fishing rods, generators, toilets, lanterns, ice-cream machines, LCD displays, bras, dancing battery-powered giraffes, fish tanks. Buyers from around the region converge at Dragon Mart and have their goods shipped to other locations in the Middle East.

Many of the Chinese workers I met at Dragon Mart had been in Dubai for only two or three years. I asked one vendor if he liked it there. He looked at me. "Does anyone like leaving home?" he asked with arched eyebrows. "We're here to make money."

Without a steady supply of cheap Chinese labor, Chinese restaurants in Dubai were forced to substitute Filipinos. But there was one glaring exception: Zheng He, a nouvelle Chinese restaurant whose chef had previously worked for the Singaporean Tung Lok group.

Zheng He was, disconcertingly, full of Chinese faces. A Chinese hostess greeted us in genteel English. A Chinese waiter from Yangzhou asked us for our drinks. A Chinese waitress patiently explained every single dish to us.

The executive chef, Leong Chee Yeng, said they had imported the Chinese waitstaff from China because they felt it was critical for the Chinese dining experience. "If you walk in and there is a Filipina hostess," he told me, "it doesn't give you a sense of authenticity."

But the food is the same, I pressed. And in either case, the chefs in the back are Chinese.

He pointed out that the experience would not be the same. "It's subconscious," he said. Others agreed. "Everywhere else, no matter food you are eating, it's always the same Filipino person. The server, whether you're at a five-star restaurant or an average one, is more or less the same," said Noor, one of my dining companions. But Zheng He was different, she said. "It doesn't even feel like you are in Dubai."

Her last comment startled me. The same thing could be said of the Ski Dubai indoor ski slope: they substitute an alternate reality.

SEOUL, KOREA

The best Chinese restaurant in Seoul is widely regarded as Palsun, in the historic Shilla Hotel, which is located against the backdrop of Nam Mountain. As one friend put it, "It's a place where future in-laws go to meet each other."

At Palsun, I met Dean Kim, a Korean-American who runs a popular chain of American-style Chinese restaurants in Seoul called Ho Lee Chow. The restaurant has a number of brightly lit, hip locations throughout the city, filled with young professionals and middle-class families. (They even serve General Tso's chicken.) To emphasize its Americanness, Ho Lee Chow manufactures its own American-style trapezoidal take-out boxes—in red, with a panda icon—instead of using the Styrofoam containers popular throughout Korea.

The day I visited, Palsun was staffed by women and men in modern black Chinese outfits, whisking around, being graciously attentive. The menu was filled with classic Korean-Chinese dishes: *tangsuyuk* (sweet-and-sour pork or beef), *mandu* (fried dumplings), *jampong* (noodles in spicy broth with seafood and vegetables), and *jjajangmyun* (noodles in black bean sauce). Korean *jjajangmyun*, which barely resembles the Chinese version, is a national comfort food and the subject of a popular rap song. The cost of *jjajangmyun* is even used in calculating Korea's consumer price index. For dessert, the restaurant offered caramelized apples. Most of the top Chinese restaurants I had visited were distinctively Cantonese in orientation, often with strong ties to the Hong Kong culinary tradition. Palsun, in contrast, was influenced by the cuisine from northeastern China, where most of the Chinese-Koreans immigrants were from.

Almost all the top Chinese restaurants in Seoul are located in hotels, Dean explained over dinner. Before Korea's rapid industrialization, which was jump-started by the 1988 Seoul Olympic games, people mostly ate at home and there were few restaurants on the street. "There was no food service industry to speak of. It only existed within hotels," he said. "Even back when I was young, twenty years ago, twenty-five years ago, if you ever wanted to get a decent Western meal you had to go to a nice hotel."

The restaurant industry depends on a population with leisure time and disposable income. It was, after all, France's nouveau riche that propelled the nascent restaurant industry after the French Revolution. (This is why so much of the dining vocabulary is derived from French: "maître d'," "hors d'oeuvres," "menu," "entrée.") Korea has only recently gotten on the restaurant bandwagon, but it has gotten on with a vengeance. Pizza, hamburgers, and French food are now offered alongside the stalwart of Chinese cuisine.

Dean explained to me Ho Lee Chow's strategy for offering American Chinese food. "The perception of Korean-Chinese food here is that it's very cheap or it's very expensive. This is the very expensive," he said, gesturing at Palsun. "It's the ambience and the service style: one dish coming out at a time. For the low end, it's more about convenience." Ho Lee Chow chose to situate itself in the middle. "Our whole premise was to build a concept that was a very casual concept, full-service, family-oriented, for daters and for gatherings, with affordable prices, right in the middle because you had this huge disparity between high and low. In order to do that, we hedged our risk by introducing a new style of Chinese food."

"Do you consider your food to be authentic?" I asked.

"We'd like to think so, that we serve authentic American-style Chinese cuisine."

VANCOUVER, CANADA

In the United States, politicians strain themselves to sprinkle Spanish into their campaigning. In Vancouver, the mayor, Sam Sullivan, makes speeches in Cantonese.

In the early 1990s, Vancouver and its suburbs, located just an eleven-hour flight from Hong Kong, were flooded with gigantic waves of Hong Kong immigrants spooked by the combination of the Tiananmen Square crackdown and Hong Kong's impending handover back to China. Their transition was not always smooth. Locals protested the Chinese-built megahomes, which, with their assertive cubic presence, still stick out from the low-slung Brady Bunch–era houses. Chinese newspapers counseled the Hong Kong immigrants about the behaviors local Canadians found most annoying: cutting down trees and paving over yards.

The new Chinese are most visible in Richmond, which, like Cupertino in the Bay Area or Monterey Park near Los Angeles, is a particular breed of Chinatown: the Chinaburb. These burbs represent the crisp, clean prosperity of postwar Asia, with little of the urban messiness of New York City's Chinatown or the prewar agricultural poverty of Hong Kong and Taiwan. Settled by immigrants armed with skilled-worker visas or hundreds of thousands of dollars in investment funds to smooth their way to citizenship, these places carry human and financial capital of the sort that economists salivate over.

With demand and supply for great Chinese food, the Vancouver region is known for some of the best Chinese restaurants outside China. The large dining halls Sun Sui Wah and Kirin offer eye-popping giant seafood and exquisite dim sum; Shanghai

River showcases an attractive open kitchen. But the place that caught my attention was Zen Fine Chinese Cuisine, voted best new restaurant in Vancouver in 2005.

Zen is hard to find, and not in the exclusive, has-no-sign-outside, edgy-nightclub way. It is hard to find because the tastefully decorated establishment is located on the second floor of a Richmond strip mall, several hundred feet down from an auto-repair shop. I drove right past it and had to make a U-turn to get back.

There is no à la carte menu at Zen. Instead the owner-chef, Sam Lau, offers a series of tasting menus that change at his whim—and he's a bit of a control freak, as artists tend to be. There are only two people in the kitchen, Sam Lau and his assistant chef, and Sam spends considerable time obsessing. Sam, who even in his forties resembles a lanky teenager, started in the restaurant business as a dishwasher at his sister-in-law's noodle shop. There, he would mop the floor while waiting for everyone else to leave, then secretly practice cooking. From that, he has become a self-taught chef of impressive scope—both refined and creative, with a Chinese foundation, European techniques, and theatrical presentation. (One dish, curried scallops and prawns, arrived in a shell surrounded by blue flames.) He has devised an astounding garlic sauce processed so as not to leave anything on your breath. Like most Chinese chefs, he prizes fresh seafood. I watched, mesmerized, as the assistant chef chopped living lobsters down the center, tossing their half bodies into a big gray plastic tray, legs and antennae still moving.

But what surprised me about Zen was the number of Chinese faces in the restaurant—both the patrons and the informative waitstaff. In fact, the friend I'd brought along was probably the only white face in the restaurant the whole night.

Fusion—or "global" and "infused" or "synergistic" or "inspired"—cuisine is not the domain of Chinese diners outside Asia. Chinese immigrants generally do not want their cuisine "fused" with any other. But at Sam's place, the clientele comprised mostly first-generation Chinese immigrants; the men had cell phones clipped to their belts and wore short-sleeved button-down shirts.

When Sam first opened his restaurant, the Chinese clients complained: Why is it so dark in here? Why are you bringing the dishes out one by one? Why are the portions so small while the plates are so big? It was a gutsy move for him to have set menus, since Chinese menus generally offer dozens, if not hundreds, of choices.

In the summer of 2006, the restaurant found its footing. It offered an eight-course tasting menu that included a half lobster, roasted quail, shark's fin soup, and flaming curried whelk at a half-off discount: only $38 Canadian (originally $75). Within days, the modest restaurant was booked every night. And the customers kept coming back. Sam had tapped into the key Chinese trait for an appreciation of fine dining: Chinese people love nothing if not a good deal.

At many fusion restaurants, I can never be sure if the food is even recognizably Chinese anymore, but I became convinced that Sam's food is genuinely Chinese, if only because his clientele is almost exclusively Chinese. Somehow, along the way, Sam has convinced a Chinese clientele and a Chinese palate to savor fine dining in a Western style.

BRAZIL

The fortune cookie trail and the worldwide hunt for Chinese restaurants intersected in an unexpected place: Brazil.

Government officials launched an investigation when in February 2004, fifteen people won the national Mega-Sena lottery—three times as many as any previous record. They feared fraud. Instead, they found an explanation met with disbelief: fortune cookies from a chain of Chinese restaurants in northeastern Brazil called Chinatown, owned by the Fong family.

Chinese food has spread around the world. Fortune cookies—and lucky numbers—are following behind.

I asked Bobby Fong, who met me at the airport, how fortune cookies had arrived in Brazil.

He smiled. "My father is a dreamer."

Bobby's father, Fong Yu, had been enchanted by fortune cookies when he saw them in America in the early 1990s. He immediately recognized their potential for his Chinese-restaurant chain in Brazil: a marketing ploy to amuse, attract, and retain customers. The same insight had occurred to Chinese-restaurant owners in California in the 1930s, when the end of Prohibition had forced them to find creative ways to retain customers in a newly competitive dining scene.

For two years, Fong Yu tried in vain to find a machine to make the cookies. A shroud of secrecy surrounded the fortune cookie industry. People did not talk. Phone directories were of no use, since the manufacturers of fortune cookie machines did not place ads in the Yellow Pages. There was no Internet to help Fong pierce though all this opacity.

Fong Yu left his business card in Chinese restaurants coast to coast—Los Angeles, Las Vegas, New York, Miami—telling people he was looking to buy a fortune cookie machine. In 1995, back in Brazil, he received a letter from a Korean-American engineer outside Boston who identified himself as a fortune cookie machine maker. It was Yong Sik Lee, whose Fortune III had revolutionized the business. Within a week of receiving the letter, Fong Yu and his wife were on a plane to New York City; they rented a car and drove up to Boston to place an order for a machine. Fong Yu shipped the machine back to Recife under severe import taxes.

Brazilians found the cookies both cute and exotic. Customers would bite into a cookie before realizing that there was a piece of paper inside. "In China, no fortune cookies," Fong Yu told me. "It's like a *pastel*! But there is no *pastel* in China." I seemed confused, so Fong Yu told his waiters to bring out a *pastel*, one of the most iconic Chinese foods in Brazil. To me, the large, flat, deep-fried stuffed bread looked South American or maybe Russian—but definitely not Chinese. "People think it's from China, just like fortune cookie," Fong Yu said, amused. In fact, the *pastel* may have been an invention devised by Japanese immigrants—not that I had seen anything like it in Japanese cuisine either. Brazil has a huge Japanese population; its most populous city, São Paulo, has the largest concentration of ethnic Japanese outside Japan. Brazil, like the United States, was built up largely of immigrants, African slaves, and whatever indigenous Indians managed to survive the European siege. Its population is a complex amalgam of Portuguese and Dutch colonizers; the descendents of slaves; Indians; plus waves of Italian, German, Japanese, and Lebanese immigrants. The intermingling of those bloodlines and cultures manifests itself even at the Brazilian breakfast table, which often includes salami, courtesy of the Italian immigrants; *tapiocas,* filled crepelike white pancakes originally made by indigenous Indians; *misto quente, a* Portuguese-style sandwich of grilled cheese and ham; and *canjica,* an Africa-influenced corn pudding.

Oddly, one nationality missing from the Brazilian mix is the Chinese, notable given the widespread immigration from China. In the second half of the seventeenth century, when the end of slavery in Brazil seemed all but inevitable, a lively debate emerged as to whether or not to import Chinese laborers to work in the fields. But the Chinese government, wary after its citizens' nasty experiences in Peru and Cuba, discouraged immigration to Brazil. The Japanese came instead. Today, the Chinese in Brazil defer to the Japanese influence on the national palate. Almost all Chinese restaurants there serve yakisoba.

• • •

After the surprising number of lottery winners, the government sent an investigator from Brasilia to Recife to interview the Fongs and visit the factory, which was located in the muggy first floor of a small building in southern Recife. Inside were two workers and two fortune cookie machines, but the inspector was interested in the stacks and stacks of fortunes with lucky numbers. "They wanted to know how we produced the random number," Bobby said.

The investigator suggested that perhaps the Fongs were pulling some funny business.

Fong Yu took offense. "I told them it couldn't be the case. After all, I didn't win any money!" He insisted, "It's a coincidence."

Before I left, Bobby offered one last thought about how fortune cookies were related to the lottery, and why people play the lucky numbers listed with the fortunes. "They both represent hope—a better life," he said. He paused, then added, "Sometimes it's an illusion."

I thought about that on the way out. An unbroken fortune cookie and an unexpired lottery ticket: they both hold promise. There is no sense of disappointment, of unfulfilled potential. It's a bit like youth. Both also ask for a small leap of faith. If you believe in the potential of the lucky number, in the upbeat fortune, you will be happier. It's a little bit of optimism packaged inside a wafer, an American import.

MAURITIUS

A tiny speck in the Indian Ocean barely over half the size of Rhode Island and located almost five hundred miles east of Madagascar, Mauritius may be best known as the original home of the dodo bird. When sailors found the uninhabited island at the turn of the seventeenth century, they encountered a three-foot-high flightless bird with a hooked beak and a naive fearlessness toward its human predators.

The dodo is now extinct, but what drew me to Mauritius were the legends of its fusion—culinary and otherwise, from its succession of Dutch, French, and British colonizers, and its Indian, Chinese, and African workers. You can indulge in octopus curry served on French bread, European cheese samosas, or chicken shawarma with coleslaw and pineapple. I had great hopes for Chinese food in Mauritius. Perhaps its fusion with other great cuisines would make for a great dining experience?

Nope.

The Chinese food itself—tiger prawns stir-fried in garlic and butter, sweet-and-sour lobster—was interesting but not spectacular. The global influence may have even made it a little worse for the wear. Nonetheless, the Mauritians loved it. Chinese restaurants are the most common type in the small island country—despite the fact that some 65 percent of the island is of Indian descent. Most of the Indian eateries were relatively casual places, and there were few "Mauritian" restaurants (those that did exist tended to cater to tourists looking for "authentic local food"). Chinese restaurants, on the other hand, spanned the entire island—from Port Louis's Chinatown to highway rest stops—though Chinese people make up only 3 percent of the population.

The best Mauritian Chinese restaurant was widely considered to be King Dragon in Quatre Bornes, owned by a third-generation Mauritian-Chinese man who had never set foot in China. When I met Ahsee Leung-Pah-Hang, the owner, I was charmed by his French accent. His grandfather had moved to Mauritius from Meixian, a town in Guangdong Province where most of the Chinese immigrants to Mauritius had come from. Ahsee himself spoke only a few phrases of Chinese. Of his six chefs, only one had been to China.

I asked him about the popularity of Chinese restaurants on the island. Why weren't there any nice Mauritian-cuisine restaurants?

"The poor people don't eat in restaurants," he said. "If you like Indian food, better to eat it at home. You can't make Chinese food." Perhaps that is the appeal ethnic restaurants offer to many people around the world: something they can't get at home.

MUMBAI, INDIA

I arrived in Mumbai (formerly Bombay) to meet friends for dinner at the most famous Chinese restaurant in all of India, China Garden. As one Mumbai resident put it to me: "It's not a restaurant, it's an institution."

For a quarter century, China Garden has been a favorite of Bollywood celebrities, Mumbai billionaires, and prime ministers. Yet it is still affordable for middle-class Indian families. If there is a godfather for Indian-Chinese cuisine, it is the owner of China Garden: Nelson Wang, a third-generation Chinese-Indian man who was born in Calcutta and given up for adoption three days later, after his father died. As one customer described him in my presence: "Chinese blood, Indian brain."

Chinese food is a great equalizer in India. It is a national obsession. When Indians are not eating Indian food, they are most likely eating Chinese food. It has been elevated to a position in one of India's fundamental food dichotomies: vegetarian versus nonvegetarian, northern versus southern, Chinese versus Indian. It is sold from hawkers' carts, in hole-in-the-walls, on the room service menu of five-star resorts, and in the finest "Indian" restaurants. McDonald's may have made inroads into India with its McAloo Tikki sandwich and Chicken Maharaja Mac, but it is swept off the table by Chinese cuisine.

Nelson is credited with having introduced Mumbai and, in fact, all of India to the Indian-Chinese fusion fare its people love: vegetarian Manchurian dishes (he wanted a very Chinese name), fried creamy corn (he hated to waste the leftover congealed corn in the fridge), fried chicken lollipops (he wished to find a way to use up chicken wings), and date pancakes (he sought a new dessert that would satisfy the Indian sweet tooth).

Starting in 1974 with only twenty-seven rupees in his pocket, Nelson worked his way up through a series of jobs in restaurants until, in 1984, he was ready to open a Chinese fine-dining establishment. China Garden became an immediate sensation.

People would wait two hours or more for a table. In an effort to turn over tables more quickly, the restaurant stopped giving out fortune cookies. (Made by a local company, they were flavored with butter instead of vanilla to cater to the Indian palate.) "They take too much time at my table," Nelson grumbled. "I give them fortune cookies, then the customers are like ha ha ha. It takes another fifteen minutes." Instead, for dessert, his restaurant offers date pancakes and honey noodles with ice cream—both Indian-Chinese classics. The honey noodles are like the deep-fried, flat chow mein noodles served in American Chinese restaurants, but coated with a sweet layer of honey and sprinkled with sesames. Without Nelson's support, fortune cookies really never took off.

As I was sitting there, interviewing Nelson, I suddenly realized that given (1) India's population, (2) the Indian passion for Chinese food, and (3) Nelson's role in Indian-Chinese cuisine, I was probably looking at the man who had influenced the Chinese dining experience for more people on the planet than any other single person.

JAMAICA

Jamaica's national motto is "Out of many, one people," a reference to how several cultures came together to produce the nation: African, Chinese, Indian, British, Spanish. The heavy Indian presence has made its way into Jamaican cuisine in the form of curries and rotis.

The Jamaican-Chinese piece of the puzzle slipped into place in the mid-nineteenth century, when Chinese immigrants arrived to work as shopkeepers and restaurant owners. Over generations they have transitioned: some have expanded their shops to retail chains; others have moved into Jamaica's most notable export, reggae music. (Bob Marley's first producer was a Chinese-Jamaican man, Leslie Kong.)

Over time, there haven't been enough Chinese cooks in Jamaica to fill the nation's demand for Chinese food. As a result, Jamaica is one of the few places where you can consistently see black men working woks.

China Express, an upscale establishment in Kingston, was one of the rare restaurants whose chef was not only Chinese but trained in China—though, like other Jamaican Chinese restaurants, it served cheesecake for dessert. I asked the manager, Bruce Chang, why Chinese food was so popular in Jamaica. "Jamaican food is not much variety," he said. "With Chinese food, you can do pork or chicken a hundred ways." That variety has allowed it to migrate around the world.

ROME, ITALY

The only good ethnic cuisine you can get consistently in Rome is Italian. This is not a tautology. After all, there is Roman cuisine, Sicilian cuisine, Neapolitan cuisine, Tuscan cuisine, Venetian cuisine.

The local attitude is "Italian food is perfect—why would you want to eat anything else?"

Italians tend to forget this, but the ingredient at the heart of their cooking was, until recently, completely foreign. Not until the 1830s did Italian cooks take the tomato, which had made its way from the New World to Europe as a botanical curiosity, and run with it as a sauce. Since then, Italians' receptiveness to other culinary influences has been decidedly more limited. Despite a history as the seat of an ancient empire that stretched from London to Constantinople, Rome has only recently experienced the phenomenon of modern immigration. (The British and French will snidely point out that it is because Italy never successfully colonized any place significant. Italians will sniff that the Britain and France are loosening their standards only to attract soccer players.) Up until the 1980s, Italy was a net exporter of labor.

The Chinese restaurants that do exist in Rome are mostly takeouts or subsist by attracting Chinese tour groups; they all serve fried gelato for dessert.

If the Chinese immigrants to Italy weren't opening restaurants, then what were they doing? Prato, an old Italian city some fourteen miles outside Florence where almost 15 percent of the population is Chinese, held much of the answer. In Prato, locals have dubbed one of the Chinese neighborhoods San Pechino, which translates to "St. Beijing," and the Chinese have adopted names like Luigi and Marco. Walk inside some of Prato's factories and you might think you're in Zhejiang, the province of China where most of the immigrants are from. The workers are Chinese. The owners are Chinese. The managers are Chinese. The pop music in the background is Chinese. But the things they are making? They are labeled with "Made in Italy."

There are two notable Chinese restaurants in Rome. A sleek establishment called Green T is unusual for ethnic restaurants in Italy because it is hip, good, and expensive. (Italians are disinclined to eat ethnic food to begin with, much less pay a lot of money for it.) The other, Hangzhou, lies at the opposite end of the dining spectrum: small, crowded, and noisy, with kitschy Mao-era decor. Nonetheless, the wait for a table can last over an hour, the crowds spilling out onto the narrow stone streets. One friend explained the appeal to me as we stood on line outside: "Being in a dive is part of the experience."

Hangzhou tops off its meals with fortune cookies; they are written in Italian, but made in Germany. It was an unexpected sighting. Sonia, the owner, was dressed that night in a bright red outfit that resembled a Chinese folk dancer's costume. She told me, in Chinese, why she imports them. "Everyone likes them. There is no one who doesn't like fortune cookies. But they are particularly, particularly American."

NEW YORK, UNITED STATES

I arrived back in my hometown hoping to discover that the world's greatest Chinese restaurant would be no more than a subway ride from my house. New York City is both a world culinary capital and a nexus for fine Chinese dining in the West. Manhattan is where Westerners discovered Sichuan and Hunan cuisine in the late 1960s and early 1970s. And New York, after all, was the birthplace of the recipe of General Tso's chicken. "The revolution was so successful that it was its own worst enemy," said Ed Schoenfeld, a Brooklyn-based Chinese-restaurant consultant. "Everyone embraced Chinese food, and the market expanded greatly. Recent immigrants could make a great deal of money. So people who did that had less training. There was a general dumbing down." Truth be told, while New York has its share of authentic Chinese dives, there are really no standout fine Chinese restaurants in New York anymore. As *Zagat* pointed out in its 2005 list of top American restaurants, "Fine Chinese dining, once the leading Asian cuisine in the U.S., seems to have stalled, with not even one Chinese restaurant reaching the Top Food Rankings."

There seemed to be hope when Ian Schrager decided he needed a Chinese response to London's Hakkasan in his upscale Gramercy Park Hotel. And what better way to answer Hakkasan than to hire its creator, Alan Yau himself? But the efforts to open Park Chinois stalled for over a year, and then, in 2007, were abandoned. Why?

One reason that many cite is also the primary cause for the stagnant state of Chinese cuisine in New York in general: Alan Yau was unable to get a visa for the chef. It is nearly impossible to get top Chinese chefs into the United States since the visa system favors superstars (like world-class geniuses and models) and skilled migrants (who need four years of college or the equivalent). Potential top chefs do not fall neatly into either category.

So Schrager turned to Yuji Wakiya, the French-influenced Japanese-Chinese chef from Tokyo. I had been impressed with his food when I'd visited that city: a combination of the delicacy of Japanese cuisine, the presentation of French cuisine, and the rich flavors of Chinese cuisine. But would he deliver the same to New Yorkers?

Diners, critics, and myself were oddly perplexed by the high-end menu at the New York Wakiya. It was not what I had experienced in Japan. I was trying to put my finger on what seemed off about the menu when a stray piece of broccoli caught my eye. Broccoli, which originally hails from Italy, is not a commonly used Chinese vegetable. The Chinese have their own version of broccoli—called Chinese broccoli, similar to broccoli rabe. China, in fact, imports broccoli from the United States, where the agricultural industry has genetically engineered stalkless broccoli (like muffin tops).

Looking at the piece of broccoli, I realized what I found disconcerting: this was a Japanese chef's perception of American Chinese food. Among more authentic Chinese dishes were stereotypes of American Chinese food gone horribly awry on fancy leaf-shaped white plates. There was broccoli, sweet-and-sour, random cauliflower, deep-fried stuff, fried rice, fried noodles, egg rolls.

Had American Chinese food suffered so much that even a haute cuisine interpretation simply made it seem comic?

At the end of my frantic travels, I landed home with lots of notes, dozens of interviews to transcribe, many ponderous food-related thoughts, and a well-tended stomach.

Now I had to decide: What was greatest Chinese restaurant in the world outside of Greater China?

Was it Davé in Paris, for being a place where people know your name, and for people whose names everybody knows? Would it be glamorous Hakkasan in London, for reinvigorating the sexiness of Chinese restaurants? Would the honor go to China Garden's Nelson Wang in Mumbai, for influencing the Chinese dining experience for more people on this planet than any other single person? Would it be Ho Lee Chow in Seoul, for repackaging "authentic" American Chinese food as something new for Koreans? Or might it be Tokyo's überexpensive Reikasai, for having the most impressive story behind its food?

During my travels, I repeatedly heard a tip from people who seemed pleased to have discovered a deep insight. "Do you know how to tell if it's a good Chinese restaurant?" they'd ask me. Then they'd lean over conspiratorially and say, "Look inside the window to see how many people eating there are Chinese."

Numerous other conversations from my trips echoed in my head: That people want a restaurant they can talk about (Melbourne). That Chinese restaurants split into camps for Chinese and non-Chinese (Los Angeles). That part of the authentic Chinese dining experience subconsciously values whether the waitstaff is Chinese (Dubai) and the patrons (San Francisco) are Chinese. That it can be appealing for a Chinese restaurant to be something of a dive and somewhat hidden (Rome).

The convergence of all these factors led me to one restaurant. But I hesitated, because the strongest argument for naming Mumbai's China Garden the world's greatest Chinese restaurant was the influence that Chef Nelson Wang has had on the second most populous country. Suddenly, looking at my notes, I realized that a technicality weakened this argument: many of Nelson Wang's Indian-Chinese dishes had been created before he'd opened China Garden. So while Nelson Wang was influential, that did not mean that China Garden was too.

Finally I felt that I could make my decision with precision. The world's greatest Chinese restaurant outside Greater China as of the early twenty-first century is:

Zen Fine Chinese Cuisine outside Vancouver—Sam Lau's modern Chinese restaurant located on the second floor of a suburban strip mall.

Why? Because it manages to uniquely balance a set of circumstances specific to the Chinese dining experience. From both the Chinese and the non-Chinese perspective, Sam Lau offers something audacious. His menu says "fine dining," but its second-story strip-mall location is not where you expect to find such fine food. Aside from the restaurants in Singapore (which is 75 percent ethnically Chinese anyway), Zen Fine Chinese Cuisine was the only modern Chinese restaurant I visited where the patronage was overwhelmingly Chinese. That is an amazing feat, since most Chinese don't want their cuisine modernized.

So Zen's Chinese clientele meant that someone who was non-Chinese could walk in and, surrounded by a Chinese staff and Chinese diners, feel like they were having an "authentic" Chinese experience in a place that, as far as top-flight food goes, is a bit of a dive. For Chinese people, Zen offers Chinese food that they cannot get in their own homes, or in many other places.

Whether Chinese or non-Chinese, downscale or upscale, diners leave Zen Fine Chinese Cuisine with a grateful stomach and a story to tell. What clinched it for me? Zen's half-price special was a bargain: an eight-course gourmet meal with squab and half a lobster. Never forget that "bang for your buck" is a hallmark of Chinese food around the world.

CHAPTER 15

American Stir-fry

There is no consistent name for "Chinatown" in Chinese. Other languages around the world have coalesced around names: *le quartier chinois* in French, *el barrio chino* in Spanish, *chukagai* in Japanese, and *Chinatown* in English, Russian, German, and Korean.

But in Chinese, the names vary. Newspapers use one name, popular speech uses another. In the Chinatown subway station in New York City, the chosen modern translation is delicately pixeled together with colorful tiles: *huabu*. I never knew this name until the Chinese characters appeared on the wall after a subway renovation, but it struck me. The *hua* in *huabu* means "Chinese," but with a sense that transcends the nation-state. After all, New York City's Chinatown has lived through the fall of two governments, a split, and a reunification just in the last century of Chinese history. *Hua* is an encompassing term, free of the fissures caused by military détentes and colonization. It is the distilled essence of being Chinese.

It is the link that ties together the Chinese I met while circling the world, where we are known as *huaqiao*, "Chinese sojourners."

With a worldwide diaspora that began in earnest two centuries ago, you can be *hua* even if you hold a passport from Singapore, the United States, or Peru. You can be *hua* even if you have never set foot in China and don't speak a single word of Chinese. The *huaqiao* label sticks, albeit technically inaccurate in many cases, as though one day we all might return, as though departure from the homeland is only temporary, even if it may last for generations upon generations. Such is the presumption of the long, muscular tentacles of Chineseness.

This book began as quest to understand Chinese food. But three years, six continents, twenty-three countries, and forty-two states later, I realize it was actually a personal journey to understand myself.

I'd never really grasped the widespread fascination with genealogy in America, since I knew exactly when my family showed up in the States. But this journey had become my own genealogical search: an investigation into how Chinese immigrants, like Chinese food, have embedded themselves in places around the world. They have adopted Italian first names, Thai last names, and, in Jamaica, Roman Catholicism (the church usually ran the best schools).

Sociologists have noted that a sense of national and cultural identity is often built on a triumvirate: blood, language and culture, and citizenship. In some countries, such as Japan, you need all three to be considered Japanese—anything less, and you're incomplete. The Japanese even call Japanese-Brazilians who return *gaijin*, foreigners.

In America, there is no blood requirement. With the Chinese, there is only a blood requirement. As I moved from culture to culture, I met Chinese people who listened to *reggaeton* and danced salsa in Peru, played guitar in reggae bands in Jamaica, and spoke Hindi in India. Yet in some sense, despite generations in other countries, we acknowledged each other as Chinese—even when we spoke no common languages.

China is the largest immigrant-producing country in the history of the world. The United States is the largest immigrant-accepting country in the history of the world. I, like the Chinese food I grew up with, sit at their crosscurrents. Look at me, and you may see someone Chinese. Close your eyes, and you will hear someone American.

Of all the people I met in my restaurant journeys, the person I most related to, the man who crystallized for me the purpose of this sweeping diaspora, was a chef named Ming Tsai. Ming's restaurant outside Boston, Blue Ginger, doesn't identify itself as Chinese, even though Ming himself is arguably the most famous Chinese-American chef of his generation. Instead, his restaurant and cooking show highlight a skillful, East-meets-West interweaving of techniques and ingredients. He draws his influences not only from China but from Japan, Thailand, Vietnam, and other places throughout Asia. His creative combinations range from the casual to the gourmet: Asian sloppy joes made with hoisin sauce (based on his mom's recipe), foie gras–morel shu mai, pork and ginger–Fuji apple chutney pot stickers. For a well-received Thanksgiving television episode (which helped win him an Emmy in 1998), he made turkey shu mai dim sum and turkey fried rice.

The first time I drove to Wellesley, I found Blue Ginger's quiet facade located on a curved street, just down from a church with a white steeple and a bell. Upon entering the restaurant, you're confronted by a wall of Mingness—including a picture from when he was selected one of *People* magazine's most beautiful people. Ming, who is now in his forties, still has the round cheeks, beguiling smile, and unself-conscious joy of a little boy. He's six feet tall with thick forearms, energetic and outgoing—an alpha male showman with mannerisms to match. He trades fist high fives with his staff. The first time I met him, I felt like I was talking to a highly articulate, intelligent American jock—only one who looked Chinese. But Ming's Chineseness manifests itself in interesting ways. He and his wife, Polly, had a feng shui expert check the site for the restaurant before they committed to buying it; he wears a piece of green jade around his neck for protection; he chats in Mandarin to the Chinese kitchen staff.

Ming is about a dozen years older than me, and his family, like mine, came to the United States by way of Taiwan and mainland China. He grew up in Dayton, Ohio, spending afternoons after school helping his mother, Iris, at her mall Chinese restaurant. He studied mechanical engineering at Yale, where he was on the squash team, but Ming wasn't a quantitative academic superstar. On one of his physics exams, faced with a question he knew he didn't need to answer to pass, he scrawled, "I don't care." As he joked to me, his motto during his senior year was *D* is for *diploma.*

Having spent his sophomore summer at Le Cordon Bleu's cooking school in Paris, he decided he wanted to be a chef. His mom told him that she just wanted him to be happy. His father agreed, adding, "You weren't going to be a great engineer anyway."

I related to Ming in part because I saw parallels between my own modest cooking efforts and Ming's sophisticated recipes— cooking grounded in Chinese tradition but heavily influenced by the cuisines of other parts of Asia, with another layer from the Euro-American tradition. Mine is an erratic hodgepodge, without the intelligence of his creations. Among the dishes I serve my friends and family: pesto pad thai with sun-dried tomatoes and marinated artichoke hearts, miso-basil marinated salmon, matzo-ball egg drop soup (great for Passover), French-style crepes filled with Korean barbecued *bulgogi,* and Vietnamese summer rolls incorporating mango, avocado, cucumber, and shredded chicken.

Cooking is like a language: the ingredients are the vocabulary; the techniques are the grammar. You can mix and match across different traditions absorbed from the people and influences you've been exposed to. I learned Thai recipes from a long-ago boyfriend whose family owned a Thai restaurant in Georgia. (He's long gone, but the recipes endure.) I learned to appreciate stuffed cabbage from a friend born in Kraków who took me to a Polish diner in Brooklyn for my birthday. I have fallen in love with dishes like seviche and *aji de gallina* from my travels to Peru and from the cooking of my half-Peruvian roommate.

But there were other similarities, ones that ran deeper than what we did in our kitchens. In one of our conversations, Ming told me, "If I can give my kids at least what my parents gave me, then that is the definition of a true success."

I reflected on his words. What his parents gave him set him apart from most of the other Chinese in the restaurant industry I had met. Many of them had told me, "We cook so our children won't have to." Ming began to cook because he wanted to, not because he had to.

Once my father brought dinner to a family friend who was too ill to leave her apartment on the Upper West Side. When he entered the building with a plastic bag of Chinese takeout, the doorman said to him, "No flyers on the floor."

My father is just a Ph.D. away from being a deliveryman. I'm just an education away from jotting down take-out orders.

In coming to the United States, what my parents gave me and my siblings is the freedom of choice. I write for a living because I want to. Sometimes I stop and think how odd it is that I earn my income wrestling with a language that my own parents struggled so much with. When I was young, my dad's company paid for him to have private lessons to remove the harsh angles of his Chinese accent. I still remember falling asleep to the sound of his practicing his short *a*—"cat," "can," "cab"—into a tape recorder, his tongue struggling to stretch out to let the vowel out. The diphthongs that slip effortlessly off my tongue are ones that my parents have to carefully parse. Whenever she read, my mother used to underline words she did not understand with a red pencil. Years later, I still randomly encounter the faded, wavy red lines under individual words or phrases in books on her shelf. These echoes of a long battle for self-improvement appear in *The Great Gatsby*, *Charlotte's Web*, the *New York Times*.

I have other friends, the children of immigrants, who veered off more standard paths, drawn by their passions. There is the Stanford-educated computer-science major who worked at Cisco for two years before quitting to become a singer-songwriter. There's my college classmate, a biochemistry major who dropped out of Harvard Business School to become a filmmaker—but not before creating an Excel spreadsheet to calculate her life happiness on different paths.

Our parents, like so many who emigrated around the world, left their homes because they wanted to give their children, and themselves, a better life. Generations later, their ambitions echo from Mauritius to Australia to Brazil, where, as in America, immigrant cultures have formed a shifting amalgam. (In Mauritius, the entire African island nation enthusiastically celebrates Christmas even though 40 percent of the country is Hindu and 20 percent is Muslim. It is a secular holiday, with no images of the baby Jesus but plenty of Santa, who wears his furry red outfit in a country that never sees snow.)

Perhaps nothing reflects that cultural convergence as subtly yet clearly as food. Today you can get soy lattes in Starbucks, tofu burgers in Costco, and Kraft sweet-and-sour sauce in a squeeze bottle in your local supermarket. Target sells a line of Asian culinary equipment and ingredients branded with Ming's name. He is not simply Target's Asian chef, he is Target's chef, period. Once, while I was sitting in the control room during a taping of Ming's show, his television producer, Julia Harrison, summed up his appeal: "He's ethnic without being exotic."

As much as the mainstream changes the immigrants, the immigrants change the mainstream. As recently as three decades ago, being American often meant distancing yourself from your immigrant ancestry. In her 1975 essay "Ethnicity and Anthropology in America," anthropologist Margaret Mead wrote, "Being American is a matter of abstention from foreign ways, foreign food, foreign ideas, foreign accents."

Even our definition of "assimilation" is changing. The old-school definition referred to how a minority blended into a majority. Now social scientists are pushing a new definition: the convergence of disparate cultures. The popularity of Chinese food shows that assimilation may no longer require that minorities be subsumed into the majority. Instead, in a country where 20 percent of the population consists of immigrants and their children, assimilation actually means convergence from all sides.

"Authenticity" is a concept that food snobs propagate, not one that reflects how people really cook and eat on a daily basis. Improvisation and adaption have defined cuisine throughout history. Tempura, which we now expect in every Japanese restaurant in the United States, was first introduced to the island country by Portuguese missionaries in the sixteenth century. Potatoes, that hearty Irish staple, were brought to the Emerald Isle by New World explorers returning home from Peru in the late

1700s. Likewise, tomatoes, the foundation of Italian cooking, also came from the New World, in the mid-sixteenth century. Chilies likely arrived in India courtesy of European sailors, forever changing Indian curries. At a certain point, that which is exotic stops being so. It becomes, in a new way, "authentic" to its new home. Chicken tikka masala was hailed as a national British original when chicken tikka was doused with masala sauce to satisfy the desire of the British people to have their meat served in gravy.

In reality, General Tso's chicken is arguably as American as it is foreign, Chinese only in the way that burritos are "Mexican" or spaghetti and meatballs is "Italian." These are "native foreign dishes"—"native" because they originated here and may exist nowhere else, but "foreign" because they were inspired by other cuisines. American Chinese food has developed its own identity—so much so that it is sold in Korea, Singapore, and the Dominican Republic as its own distinct cuisine.

In crisscrossing the country, I visited Jamaican-Chinese restaurants in Miami, Korean-Chinese restaurants in Los Angeles, Mexican-Chinese restaurants in San Jose, Indian-Chinese restaurants outside Chicago, and halal Chinese restaurants in Brooklyn.

When I stopped into an Indian-Chinese restaurant, the Indian-American customers told me that Chinese food is a taste of home more so than Indian food itself. After all, they can always cook Indian food in their own kitchens, even when they live outside India. But Chinese food served Indian style? That is something truly from India. These restaurants are authentic to those who want to be reminded of their native lands.

Even as our world and nation cycle through ideological battles with treacherous fault lines, the blurring boundaries of cuisine provide one of the few constants. Good recipes, like good ideas, circulate. They are carried in the minds of the millions of individuals who cross borders every year. Certain ideas simply stick: Why limit seaweed and vinegared rice to wrapping raw fish? Why limit tortillas to tacos?

Food is an intimate language that everyone understands, everyone shares. It is the primary ambassador of first contact between cultures, one that transcends spoken language. Food crosses cultural barriers. It bridges oceans. Becoming competent in a foreign language takes a lot of time, and learning a culture's history and literature requires a great deal of effort. But everyone can immediately have an opinion on food. More Americans have eaten pad thai than can tell you whether Thailand has a king. (It does.) And more people eat Chinese food regularly than can name a single famous Chinese poet or painter. Chinese restaurants have served as frontline cultural embassies for the Chinese and other Asians in America, paving the way for Japanese sushi, Indian curries, and Vietnamese *pho*. Willingness to try new foods is a lucid reflection of one's curiosity about and acceptance of other cultures—and this exposure has stimulated an appetite for travel, as well. If you can eat the food of a country, it seems less foreign.

Food is also one of the most easily preserved aspects of cultural heritage through the generations. I think of all my Italian-American friends who speak Spanish better than Italian, thanks to high school language classes, but who still know how to make a terrific tomato sauce. Many of my Jewish friends can make matzo-ball soup yet cannot recite the Hebrew alphabet. I have no idea whether my grandchildren will speak Chinese, but I feel certain they will know how to make fried dumplings.

The convergence emerges in tiny rivulets, through weddings, music, and holidays. I don't have enough fingers to count the number of Hinjew weddings between my Indian and Jewish friends. Sometimes, they walk around the fire and then stomp on the glass. Hip-hop artists like Dr. Dre and Jay-Z have sampled Indian bhangra rhythms. Chrismukkah has been elevated to pop-culture status with its appearance on *The O.C.* and tongue-in-cheek products like matzo-bread houses and menorah-emblazoned Christmas-tree ornaments.

In kindergarten, when we learned about Ellis Island we were taught that America was a melting pot—everything blended together into one massive swirling pool, a term popularized by a 1908 play of the same name. By the time I got to middle school, that analogy had fallen out of favor. Suddenly, instead of being one big amorphous fondue, America had become a tossed salad, its distinct, disparate pieces jumbled together.

I would like to propose another food-related analogy. (In a book about Chinese restaurants, how can I resist?) We are a stir-fry; our ingredients remain distinct, but our flavors blend together in a sauce shared by all.

CHAPTER 16

Tsujiura Senbei

I had never found anyone as obsessed with fortune cookies as I was until I arrived in Japan and met Yasuko Nakamachi. A researcher at Kanagawa University, she had spent six years following the global fortune cookie trail from the United States to Japan and back to the United States.

She had first encountered the cookies in New York City Chinese restaurants some two decades earlier. Amused by the cleverness of the idea, she thought, *Chinese people really come up with the most interesting things.*

But a few years later, while reading a Japanese book on confectioneries, she stumbled upon a reference to a regional snack—Japanese cookies folded around little pieces of paper. Intrigued, she traveled to Ishikawa, on the opposite side of the island, to see the cookies being made in local shops for the New Year's festivities. She thought they were a local snack until she made a visit to Kyoto in 1998. While walking the narrow roads near the shrine, she saw a number of small, family-run Japanese bakeries selling cookies with a familiar shape. They were exactly like fortune cookies. But the bakers called them *omikuji senbei* ("fortune crackers") or *tsujiura suzu* ("bells with fortunes"). She also heard them called *tsujiura senbei*. At that point she knew it in her heart: fortune cookies were originally Japanese. She would find the connection.

She spent years sifting through Edo- and Meiji-era documents from various historical archives, a difficult task because the Japanese language had evolved, shifting away from Chinese characters and toward phonetic systems that allowed the incorporation of Western words. She found references to *tsujiura senbei* in nineteenth-century Japan, described as brittle cookies that contained a fortune in a fictional work by Tamenaga Shunsui, a humorist who lived between 1790 and 1843. In the story "Haru no wakagusa" ("The Young Grass of Spring"), a mischievous character named Mamehachi tries to placate a pair of women with the cookies. The snack was also mentioned in notes by Edward Morse, an American zoologist visiting Japan; in an 1883 Japanese publication, he described *tsujiura senbei* as being crisp, sweetened with molasses, and "tasting like ginger snaps without the ginger."

Then a breakthrough: a reference to an old drawing of a *tsujiura senbei* shop from a modern artist. She went to the national library, which had one of the few remaining copies of the book in which the artwork appeared, and found an 1878 print of a man grilling *tsujiura senbei*. This was the drawing Gary Ono had shown me while I was doing fortune cookie research in Los Angeles.

The illustration accompanied a fictional story about a man who was looking for work and finally landed a job making the cookies. In the drawing, the sign above the store read TSUJIURA SENBEI in hiragana phonetic script. The big bucket of the cookies was also labeled TSUJIURA SENBEI, and the man was using the same type of grill she had seen in Kyoto's bakeries. It was a lucky needle to find in the haystack of historical documents. "It's very rare to see artwork of a thing being made," she told me.

Yasuko led me, via a series of commuter trains, to a little town outside Kyoto called Fukakusa. We ended up near the Fushimi Inari Taisha shrine, one of the most prominent in Japan. The visitors who flock to the shrine pray for health, more so than happiness. To call the gods, they often clap twice and ring what appears to be a massive jingle bell with a long rope.

The narrow street leading to the shrine was full of family-owned confectionery shops whose open storefronts showcased their wares in dazzling, elaborate displays. As we walked down the road, I saw them. The resemblance was uncanny and undeniable.

If the American fortune cookie is a yellow Pac-Man, these were Pac-Man's bigger, browner older brothers. Darker and shinier, they also had the store's logo imprinted on them—a fox jumping over a gate, which derived from the Shinto tradition of seeing the fox as the messenger of the gods.

A young man sat behind a line of round iron grills, folding the brown wafers around little slips of paper as they became ready—but not inside the cookie, just between its outer folds. If not for the absence of the kimono, he and his equipment would have looked just like the etching from the nineteenth century.

I took one of the cookies in my hand. It was significantly heavier than an American fortune cookie. It was thick, crunchy, but not crisp. A short, initially sweet taste quickly melted into a dense, slightly nutty flavor. I sifted the flavor on the tip of my tongue. I recognized one of its constituents as sesame, but something else was entirely unfamiliar. The store owner then showed me a big yellow tub full of a beige paste. "White miso," he said. They flavored the cookies with fermented bean paste, and this also helped give the confections their dark color.

I had traveled eight thousand miles, by plane, train, and foot, to try a cookie.

The family originally called them *suzu senbei,* or "bell crackers." Yasuko theorized that the cookies may have been shaped like the bell in the shrines, so that visitors could keep them as souvenirs of their trip.

The young man behind the hot grills, Takeshi Matsuhisa, explained that originally, in the Showa period, many confectionery stores had offered candies that came with little fortunes inside them. "Then the companies realized it wasn't such a good idea to put pieces of paper in candy, so they all disappeared," he said. He surmised that the fortunes in the bell cookies were the vestigial remains from that era.

His father, who was sixty-nine, remembered that when he was a child, a large flow of Chinese people had come to observe all the bakeries. "Were they Chinese or Chinese-American?" I asked. He shrugged. He didn't know. All he could say was that they had spoken Chinese.

I asked if they had ever seen American fortune cookies. Only in pictures and movies, they responded. So I brought out a handful of American fortune cookies and handed one each to Takeshi's father and the mother, using both hands and making a slight bow. Mrs. Matsuhisa opened the package, cracked the cookie in two, and popped one half in her husband's mouth.

"Oh, it's made well," he said as he chewed.

"It's very light," she agreed. She broke off another piece and handed it to her son, Takeshi, who bit it and said, "It's very interesting."

Tasting butter or oil, they surmised that this would make the mixture nonstick for the machines. Their batter didn't use butter, so Takeshi had to pry each wafer from his grill with his hands and a pick.

The American cookies didn't have miso in them, which is

why they were yellow, Takeshi said, examining the color. The three of them then discussed what kind of grill they would use for something that small and thin.

The fact that the Japanese still make the cookies by hand is evidence that they were the originators, Takeshi conjectured. You create the product first; then, if it's popular, you create the machine. "That's why I think the Japanese fortune cookie came first," he said.

The practice of inserting fortunes is common in the Japanese culture, Takeshi continued. They didn't think to market it as anything unusual, whereas the Chinese didn't have that kind of tradition, so they found it novel. He smiled, admitting, "It was the Chinese who popularized fortune cookies. They're the ones who seized the opportunity." Now his family business had benefited, too. The increased interest in the American fortune cookie had drawn more Japanese customers, from as far away as Tokyo, to buy their cookies.

We now knew that the fortune cookie had originated in Japan, but there was still one final mystery. I wondered out loud: Almost all the people who claimed to have created the American fortune cookie had Japanese roots—so how had the Chinese managed to take over the fortune cookie business?

"When Japanese-Americans were interned during World War II, they had to leave all their equipment behind," Yasuko pointed out in Japanese.

As her words were translated, all the pieces in my quest came together. Of course. How could I have missed this? I had a flashback to my first conversation with Sally Osaki, on the phone, and her telling me that when she'd been a child the original fortune cookie messages had been in Japanese. But at one point they had become English: "By the time we came out of camp." The fortune cookies had changed by the end of the war. I recalled that the Japanese-American confectionery shops—Ben-kyodo, Fugetsu-do, Umeya—had all closed when their owners were "relocated."

Later, I looked back over all my notes, reviewing dates, anecdotes, and stories, trying to fit the pieces of the puzzle together.

The popularity of Chinese cuisine grew tremendously during World War II; after Japan invaded China and China became an American ally, the national perception of the Chinese threat gave way to sympathy. In addition, the wartime rationing of meat enhanced the appeal of Chinese dishes, which made a little meat go a long way. San Francisco's Chinatown quadrupled its business between 1941 and 1943. The tide of public opinion turned. The Chinese Exclusion Act of 1882 was repealed in December 1943, opening the door for an eventual flood of Chinese immigrants (and additional Chinese restaurant owners). In 1946, the United States Office of Price Administration delisted "Chinese fortune tea cakes" from its price control list, which tells us that (1) by the end of the war, the cookies were identified with the Chinese, (2) they were known as "tea cakes," and (3) they were popular enough to warrant having been listed by the Office of Price Administration in the first place.

Although the interned Japanese were released by 1945, it took years for the families to rebuild their lives. Many of the business owners had lost everything. It wasn't until 1948 that Benkyodo was up and running under family control, Gary Ono believes. During that time, a number of Chinese fortune cookie makers sprung into existence—like Lotus, which opened in 1946. A sharp rise in demand at Chinese restaurants combined with a lack of Japanese bakers gave Chinese entrepreneurs an opportunity to step in. One of America's beloved confections emerged from one of the nation's darkest moments.

CHAPTER 17

Open-Source Chinese Restaurants

McDonald's and its golden arches represent an epic achievement of twentieth-century-America, the story of highways, homogenization, and a nation in a hurry. The standardization of menus, decor, and experience is regarded as a postwar organizational triumph, coordinated from the company's Oak Brook, Illinois, corporate headquarters. Chinese restaurants—which outnumber McDonald's franchises in the United States by two to one—have achieved largely the same effect, but without a central nervous system.

This is something Monty McCarrick, the Wyoming truck driver and Powerball winner, discovered long ago in his hauls across the country. Chinese food has become an American comfort food in part because it is so predictable. While there are a few scattered chains, such as Panda Express (which operates one thousand restaurants nationwide from Rosemead, California), and some impressive banquet halls, like Jing Fong in New York

City, the vast majority of Chinese restaurants are in fact mom-and-pop establishments.

Yet at times it seems that America's Chinese restaurants operate as a single giant, pulsing entity, a lively example of one of the most fertile research areas for biologists, sociologists, and economists: spontaneously self-organizing networks. The principles that govern any colonies, slime molds, and the growth of the Internet also extend to Chinese restaurants; from local actions emerge collective wisdom.

McDonald's has spent billions on advertising over the years to establish its brand. Today, a red-haired, floppy-shoed clown and the bright yellow M evoke strong nostalgic sensations in the chain's customers. Chinese restaurants have spent but a fraction of that sum (much of it on disposable take-out menus), yet they've left an equally indelible imprint on the American culinary psyche. Walk into any Peking Garden or China Buffet and you know you can get a reasonably tasty meal, served in healthy portions, for somewhere between five and ten dollars, no matter what region of the country you may be in.

While there are authentic Chinese restaurants in the Bay Area, New York, and Los Angeles for people whose taste buds have escaped the gravitational pull of homogeneity, in a large swath of the country, American Chinese food has become its own brand. What Chinese restaurant menu doesn't offer beef with broccoli, sesame chicken, roast pork lo mein, fried wontons, egg rolls, and egg drop soup? Somewhere, sometime, someone decided that these were going to be the standard-bearers of Chinese cuisine in the United States, but not through the focus groups and market testing American food corporations rely on. This standard was created through decisions on the local level.

Good ideas have historically rippled quickly through the Chinese-restaurant system, carried by word of mouth and by the experiences of the streams of dispersing immigrants.

Fortune cookies traveled eastward from California. General Tso's chicken traveled westward from New York. Philly cheesesteak rolls traveled out from Pennsylvania. Nor do the ideas center just on food. Behind the country's Chinese restaurants sits a vast unofficial network of zodiac place-mat printers, restaurant suppliers, and employment agencies that propagate the same standards. Kari-Out makes the majority of the soy sauce packets in the United States. Fold-Pak manufactures two-thirds of the take-out containers. A handful of Chinese menu printers in New York's Chinatown, under the Manhattan Bridge, supply millions of menus a year throughout the eastern United States. Another set of printers in California does the same for the West. A single set of photos—with a lavender backdrop, floral dishware, and white baby's breath flowers—has become the dominant motif on the brightly lit menu boards in restaurants run by the Fujianese. The same exact picture of beef with broccoli will greet you in restaurants in Bensonhurst, Brooklyn; Hiawassee, Georgia; and Madison, Wisconsin.

Then there are the many restaurants inspired by Misa Chang's idea of scattering menus to promote door-to-door delivery—a campaign powerful enough to spread beyond the Chinese establishments.

With Chinese restaurants, as with open-source software development, the best ideas bubble sideways. In the end it pays to be part of the informal system even if you don't have exclusive claim to your own innovations. The entire system benefits.

If McDonald's is the Windows of the dining world (where one company controls the standards), then Chinese restaurants are akin to the Linux operating system, where a decentralized network of programmers contributes to the underlying source code. The code is available for anyone to use, modify, or redistribute freely. When I ran this comparison past Jimmy Wales, the

founder of Wikipedia and an observer of open-source collabora-
tions, he got excited during our instant-messaging conversation,
typing:

```
totally
open standards
there is a lot to the analogy.
if there is no one body enforcing stan-
dards, won't it be chaotic, won't the cus-
tomer be confused, won't every restaurant
be completely different?
but no
what you get is a set of remarkably similar
places
with some experimental variations for
innovation
and innovations spread rapidly
there are dozens of companies selling linux
distributions
and you would think they might all be radi-
cally different
but they all tend to follow certain broad
standards
```

The speed at which these ideas can spread is breathtaking.
Chop suey—an American creation—blew across the country in
less than a decade, starting around 1896. After World War II,
the fortune cookie went from a regional curiosity to a national
phenomenon in about the same time span.

General Tso's chicken, too, conquered America and became
such standard menu fare that by the mid-1980s, the once foreign and oddly spelled name General Tso rolled off people's
tongues with ease. (Where it didn't, the local restaurateurs

shrewdly renamed it after General Chow, General Tao, or General So.) In contrast, McDonald's began the rollout of its own crispy battered and fried chicken bits accompanied by palate-pleasing sauces, Chicken McNuggets, in 1980—but only after a decade of failed experimentation at headquarters with other chicken products, including chicken pot pie and fried chicken with bones. When the product did come out, two of the original four McNugget sauces—sweet-and-sour and hot mustard—were Chinese-influenced.

Just how do these ideas leap so vigorously from restaurant to restaurant? Some travel along village and family connections. Some ideas are spread as immigrant restaurant owners disperse across the country. (Intrigued by the Philly cheesesteak rolls in Georgia, I quizzed the owner. It turned out that the family had moved from Philadelphia.) Some are carried by the restaurant workers who move by bus and plane from state to state. Some are popularized through such industry publications as *Chinese Restaurant News*. Some are promoted in part by "defensive copycat syndrome." Eugene Lee, whose father, Kam Lee, owned one of the first New York printing companies to specialize in take-out menus, said, "If someone introduced another dish, then the nearby restaurants would feel threatened and they would also add it onto their menu as a way to compete."

He told me how restaurant owners would physically copy one another's menus, making mock-up samples that were cobbled together from their competitors'. "They would cut out single lines at a time and they would reposition it in the order they wanted it. It was complete cut-and-paste," he recalled.

"Everyone just wanted to take on so many more dishes," he added. "I remember watching the frequency of the dishes just growing." As a result, the standard Chinese menu ballooned from fifty to one hundred to two hundred menu choices. "I wanted to redesign the menus for them. The more I wanted to change it, the more they were like, 'No no no no no,' " he said. "It's a psychology of comfort—that where they came from everything was the same."

Paul Epstein, the president of Kari-Out, the restaurant supplier and soy sauce manufacturer, described the phenomenon as "massive communications." The restaurants pass along information so smoothly that it would make for an impressive knowledge-management case study. "We call it the tom-tom effect," Paul said. "The tom-toms will beat in New York. If something happens in New York, they will find out in Ohio.

"They find a formula that works and duplicate it," he added. In fact, the system works so well that the Chinese have copied themselves in another cuisine: Mexican. In New York City, Chinese-run Mexican takeouts carry the hallmarks of their Chinese brethren: yellow skins, neon lights in the windows, photos of the dishes, Chinese faces behind the counter. The formula is the same, only the cuisine is different—fajitas instead of fried rice, guacamole instead of duck sauce.

These self-organizing Chinese systems are not just limited to the United States. Across the world, many countries seem to have their go-to Chinese dishes: Manchurian chicken in India, crispy shredded beef in England, a fried *pastel* in Brazil, *jjajang-myun* noodles in Korea, and Hainan chicken in Singapore. Those networks are strong in large part because different parts of China map to different parts of the world: Wenzhou to France; Chaozhou to Thailand; Hong Kong to Britain and Canada; Shandong Province to Korea; the southern Fujianese (or Hokkien) to Indonesia, the Philippines, and other parts of Southeast Asia; and Hakka immigrants to India. Their efforts represent the glocalization—global localization—of Chinese food.

So perhaps it was only in the hands of the Chinese immigrants that fortune cookies, a Japanese product, could have become an American phenomenon. This idea is accepted by some descendants of the Japanese families who were involved in the introduction of the American fortune cookie. A lot of people ask Doug Dawkins, Makoto Hagiwara's great-great-grandson, if he regrets that his family didn't make money from the fortune cookies his ancestor introduced in the Japanese Tea Garden, but he has adopted a generous attitude. "New cultures arise from old cultures in combinations," he told me. "I think it's great. I really don't think the fortune cookie would have taken off if it hadn't been popularized in such a wide venue." He added, "If the family had decided to sell fortune cookies, they would never have done it as successfully as the Chinese have. I give them credit for it."

Gary Ono wishes that Americans would understand the role that Japanese establishments played in introducing the fortune cookie, but even he respects the role of the Chinese. "I personally don't oppose the term 'Chinese fortune cookie' because it was the Chinese who borrowed the fortune cookie from the Japanese and refined it. They marketed it better. They put a better spin on it, and that is how it got world popular and ubiquitous."

American corporate food lore is filled with figures like Ray Kroc of McDonald's, Howard Schultz of Starbucks, and Asa Griggs Candler of Coca-Cola: strong personalities with a vision who established powerful culinary brands. Chinese food in America has no such dominant figures, yet it is no less a powerful presence in Americana. Instead we meet micropersonalities: Misa Chang of delivery, Edward Louie of fortune cookie machines, Chef Wang and Chef Peng of General Tso's chicken, and the mysterious Lem Sen of chop suey. Though they may be at best footnotes in history, they were forward-thinking individuals who had an intuition as to what the American market wanted. The network did the rest.

CHAPTER 18

So What Did
Confucius Really Say?

One last phone call brought me to the end of the lucky-numbers trail. I called Kari-Out, the Chinese-restaurant distributor, and asked, Who makes your fortune cookies?

"Wonton Food," one of the Epstein brothers said.

Wonton Food, the Brooklyn-based company that had grabbed headlines when it tried to sell fortune cookies in China in the early 1990s. Wonton Food is the largest fortune cookie manufacturer in the United States, at least twice as big as its nearest competitor. It churns out more than four million cookies a day—more than a billion cookies a year. All of which have lucky numbers inside them.

I hung up, Googled "Wonton Food," called the number listed on the Web site, and left a message. A vice president named Derrick Wong called me back.

Tennessee Lottery officials had sent me a scanned image of one of the fortunes, "All the preparation you've done will finally be paying off," with the sequence of numbers written underneath; they'd gotten it from a winner who had kept the slip of paper in his wallet. I sent Derrick the image via e-mail while we were on the phone.

"That's ours," he said with a note of recognition, as soon as he opened the file.

And there it was. The trail of the fortune cookie had led me from Iowa to California to Japan and back to New York City, some ten traffic-congested miles from my home.

Derrick explained why he could be so sure. It wasn't the words themselves but the paper they were printed on. "We are the only one that has the hole in the middle," he said. The dimple was the mark of the paper cutter, Derrick told me, as the fortunes were sliced off a big roll.

Where did they get their lucky numbers from? I wanted to know.

"We just have those numbers put in a bowl and pick them out," he explained. "I picked a lot of numbers by myself."

Generating number sequences can be quite labor-intensive, so Wonton Food takes a shortcut: the same sequences are repeated on different fortunes. In addition to "All the preparation you've done will finally be paying off," other winners got their Powerball numbers on messages that said "Your co-workers take pleasure in your great sense of creativity" and "The stars of riches are shining upon you." Wonton executives were thinking of moving to a more efficient, computerized random-number generator.

Who writes your fortunes? I asked.

Well, that was a sad story. Their main writer had been one of their executives, Donald Lau, who had been with the company since the 1980s. The fact that he was the only employee who spoke fluent English made him the de facto fortune cookie writer. At his peak he wrote maybe a hundred fortunes a month. The effort drained him. A decade into his soothsaying career, Lau became stymied by writer's block. He retired as their chief fortune cookie writer in 1995. "He told me it was the hardest job he ever got," said Derrick. "He ran out of ideas. He can't write anymore."

Since then Wonton Food has worked mainly with outside contract writers. When I inquired about them, Derrick immediately became tight-lipped. "It's one of the things I can't discuss," he said. "It's private and competitive."

Fortune writing is taxing, Donald Lau explained later, at the company's headquarters in Brooklyn, when I met up with him and Derrick. The epigrams have to be short enough (about a dozen words) to fit in a half-inch by two-inch slip of paper. Plus, a happy tone is required. "At the end of the meal you don't want people to be angry at the restaurant," Donald said. I pointed out that these days, fortune cookies are more like food-for-thought cookies or wisdom cookies. Fortune cookies hardly contain fortunes anymore. Derrick agreed. "You limit yourself in a tight corner if you go in that direction," he said. After all, there are only so many things you can augur about: love, business, health.

When word got out that Wonton was thinking of switching to computer-generated numbers, it caused a consumer backlash. One e-mail from a customer in Cranston, Rhode Island, urged them not to switch:

> For some reason you workers picked the right combination for 110 people. It kind of restored my faith in a higher spiritual consciousness that the Chinese seem to embody. A wisdom that Westerners do not have. Will it ever happen again in such a way? Perhaps not, but sometimes life hands you a thrilling surprise and all because you believed in something unexplainable. With the addition of computers, you will have taken away any chance of human connection. You will now be taking

away the chi. Now I do not kid myself into believing you hire only Chinese workers or even Asian workers, so I do not think there is a red and gold room full of tiny women with bound feet or austere fu-manchued men with long nails dressed in silken robes, but it is enough for me to know that another person's life force is communicated through a slip of paper. I want to keep believing in the Ancient Chinese Secret.

Wonton Food stayed with handpicked numbers. Every time its workers update their inventory, one man spends his entire day picking numbers by hand.

Maybe there is something to the concept of fortune cookie chi after all. Lightning apparently *can* strike twice in the same place. Powerball investigators had called up Wonton Food again. Another inordinately high number of five-of-six winners had popped up in a May 2005 drawing—eighty-three people. Again officials had traced the sequence to fortune cookies from Wonton Food. "They wanted to verify the numbers," said Donald. "They asked me to submit the original slip." That would be twice in a year that Powerball had matched five of six Wonton Food numbers. Donald wryly commented, "We're going to work on Mega Millions next."

Soon I turned the conversation to Wonton Food's attempt to make fortune cookies in China in the mid-1990s. The conversation suddenly became somewhat stilted. Businessmen don't always like to talk about failed ventures. Derrick admitted, "The project didn't work out. It's very difficult in China. There is no market over there." As another executive put it, fortune cookies were simply "too American a concept."

Too American?

As I left Wonton Food, I wondered, Just how American are

fortune cookies anyway? What made them take off in the United States when they could barely get a foothold in China and are only a regional treat in Japan?

Perhaps the inventor of the Fortune Album, a $9.95 keepsake holder for lucky fortunes, would be able to elucidate things for me. Upon entering Michael Moskowitz's home in Fort Lauderdale, I was immediately struck by two things: the stack of large cardboard boxes pushed up against the wall of his living room and the vast array of litter boxes and cat cushions scattered throughout the house. The boxes contained hundreds of unsold albums, each with forty-four inside. Nine cats, almost all previously homeless, shared the two-bedroom apartment with Moskowitz, twenty-seven years old. Mike said he had long had an affinity for fortunes, collecting them through childhood. He had attached five of the small slips of papers to the final page of his college application to Wharton, each one hinting that he belonged at the school. He got in.

While at Wharton, he and his friends ate at a local Chinese restaurant called Beijing at least once a week. He prided himself in being the one at the table who got the best fortune at the end of the meal. "I would randomly take one and they would randomly take one. I'd get the good one and they'd get the crappy ones," he explained. By graduation, he had amassed a large collection of fortunes, but they were all fluttering about in manila envelopes. To hem them in, he came up with the idea of creating a fortune album for himself. He found a designer and a subcontractor in China through Alibaba.com. The main problem: the minimum order from the Chinese manufacturer was one thousand albums. In order to get his one fortune album, he had to order 999 extra.

Mike was far from making back his $7,000 investment, but he was fervently proud of his album, independent of its bottom line. We sat down on his couch and Mike showed me some of his favorite fortunes:

Simplicity of character is the natural result of profound thought.

Discontent is the first step in the progress of a man or a nation.

Remember, being happy is not always being perfect.

If you follow it, you realize that unsatiable desires don't lead to happiness.

"They are all true; it depends whether or not you internalize them," he said.

Fortunes appeal to him precisely because they provide pithy guidelines for life. "I like the thought-provoking ones, maybe ones that have some self-improvement attached. I used to, when I was younger, be into personal growth. I always strove for perfection at least in an ideal sense. You'd read a book on personal growth. To some extent, I felt it was in one ear and out the other," he said. But fortunes were easier to tackle. "I came up with the philosophy of the one-liners. If you could get one line of a piece of advice, then you can carry that one sentence or phrase with you when you have to confront split-second decision making." For people who don't have time to contemplate the life well lived or read Confucius, Immanuel Kant, or Aristotle, fortune cookies provide the Cliffs Notes version of wisdom.

I sought out another man: a performance artist named Marcus Young who, in 2004, had distributed some ten thousand fortune cookies with bizarre, often nonsensical messages through six Minneapolis-area Chinese restaurants. A twenty-three-hour Chinatown bus ride to Minneapolis left me in the parking lot of a local Leann Chin's restaurant, our rendezvous point.

Marcus was a child of the Midwest, having grown up in Des Moines, where his parents, who emigrated from Hong Kong, had been among the string of owners in the King Ying Low restaurant's hundred-year history. There he had been introduced to the fortune cookie. "Growing up, I thought they were Chinese. Growing up, there are all sorts of confusions. What is China? You got these filtered images from the media. Everything is confusing when you are a kid and you are Chinese and growing up in Iowa."

Fortune cookies were an important part of the Youngs' restaurant. People would burn a good fortune in an ashtray, believing that it was the only way it could come true. Other argued that the cookie had to be eaten before you read the fortune for it to come true. The customers also believed in second chances. "I remember people asking for a second fortune cookie if they didn't like the first one," he said.

Despite the ubiquity, there is something deeply personal about fortune cookies. "It's like opening a present," Marcus told me. "It's just for you. It's in front of your eyes. The cookie breaks, like a door which opens; then there is this magical piece of paper." Inserting himself into that ritual gave him a sense of power, he said: "It's a little like playing God, if you get to be creator of fortunes for people. That's really what God does—but a very modest God, the God of fortune cookies."

Marcus had trained as a musician, but he wanted his art to be more experimental, art that became infused with reality— where, as he put it, "You can't really figure out what is art and nonart." During his "performance," Marcus pretended to be a busboy and wandered the restaurant filling water glasses as the customers were finishing their meals and opening their cookies. (Busboys, he notes, are invisible—especially in Chinese restaurants.) The fortunes were strange. Some were enigmatic: "Buy a door. Sell a door. Open a door. Close a door. Adore a door. Ignore a door." Some were wistful yet pessimistic: "Dream of a place that will never be. Dream of a happiness that will never be. Dream of a peace that will never be." Some were confoundingly simple: "Wait." And some were simply nonsensical: "Half a prayer for waking up and using the toilet and the dead animal on the road." Not surprisingly, the fortunes drew confused, amused, and angry responses from the customers.

He was fascinated by the public reaction to his art project. "I thought people looked at fortune cookies as just fun, but they take it more seriously than that. At least some do," he said. In one case, a woman got very upset at her fortune. She walked up to the register and asked for her money back, then gave the owner an ultimatum: "If you continue to use these cookies, I'm not coming back to the restaurant."

Americans expect good fortunes; it goes along with our general sense of entitlement. This demand offers clues to the secret of American fortune cookies, but it weighs heavily on two men who are no longer speaking to each other. One, Steven Yang, is Shanghai-born and works out of a warehouse in an industrial area in San Francisco; the other, the Korean immigrant Yong Sik Lee, sells fortune cookie machines from outside of Boston.

More than a decade ago, fortune cookie manufacturers around the country realized that their core competency lay in food production, not professional soothsaying. So dozens of them outsourced their message writing. Aside from those in Wonton Food cookies, nearly all the fortune messages you encounter in the United States will have passed through either Steven Yang or Yong Lee.

These two men figure in what is perhaps the harshest drama in fortune cookie history. Steven once worked for Yong as a salesman. Yong holds the patent for the first fully automated fortune cookie machine, which he filed in 1981. (It was one of Yong Lee's machines that made its way to Brazil.)

Aside from the machines themselves, Yong Lee's biggest contribution to fortune cookies in America may be the elimination of Confucius from inside the crispy vanilla wafers. When he first started the business, Confucius said a lot. "Confucius is the best-known philosopher, respected, a good person. Making a joke out of him is not right," he told me. "I don't think it's nice to say 'Confucius say.' I took them all out. That set a trend." His other contribution? Yong Lee added the smiley faces.

Somewhere along the way, Steven decided that there was more money to be made in supplying the fortune cookie papers than in selling the machines. Machines are sold only once, but the messages are needed on a continual basis; it's the confectionery equivalent of the razors versus blades business model. He apparently won (or stole, depending on who is doing the telling) customers from Yong Lee. But instead of starting from scratch, Steven copied Yong Lee's repertoire of fortunes wholesale—typos and all. "We no longer talk," said Steven. Then, by focusing mainly on the fortunes themselves and implementing some innovative packing techniques, he overtook Yong's business.

In the earliest days, fortunes were awkward—full of misspellings, grammatical mistakes, and cultural faux pas. Diners often complained, and that displeasure made its way back up the supply chain. "Customers complain to restaurant, restaurant complain to wholesalers, wholesale companies complain to manufacturers, manufacturers complain to me," Steven said. Then he and his daughter, Lisa, had to comb through their plates, which each had 160 fortunes on them, hunting for the errant message. "If one is wrong, you have to reset it. The plates are very expensive."

Steven Yang ships out 3.5 million fortunes each day, every day, over a billion fortunes a year; they travel the country in compact black boxes. He and his wife, Linda, can't take a day off, because the demand from the companies is incessant. He has a droll sense of humor and an (only somewhat) exaggerated sense of his role in American society. "If one day I couldn't do this anymore, if I retired or died, it would be a big problem for America," he pointedly told me during a visit. "The papers would certainly write about it: 'Fortune Cookie Man Dies.' " Steven's position in the fortune oligopoly is impressive, given that he doesn't speak much English. Instead, he has help from his daughter, Lisa, a sweet-tempered twenty-something girl who majored in finance at San Jose State.

Fortunes are tricky things. People are easily offended. You have to eye the messages with the same precision and sense of paranoia as an adult trying to childproof a home—taking into consideration the possible recipient's gender, age, body type, and religious outlook.

"You will soon meet handsome young man" caused problems, Yong Lee told me. "We took that message out because old ladies in southern states complained quite a bit." They were old. Why would they want to meet a young man?

Other fortunes that have drawn complaints, and the complainers:

"Lighten up a bit": a man and his wife, both overweight.

"You will soon inherit a large sum of money": people who interpreted it as auguring the death of a loved one.

"It's your turn to pick up the check": Californians guffawed; southerners found it gauche.

"Women marry because they don't want to work": an irate fiancée in the 1950s.

"Don't kill a chicken for an egg": people who had obviously never heard of the parable of the goose who laid golden eggs.

"You'll be going on a long voyage": a woman whose husband died shortly after getting that message.

Anything religious: anyone not religious.

During my visit, Steven had just received another complaint about a fortune: "Be as sexy as you want to be." Lisa knew that their quality control would have caught that one. When they hunted through their printing plates, it turned out to have come from a customized list that had been put together by a cookie manufacturer himself. I would never have let it get by, she insisted.

I met with Yong's son, David, on the Google campus, where he works in strategic planning. David was discreet in his comments about Steven Yang, but it was clearly a prickly topic. Since David had a degree from Stanford Law School, I inquired about the copyright issues around the stolen fortunes. "You have to actively copyright it to sue for statutory damages," said David. "I'm not sure it would be worth it to take it to court." He'd already calculated it: "How much damage is really there at two cents a fortune, three cents a fortune?"

It wasn't about the money anyway. "It was more a breach of trust," he said.

David echoed many of Steven's thoughts on fortune writing. Fortunes have become trickier to write because they have to apply to a broad audience all across America. In America, they work best when they are life-affirming, he noted: "It's about the possibilities of life." The best kind say things like "Dance as if no one is watching." (Another fortune writer told me his favorite fortune was "Don't be afraid to dance badly.")

"No one wants to read a fortune that says you are soon going to lose a loved one," he told me. Things are different in Asia, where fortunes are more of a mixed bag, he said: "They take the good with the bad."

• • •

Did Asian cultures really accept unfortunate fortunes? I wondered as, with Yasuko Nakamachi, the Japanese researcher, I visited the original Japanese shrine that had inspired today's modern fortune cookies. Once isolated and difficult for pilgrims to get to, today the sanctuary is a five-minute walk from a commuter rail station outside of Osaka.

The Hyotanyama Inari shrine was the originator of the *tsujiura* method of telling fortunes—the *tsujiura* of the *tsujiura senbei*. I was greeted by a sixty-nine-year-old priest dressed in stiff purple and white robes; he had originally worked as a chemical engineer, but when his father had died three decades ago, he had inherited the shrine. The priest sat us down in the reception area and had an assistant bring out green tea and cookies that I noticed resembled flattened fortune cookies.

The *tsujiura* method of telling fortunes was based on the patterns of pedestrian movements, he explained. After a while it had become quite famous, so vendors began selling fortunes around Japan to those who couldn't make the trek to the shrine. The cookies came later, as shrewd bakers took advantage of the *tsujiura*'s reputation to promote their confections.

The priest led me to the front of the shrine. He filled out a white form on a clipboard, writing down my name, my age, and the date. It was not unlike being in a doctor's office, only he was dressed in white and purple robes and it was my fate he was divining.

Ring the bell and pray for something, he told me. I rapidly contemplated my choices. The three things people care most about are health, career or money, and love.

I thought carefully about what my parents had taught me and scribbled, "Good family."

He told me to pull the rope and toll the large bell suspended above to call the gods; then he gave me a canister so I could pick out a stick with a number on it. I drew the number 1. He led me around the edge of the property to the first stone, where he turned me toward the street.

Wait for the first person to pass, he said.

A moment later, a young man wearing a blue suit whizzed by on a bicycle.

The priest eyed the man and filled out the boxes in the clipboard: the passerby's age, direction, gender, and method of transportation. He studied it for a second, then told my fortune to my Japanese friend Tomoko, who burst out laughing.

"He said the young man on the bicycle represents men in your life, or a man in your life. He's on a bicycle. If you are too slow you won't catch up to him."

The priest also warned me about my liver.

"My liver? I don't even drink," I whispered to Tomoko.

"I know, isn't it ironic?"

As we were leaving, we handed the priest an American fortune cookie. The second he saw it, he said, "Oh, that's Japanese! It's from Kyoto."

No, it's from New York, we told him.

He cracked the fortune cookie open and took out the slip of paper, which read: "Pessimism never won any battles."

He nodded when we translated it for him, saying, "I agree with that."

The fortunes in American cookies are almost uniformly positive, I told him. He looked aghast and vehemently shook his head. "No, no, no!" he said. "That's unimaginable!" Fortunes have to be good as well as bad, he explained. Life isn't all happy. You have to have bad messages and bad fortunes because that is how you change course to save yourself. The point of a fortune is to give you direction in life. If it's always good, there is no critical feedback. "If it is all happy fortunes, that's wrong," he said. He compared life to scientific lab work: "When you are in your lab, it's not always success after success. You have a lot of setbacks."

So why don't Americans like negative fortunes? we asked him.

The priest considered the point out loud for a bit. Finally he gave me this observation: "Because they don't like to think about the past."

I mulled over why Americans love fortune cookies so much, whereas they barely register on Japan's confectionery landscape. "I wonder if it's because in Japan, you can get fortunes anywhere. It's pretty easy to get candies with fortunes and toys and gums with fortunes," Yasuko said. "Here, you can go to a shrine," she noted. America has its palm readers, psychics, and astrologers. But it's all a bit New Agey, as unfamiliar as Kabbalah and Buddhism. In contrast, fortune cookies are a safe mainstream source for fortunes. Who doesn't go to Chinese restaurants?

I was surprised by how few fortunes they had at the Matsuhisas' bakery outside Tokyo—only twenty-three. And they had been using the same ones for decades. What happens if someone gets the same fortune again? I asked.

"Japanese people, if they get the same fortune twice, then it really is their fortune," she said. "They think to themselves, That really is my fate."

She added, "In America, it seems like they are trying to come up with new fortunes all the time. In Japan, the older the fortune, the better. The older the fortune, the more valuable it is. There is no effort to get rid of that or update that."

There is a steady pressure to keep the messages in American fortune cookies fresh and up-to-date. Americans hate getting the same fortunes. it makes them feel less unique.

So what did Confucius really say?

I downloaded a translation of the *Analects* (known as *Lun Yu* in Chinese) and read through it, trying to glean bits of wisdom. It turns out that Confucius said a lot, but only a fraction of which would resonate with an American audience. There is a lot about virtue, filial piety, and ruling small kingdoms. What did Confucius not say? "May you live in interesting times." Nor did any Chinese sage. Though the maxim is often cited as an ancient Chinese proverb, scholars have scoured Chinese literature and not found any evidence of it.

I took diligent notes, finding a few gems scattered throughout the *Analects*. My favorites included "Learning without thought is labor lost; thought without learning is perilous" and "To see what is right and not to do it is want of courage."

After hours of study, I'd found fewer than forty maxims that fit the dozen-word rule—not quite enough to fill one-quarter of one of Steven Yang's plates.

The same month, I went out to lunch with my mom to gain a modicum of understanding of Chinese philosophy and classics. My mom had been a high school literature teacher before moving to the States. She handed me two comic books filled with Lao Tzu's sayings translated into English: this was Chinese Classics 101 for the Xbox generation. Lao Tzu is a better source for pithy aphorisms than Confucius, my mom explained. Confucius was more concerned with governing; Lao Tzu was focused on self-improvement. She had also brought a book of Chinese proverbs, and flipping through the two books revealed some contrasts between English and Chinese. English speakers use the expression "The squeaky wheel gets the grease." But my mom pointed out the Chinese perspective for getting one's due: "*Qiang da chutou niao,*" she said. The bird who sticks its head out gets shot.

Then she read off a whole bunch of proverbs that just sounded odd to my American ears. "When in a melon patch, do not bend down and tie your shoes. When under a plum tree, do not adjust your hat."

Huh?

She glanced up. "It means 'Don't do anything that looks suspicious even when it's not.' "

Oh. *Obviously.*

Other Chinese proverbs were stranger: "Three people can make up a tiger," "Fingers can't all be the same length," "Killing the chicken to scare the monkey." I found that some of these made even less sense to me than "You can't have your cake and eat it too" does to a nonnative speaker of English. (My Chinese friends have wondered, "Don't you need a cake in order to eat it?")

Common wisdom from one culture is perplexing in another.

Real Chinese proverbs—not the kind that come with the bill—are largely the heritage of thousands of years of China's illiterate, oral, peasant-based culture, according to Professor John S. Rohsenow, who spent years compiling a comprehensive dictionary of Chinese proverbs. Western culture used to have more proverbs (when it was more oral and illiterate and agricultural). Elizabethan England was soaked with them, but they have since declined. James Obelkevich, another researcher who has done work in proverbs, argues that they disappeared in part because proverbs put the collective before the individual and external rules before self-determination. The increasingly educated and middle-class British population disdained proverbs for their lack of independent thought.

At lunch I asked my mom how she felt about her children. "Do you wish our thinking was more Chinese?"

I expected her to talk wistfully about the old country and old traditions and old ways.

Instead, she blinked. "Not really," she said. "The Chinese have some strange ideas." Among them, she noted, is that the parents are always right. "Dad and I aren't like that," she said. They would rather be fair than right.

But it's been hard. In China, you have to obey your parents, she reminded me. I thought back a decade. When my grandmother died in her hometown, my father and mother had to crawl along the streets of the town sobbing. My aunt had given them knee pads to wear, hidden, underneath their pants. My brother, the firstborn son of the firstborn son, had to kneel during the entire funeral service.

In America, it's the opposite, my mom said. In Chinese culture, you criticize your children to make them better. (Why did you get only a 97 on the test? You need to lose weight. Your piano playing needs practice.) Here, you have to affirm your children's self-esteem. "We've had to recalibrate our thinking," she said in Mandarin. "It's not easy."

Earlier during lunch, I'd mentioned a Chinese-American friend who'd felt unloved by his parents because they had been distant when he was growing up. My mother's response: American children can't understand the Chinese expression of love through sacrifice.

When I'd visited his fortune cookie printing shop, Steven Yang had commented on the same thing. "Chinese have a bigger sense of self-sacrifice. Americans are about self-enjoyment, not self-sacrifice," he'd said. "We have this concept of sacrificing for the next generation. I don't think Americans really have this concept. They are about themselves." Or as my friend Jimmy Quach once said, Chinese parents are so good at deferring gratification, they sometimes defer it to the next generation.

After lunch, my mom sent me an e-mail, typed in her charming but haphazard way: "The Chines Americans can not feel the love deeply. Only take huging and 'verbal love' as love." She wanted me to transmit this concept to my friend. "Try to see thing from different angles. You people have been influenced by the American culture too much, the TV show the media and all. Remember, thinking of the percentage of the parents pay for the college tuition between the Chinese and the American. So, do you think huging is love, and paying bill is not? And remember, we are the new Immigrants in the country."

Only a fraction of the many Chinese proverbs can transcend cultural barriers and language. All the fortune cookie writers I interviewed talked about the incessant pressure to come up with new fortunes. Back in the heyday of the fortune cookie boom, during the 1950s and 1960s, a handful of fortune writers looked to the East for their inspiration, drawing from the *I Ching,* Confucius, and Chinese proverbs, but others did not. Twixt, Wonton Food's predecessor in New York, once invited the National Association of Gagwriters to submit fortune cookie sayings. Others combed the works of such Western philosophers as Goethe. Still others looked more locally—to the people they did business with, for instance. The Hong Kong Noodle Company agreed to buy paper from Moore's Business Forms only after the company salesman agreed to write fortunes. In the 1970s, the primary scribe was a twenty-something Mexican-American named Faustino Corona.

Chinese sages stopped spewing their aphorisms centuries ago, but the American appetite for pithy, exotic maxims has not stopped. In 1959, Twixt had a repertoire of but one thousand fortunes. Today, Wonton Food's database exceeds ten thousand.

So then, where were the fortune cookie writers getting their inspiration from?

Poor Richard's Almanac, the Bible, a book of Jewish proverbs, and song lyrics, said Greg Louie of the Lotus Fortune Cookie Company. "I don't think we had a Confucius at all," he remarked.

A book called *The Great Thoughts* by George Seldes, which

compiled sayings from a lot of the movers and shakers in intellectual history, said Russell Rowland, who churned out seven hundred fortunes for Steven Yang.

Astrology books, said Donna Jackson, a speech pathologist from San Diego; she'd approached Steven Yang after being irked by ungrammatical fortunes. This helps account for all those fortunes that ascribe personal qualities to the reader: "You are generous and kindhearted to others."

Movies, inspirational Hallmark-type sayings, and forwarded e-mail messages, said Lisa Yang, Steven's daughter. "If I was watching a movie and they came out with a very neat line that got stuck in my head, I would end up writing it down," she told me. She'd gotten a lot of chain letters in college; she liked the ones that were touchy-feely.

This all coalesced for me one Thanksgiving, when I headed to New Mexico to visit a lone Powerball restaurant just north of Albuquerque in Bernalillo. My friend Josh Yguado, his parents, and I trekked to Guang Dong Chinese Restaurant, which had given a local police sergeant his lucky Powerball numbers. At the end of the meal, when the requisite plate of fortune cookies was placed in front of us, we each plucked one, cracked it open, and began the sequence of reading our fortunes around the table.

Mine was bland and forgettable. Then Josh's mom read hers: "Do or do not. There is no try."

I looked up with a mixture of recognition and disbelief. "Oh my God. That's from *The Empire Strikes Back*," I said. I knew the scene by heart, one in which Luke Skywalker struggles with his Jedi knight training on the mist-shrouded planet of Dagobah.

Yoda our new Confucius is.

The purpose of fortune cookies became startlingly clear to me then: this is Western wisdom recycled for an American audience. The Chinese are just the middlemen.

Acknowledgments

A personal literary project like this has a long trajectory, starting with the phone call where someone first asks, "Have you ever thought of writing a book?" Over the past four years it has become so intimately intertwined with my daily life that the contributions I acknowledge are not only for content but emotional support, as a wisp of an idea morphed into a finished product.

This book as you hold it would not have been possible without the amazing Jonathan Karp, who was the insightful editor everyone told me he would be. He saw the potential for this book more than even I did, and gave me both the road map and the encouragement toward fulfilling it. I must hug my agent, Larry Weissman, and his wife, Sascha, who got the book almost immediately when they heard the idea, shaped a beautiful proposal, and put me in the right hands at Twelve. I could not have wished for a better publicist than Cary Goldstein, whose reputation precedes him. Bonnie Thompson's copyediting astounded me with its grace and precision.

A number of people took considerable time out of their busy lives to improve the draft manuscript once it was in hand: Jimmy Quach, who put together the giant insight that made the book come together; Tim Wu, for spewing his usual brilliant observations on food and other things; Hugo Kugiya, who gave thoughtful writerly feedback on my chapters; Nate Gray, Charlie Delafuente, and Juliet Chung, who devotedly line-edited the book, smoothing sentences in ways that made me smile; and Jennifer Stahl, whose dedicated fact-checking saved me.

Of all my friends who jumped in on this project, Tomoko Hosaka stands out for her willingness to immerse herself: arranging everything in Japan, taking pictures of Chinese restaurants, and lugging hundreds of Japanese fortune cookies across the Pacific. We are two children of immigrants who met here, and we have not let the Chinese/Japanese fortune cookie dispute get between us.

From here on, the thanks are listed roughly in chronological order by stages of the project: Michael Nagle, the photographer whose quest for a photo essay on Chinese immigrants started us on the journey toward Hiawassee; Michael Luo, the first person I told about my idea, a partner in conception and the originator of the most brilliant title, "The Long March of General Tso," which remains a chapter name; the late Gerald Boyd, who shaped many young careers, for giving the initial okay on the Hiawassee story; Jon Landman, who saw the potential even though I was not a metro reporter and handed me over to Wendell Jamieson, who was a great editor for that original story and subsequent work. A number of generous people made that first story on Hiawassee possible: the family that let me into their lives; their generous neighbor Jane Chianinni; and McConnell Church.

In addition to the people who directly appeared in the book, I must thank those who gave me a significant body of leads in my research, including Betty Xie of *Chinese Restaurant News,* Cynthia Lee of the Museum of Chinese in the Americas, Harley Spiller for his amazing menu collection, Indigo Som and her Chinese restaurant quest, and Jacqueline M. Newman of *Flavor and Fortune.* I was inspired by the work of academics and other journalists: Ted Anthony, who first found General Tso's family; Ko-Lin Chin, who studied Chinese smuggling and took the time to talk to me; Samantha Barbas, who examined chop suey in depth; Zai Liang, for his work on the Fujianese; Mimi Sheraton, for her early reviews on the great New York Chinese restaurants; Lisa Hsia, for her paper on the early days of Chinese restaurants; Cheuk Kwan, for his restaurant documentaries; and Peter Kwong, who wrote the first book that opened my eyes to the Chinese in America.

Many random Chinese restaurant tips made their way into the book from many sources: Paige Craig, for being the first to let me know about Chinese restaurants in the Baghdad Green Zone; Derek Shimoda, for fortune cookie leads; Gabriel Sherman, for the NASA tip; Roman Roman, for pointing me to Mexicali; Jonathan Zittrain, for the observations on Jewish bar and bat mitzvahs; Tom Scocca, who let me know about his college roommate's grandfather who headed Fold-Pak; Andy Revkin, for putting me in contact with McMurdo Station in Antarctica; Alicia Mundy, who exclaimed, "You have to write about the kosher duck scandal!" as soon as she heard about my book.

On the library and research front, I thank Abby L. Yochelson of the Library of Congress for pulling many documents; Lynne Oliver of foodtimeline.org for tracking down Fold-Pak when I could not; and Austin Lavin, Zak Stone, Lulu Zhou, Tim Wu, and Chris Thorpe for pulling things that I didn't have access to. And a very, very big thanks to Trey McArver for PDFing lots and lots of documents.

Many publishing industry people took the time to give me advice when I was still figuring my way around: Liz Nagle, Ben Loehnen, Douglas Stewart, Jennifer Joel, Tim Duggan, and David Black.

A number of authors were generous with their advice: Warren St. John, Benoit Denizet-Lewis, Stephen Dubner, Sasha Issenberg, Dana

Vachon, Alicia Mundy, Bob O'Harrow, Brendan I. Koerner, Taylor Clark, and Ben Wallace.

Many people around the world helped me on a quixotic hunt for lucky numbers and the world's greatest Chinese restaurant, either by opening up their homes, doing local research on my behalf, or both: Rose Murphy in Vancouver; Matthew Funk in Singapore; the Yguado family in New Mexico; Amy Morrow (now Gerlicher) and Ben Gerlicher in Phoenix; Antonio Regalado in Brazil; Thomas Crampton and Thuy-Tien Tran in Paris; Nikhil Chandra in London; Matthew Santaspirit in Rome; Gillian Wu and her family in Toronto; Ben and Lydia Choi in the Bay Area; Bernard Chang in San Francisco; Janet Chang (now Tseng) and Kien-Wei Tseng in San Jose; Stephen and Ming Hsu Chen in the East Bay; Alice Chen in Chicago; Brendan Kredell in Chicago; Yilu Zhao in Boston; Steve Schwartz and his family in Mauritius; Jason Begay in Gallup, New Mexico; Chris Thorpe in Boston; Matt MacInnis in Beijing; Thomas Henningson in Shanghai; Mark Zavadskiy in Hong Kong; Walter Miller in Mexico; Julio Villenueva and Eugenia Mont in Peru; Patrick Ventrell in Colombia; Rungtip Tangparimonthon in Bangkok; Joshua Polacheck in the Dominican Republic; and Wang Wei in Changsha.

I'm thankful to those who helped with translating and local research: Fernanda Santos for Portuguese translation and tracking down Fong Yu; Iara Luchian for translating in Brazil; Emily Vasquez for help with Spanish; Juro Osawa for helping in Japanese; Yilu Zhao, Charlene Wang, and Mom for translating Chinese; Daniel Bloom for finding Chef Peng in Taiwan; Alexandra Lee in Jamaica; Yuko Morikawa for translating the Japanese documents.

My research was smoothed by talented programmers I have never met but who brought us Google, Google Maps, Google Scholar, Pro-Quest, and Kayak—all tools I used extensively in assembling this book. And in a nod to the old as well as the new, the New York Public Library was an amazing resource and writing sanctuary that opened up the world of history not yet captured digitally. (The magnificent reading room is the photo on my Treo.)

And thank you to Nina Subin and Chinatown Brasserie for helping with the perfect (and last-minute) author photo.

Writing a book while working full-time would not have been possible without the patient understanding and support from others on the metro desk at the New York Times: Susan Edgerley and Joe Sexton, metro editors; Daryl Alexander for working out my scheduling snafus; Anahad O'Connor, Timothy Williams, and Manny Fernandez for willingly trading shifts with me so I could hunt for Chinese restaurants;

my immediate editors, Pete Khoury, Denise Fuhs, Karin Roberts, and Ian Trontz, for understanding when my planes arrived late.

Many colleagues at the *New York Times* had early and continuous enthusiasm for the project, which kept me going: Sewell Chan, whom I have known and worked with since seventh grade; Amy Harmon; Cate Doty; Richard Oppel; Karen Arenson; David Chen; Edward Wong; Yilu Zhao; Verlyn Klinkenborg; Damien Cave; Nick Confessore; Eric Dash; Campbell Robertson; Rachel Swarns; Lynette Clemetson; Julie Bosman; Maureen Dowd; Nick Fox; Kathleen McElroy; Manny Fernandez; Andy Revkin; Eric Schmitt; Jill Abramson; Rick Berke; and many others.

Many readers of the proposal offered good insight: Jay Dixit, Chris Thorpe, Tim Wu, Chris Kirchoff, Eugene Lee, Zak Stone, Max Levchin, Charlie Savage, James Hong, Mike Epstein, Yiyun Li, Lulu Zhou, Josh Schanker, Mark Glassman, Charlotte Morgan, Alison Seanor, Alexis Ohanian, and Javier C. Hernandez. I must also thank Alexis Ohanian, Eugene Kuo, and Eugene Lee for doing creative graphics work.

On the writing front, Sugi Ganeshananthan gave me pep talks on caring about each and every sentence, while Verlyn Klinkenborg and Anne Hull both opened my eyes to the possibilities of prose.

My friends and roommates were supportive and patient when I disappeared for weeks and weekends, hunting for great Chinese restaurants and fortune cookies: Jay Dixit, Rachel Metz, Jessica Luterman, Robin Stein, Kathryn Shouyee Yung (who will always be Shouyee to me), Braxton Robbason, Donald E. Lacey, David L. Hu, Anders Hove, Emily Vasquez, Maria Kim, Eric T. Lee, Bernard Chang, Pawel Swiatek, Paul Craig, Camberley Crick, Matthew Funk, Eli Pariser, Arianna Cha, Garrett Therolf, Brendan Kredell, Christian Bailey, and David Lat. I'd like to say thanks to Daniel J. Hemel for promising to start my fan club; Bobby Lee for reincarnating Hubba Bubba, my purple hippo, whom I thought had been lost forever when he was kidnapped in Cuzco; and Josh Yguado for the late-night cross-continental phone calls that kept me from being lonely.

My siblings, Frances and Kenny, have had a lifetime of dealing with a big sister who wants to share the big bowl of noodles. To you both: this book is really about us and our parents, to whom this book is dedicated.

There are three people whose presence I will treasure throughout my lifetime. Adam S. Hickey and Matthew W. Granade have alternately believed in me and put up with me with biting humor. As we move through time and space, the strands of friendship and common experience will stretch but continually bind us together. Lastly, many thanks to CAT, whose devotion translated into both having the patience to take my panicked three A.M. phone calls and the honesty to tell me when my writing sucked.

Notes

Prologue: March 30, 2005

The original interviews for this piece—with Chuck Strutt, Rebecca Paul, Derrick Wong, and James Currie—were conducted in May 2005 and were used soon thereafter in a short piece of mine called "Who Needs Giacomo? Bet on the Fortune Cookie," which ran in the *New York Times* on May 11, 2005, page A1. I again interviewed Rebecca Paul in Nashville, Tennessee, in March 2006 and Chuck Strutt and Sue Dooley in Des Moines, Iowa, in July 2006.

Chapter 1: American-Born Chinese

The statistic on the number of Chinese restaurants is provided by *Chinese Restaurant News*, an industry publication; as of 2007, there are more than 43,000. The number of McDonald's, Burger Kings, and KFCs is derived from the counts from the corporations themselves.

The information about chop suey showing up in World War II cookbooks on page 10 is drawn from page 79 in Harvey Levenstein's *Paradox of Plenty: A Social History of Eating in Modern America* (University of California Press, 2003).

As of 2007, Wok n Roll Chinese restaurant, mentioned on page 9, is situated at 604 H Street NW, which is the location of the former Mary Surratt boardinghouse, where Abraham Lincoln's assassination was planned.

The story about Jonas Salk and Chinese food on page 10 is from a letter to the editor, "Dr. Salk's Brain Food," submitted by Yee Yuen Lee of Mount Lebanon to the *Pittsburgh Tribune-Review*, April 21, 2005.

The reference to the Freedom Riders eating at a Chinese restaurant on page 10 has been cited in numerous firsthand and contemporary accounts, and is available in "A Brief History of the Freedom Riders" by David Lisker, written in 2001, available online at http://www.freedomridersfoundation.com/brief.history.html.

President Eisenhower's relationship with Sun Chop Suey Restaurant on page 10 is documented in "Eisenhowers Keep Yen for Chop Suey," *New York Times*, August 2, 1953, page 44.

The information about Peking Gourmet Inn's bulletproof window on page 10 is from an interview conducted with the owners in February 2006.

The interview with Jim Ye took place in Arizona in November 2006. The interviews with the P. F. Chang staff took place in October 2005. The interviews at Trey Yuen, in Louisiana, took place in November 2006. The interviews at the McCarricks' home took place in Wyoming in July 2006, as well as before and afterward on the telephone. The interviews at the Oriental Chow Mein factory took place in 2005.

Chapter 2: The Menu Wars

The information about Misa Chang is drawn from interviews with Misa and Eric Ma in September 2005 and again in August 2006, as well as earlier news articles. These included an excellent extensive piece, "The Chinese Menu Guys," by Jane H. Lii in the *New York Times*, July 28, 1996, section 13, page 1; "Neighborhood Report: Upper West Side—Update; The Menu Wars, Continued" by Emily M. Berstein, *New York Times*, January 2, 1994, section 13, page 6; "Neighborhood Report: Upper West Side—Update; Empire Szechuan Fined over Menus," unsigned *New York Times*, March 20, 1994, section 13, page 7; and "Chinese Food Places Vying on Delivery" by Fred Ferretti, *New York Times*, July 20, 1983, section C, page 3.

Chapter 3: A Cookie Wrapped in a Mystery Inside an Enigma

The recounting of the 1983 San Francisco fortune cookie trial is drawn from interviews with Sally Osaki in March 2006, documents provided by participants, and contemporaneous news accounts at the time. These news accounts include: "S.F., You'll Be Happy to Know, Is the Home of the Fortune Cookie" by Ken Wong, *San Francisco Examiner*, October 28, 1983, page B11; "The Judge

Was One Smart Cookie in Handling This One" by Bob Lyhne, *Peninsula Times Tribune,* November 1, 1983; and "Judge Settles S.F.-L.A. Clash—S.F. wins" by Sheri Tan, *Asian Week,* November 2, 1983.

Note that while some news accounts attribute the anecdote about the Japanese women's outing to Chinatown to Sally Osaki herself, it is actually an account from Kathleen Fujita Date that was recounted by Sally at the trial.

The explanation for how World War II soldiers passing through San Francisco played a role in the spread of the fortune cookie is drawn from accounts from fortune cookie manufacturers in a piece called "Inside the Fortune Cookie" by Franz Gustafson, available in the San Francisco Public Library historical archives' fortune cookie file. The name and date of the publication is unclear from the clip; however, judging from the content, it likely appeared in the mid-1970s. Other historical accounts about the rising popularity of the fortune cookie are drawn from the following news sources: "Ah So! Sales Boom for Fortune Cookies: Messages Go Modern" by Michael Winger, *Wall Street Journal,* August 12, 1966, page A1; "Cookie's Origin Leaves Asian-Americans Bantering" by Ginny McPartland, *Sacramento Bee,* final edition, January 24, 1990, Food 13 (Kathleen Fujita Date's account of her mother sharing fortune cookies with a Chinese restaurant owner in Chinatown); "The Inside Story of the Fortune Cookie Craze" by Leslie Lieber, *Los Angeles Times,* June 7, 1959, page 125 (which provides the late-1950s estimate of 250 million fortune cookies produced annually); "Psst! Filthy Fortune Cookies? Yup, They're Selling Like Hotcakes" by William McAllister, *Wall Street Journal,* March 3, 1972, page A1 (where the Transamerica protest anecdote is drawn from); "Rising Fortunes" by Armand Schwab Jr., *New York Times,* November 27, 1960, page SM84 (on the use of fortune cookies at the 1960 Democratic convention); "Cookies and Song Enliven City Race" by Eric Pace, *New York Times,* September 4, 1965, page 46 (regarding Abraham Beame in his 1965 mayoral race); "Daley Gets Cookies," *Chicago Tribune,* March 25, 1972, page N15.

Interviews with Sally Osaki, Douglas Dawkins, and Sue Okamura were conducted in San Francisco in March 2006.

Chapter 4: The Biggest Culinary Joke Played by One Culture on Another
The following academic works were instrumental in my understanding of chop suey and the early perception of Chinese food in America: "Chop Suey: From Chinese Food to Chinese American Food" by Renqiu Yu, *Chinese America: History and Perspectives* (1987): 87–99 (the journal is difficult to find, and as far as I am aware, there is no digital copy available); "I'll Take Chop Suey: Restaurants as Agents of Culinary and Cultural Change" by Samantha Barbas, *Journal of Popular Culture* 36, no. 4 (2003): 669–87; "Eating the Exotic: The Growing Acceptability of Chinese Cuisine in San Francisco, 1848–1915" by Lisa Hsia, published in *Clio's Scroll,* the undergraduate history journal at the University of California, Berkeley, vol. 5, no. 1 (Fall 2003): 5–30; and Harvey Levenstein's *Paradox of Plenty: A Social History of Eating in Modern America* (New York: Oxford University Press, 1993).

For an early perspective on Chinese food, the digitization of early newspaper archives through ProQuest and other services proved extremely useful, both in finding early citations of phrases like "chop suey" (in various spellings) and "Chinese restaurant," as well as seeing the jump in frequency of those phrases that took place after 1896.

Other works that were more specifically helpful included *Alas, What Brought Thee Hither? The Chinese in New York, 1800–1950* by Arthur Bonner (Madison, N.J.: Fairleigh Dickinson University Press, 1997), which is an excellent distillation of early media coverage of the Chinese in New York; *Pigtails and Gold Dust: A Panorama of Chinese Life in Early California* by Alexander McLeod (Caldwell, Idaho: Caxton Printers, Ltd., 1947); "Chinese Food and Restaurants" by Alice Harrison in the old out-of-print magazine *Overland Monthly,* June 1917, pages 527–32; "Cathay on the Coast" by Idwal Jones in the *American Mercury,* August 1926, pages 453–60.

Information about particular anecdotes follows: The health inspector's search for rats on page 50 comes from "Mott Street Chinamen Angry: They Deny That They Eat Rats; Chung King Threatens a Slander Suit" in the *New York Times,* August 1, 1883, page 8. The information about Taishan's disasters on page 51 comes from Madeline Yuan-yin Hsu in *Dreaming of Gold, Dreaming of Home* (Palo Alto, Calif.: Stanford University Press, 2000) on page 25, where she cites "Chinese Emigration, the Sunning Railway and the Development of Toisan" by Lucie Cheng, and Liu Yuzun, with Zheng Dehua, in *Amerasia* 9, no. 1 (1982): 52–74, page 62. The reporter quoted about the standard "Chinese bill of fare" is from "Restaurant Life in San Francisco," *Overland Monthly* (November 1868). The description about beans comes from "Chinese Food and Restaurants" by Alice Harrison in *Overland Monthly*, June 1917, pages 527–32. The writer describing Chinatown after the earthquake on page 53 is D. E. Kessler in "An Evening in Chinatown" in *Overland Monthly,* May 1907, pages 445–49.

Mark Twain's account on 54 comes from *Roughing It,* which has been published in many versions. In the 1972 University of California version, his description of Chinese food starts on page 353. The story about the judge, defendant, and chopsticks on page 54 comes from "Good Fortune Since the Gold Rush, Chinese Food Has Added Spice to American Life" by Bryan R. Johnson, published in the *Chicago Tribune,* February 17, 1988, and reprinted from American Heritage Inc.

The anti-Chinese document on page 55 is *Some Reasons for Chinese Exclusion: Meat Versus Rice, American Manhood Against Asiatic Coolieism—Which Shall Survive* by Samuel Gompers and Herman Gutstadt in affiliation with the American Federation of Labor (Washington, D.C.: GPO, 1902). The document was submitted to the U.S. Senate as Document No. 137.

Statistics on restaurant workers between 1870 and 1920 and restaurants between 1900 and 1920 on page 57 are taken from Ronald Takaki's superb *Strangers from a Different Shore* (Boston: Little, Brown, 1989; revised 1998), page 247.

The statistics on New York City restaurants in 1885 is taken from *Alas! What Brought Thee Hither? The Chinese in New York, 1800–1950* by Arthur Bonner (Madison, N.J.: Fairleigh Dickinson University Press; 1997), page 71; the 1903 statistics are from page 105.

The employment statistics on page 57 come from *The Chinese in America* by Reverend O. Gibson (Cincinnati: Hitchcock and Walden, 1877).

The fact that New York City had gone chop suey mad on page 57 is from a "Heard About Town" column in the *New York Times,* published on January 29, 1900, page 7.

Information on the Chicago City Council investigation on chop suey comes from "Investigates High Costs of Chop Suey, Chicago Council Grills Bewildered Orientals" in the *Boston Globe,* November 18, 1920.

The story about the fifteen-year-old Chicago girl stealing $3,400 from her parents for chop suey is from "Tells of Chop Suey Orgy" in the *New York Times,* May 2, 1923, page 21.

The anecdote about Luchow's new spelling on page 58 comes from "Umlaut Spells Difference in Chow on 14th Street" in the *New York Times,* September 6, 1952, page 14.

Li Hongzhang's visit on page 60 comes from "The Viceroy Their Guest: Ex-ministers to China Entertain Li Hung Chang," *New York Times,* August 30, 1896. The statement of chop suey first becoming popularized in New York City found on page 64 is based on work done by John Kuo Wei Chen, a Chinese American historian who has examined menus, historical photographs, and newspaper accounts from that era.

Chapter 5: The Long March of General Tso

This chapter was largely inspired by Ted Anthony of the Associated Press and his piece "Chinese Takeout Menu Legends: General Tso—warrior, innovator…chicken?," which was transmitted July 24, 2004. Ted's advice and guidance concerning Sichuan and Shanghai food was immeasurably critical for this chapter.

The account of the great Chinese chefs in New York City in the late 1960s and early 1970s is reconstructed from interviews and news articles of the era.

Michael Tong was originally interviewed about General Tso's chicken in December 2004. Bob Lape, formerly of ABC News, was interviewed in August 2005. My trips to Hunan and Taipei took place in October 2006.

Chapter 6: The Bean Sprout People Are in the Same Boat We Are

The interview with Greg Louie of Lotus was conducted in November 2004, before Lotus closed. The anecdote about Edward Louie's account of how to market fortune cookies as exotic was drawn from "Ah So! Sales Boom for Fortune Cookies: Messages Go Modern" by Michael Winger, *Wall Street Journal*, August 12, 1966, page A1.

Chapter 7: Why Chow Mein Is the Chosen Food of the Chosen People—or, The Kosher Duck Scandal of 1989

This account of the kosher duck scandal is based on interviews with Michael Mayer conducted in March 2006, as well as several third-party news accounts, especially Alicia Mundy's piece "The Case of the Smoking Duck: Moshe Dragon Chinese Kosher Restaurant Investigation," *Regardie's* 10, no. 8 (April 1990): 86; the article ran at a very entertaining 8,218 words.

These other pieces also supplemented the *Regardie's* piece: "The Strange Case of Moshe Dragon Restaurant" by Judith Colp, *Washington Times,* March 15, 1990, page E1; "In Kosher Conflict, the Duck Stops Here; Rabbinical Council Under Fire for Handling of Chinese Restaurant" by Eugene L. Meyer, *Washington Post,* June 20, 1990, page C1; and "Is Everything Kosher with Moshe Dragon's Duck?" by Ruth Sinai, Associated Press, July 4, 1990.

My chapter also draws on contemporaneous coverage by *Washington Jewish Week,* available in bound volumes at the *Washington Jewish Week* offices in Silver Spring, Maryland. In chronological order, these included: "Chinese Kosher Clash at Moshe Dragon: Food Fraud or Frame-up?" by Judith Colp, September 14, 1989, page 3; "Moshe Dragon Mashgiach Fired" by Judith Colp, September 28, 1989, page 2; "Moshe Dragon Inquiry Nears End" by Jon Greene, November 18, 1989, page 3; "Moshe Dragon Exonerated of Kosher Wrongdoing" by Jon Greene, December 8, 1989, page 3; "New Charges Rock Moshe Dragon" by Jon Greene, April 5, 1990, page 27; "Rabbis Face New Questions Over Kosher Pancake Flap" by Jon Greene, April 12, 1990, page 11; "Conservative Rabbis Split on Moshe Dragon" by Jon Greene, April 12, 1990, page 11; "Maryland Attorney General's Office Reviewing Moshe Dragon Charges" by Jon Greene, April 19, 1990; "Moshe Dragon," letter to the editor submitted by Lazer Fuerst of Rockville, Maryland, May 17, 1990; "Unorthodox Practices: Washington's Kosher Food System Is Flawed, Critics Charge, and It May Be on the Brink of a Movement Toward Reform" by Jon Greene, May 31, 1990, page 5; "Washington Board of Rabbis Voices Support of Moshe Dragon" by Jon Greene, June 14, 1990, page 7; and "The Saga Continues: Why Moshe Dragon's Last Mashgiach Quit" by Jon Greene, June 21, 1990, page 5.

The role of Chinese food in American Jewish culture drew its inspiration from two academic papers. The first is Hanna Miller's "Identity Takeout: How American Jews Made Chinese Food Their Ethnic Cuisine," *Journal of Popular Culture* 39, no. 3 (2006): 430–65. The second is the oft-cited granddaddy on Jews and Chinese food: "New York Jews and Chinese Food: The Social Construction of an Ethnic Pattern" by Gaye Tuchman and Harry G. Levine, *Journal of Contemporary Ethnography* 22, no. 3 (October 1993): 382–407. It is available online at http://soc.qc.cuny.edu/Staff/levine/NYJews-and-Chinese.htm.

The anecdote about the protest sign reading "Down with chop suey! Long live gefilte fish!" on page 97 is from *Getting Comfortable in New York: The American Jewish Home, 1880–1950* by Susan Braunstein and Jenna Weissman Joselit (New York: Jewish Museum, 1990), page 215; I found it quoted in Miller.

I made visits to Chai Peking in January 2006 and Soy Vay in March 2005. I visited Kaifeng, China, in October 2006.

In addition, I had many conversations with Jewish friends around the country to build up my understanding of the role of Chinese food in their families' lives.

Chapter 8: The *Golden Venture:* Restaurant Workers to Go

Interviews with Michael Chen were conducted in Dublin, Ohio, in June 2006. The visits to Houyu and Shengmei in Fujian were conducted in October 2006. The visit to Bangkok was conducted in December 2006. The visit to the Dominican Republic and the interview with "Naum" was conducted in May 2006.

Information on the Fujianese immigration routes was drawn from numerous academic sources, including the book *Global Human Smuggling: Comparative Perspectives,* edited by David Kyle and Rey Koslowski (Baltimore: John Hopkins University Press, 2001). Among the essays that proved extremely useful in the book are "From Fujian to New York: Understanding the New Chinese Immigration" by Zai Liang and Wenzhen Ye, and Peter Kwong's "The Impact of Chinese Human Smuggling on the American Labor Market." Additionally, I drew insights from *Smuggled Chinese: Clandestine Immigration to the United States* by Ko-Lin Chin (Philadelphia: Temple University Press, 1999). Interviews with Zai Liang, Peter Kwong, and Ko-Lin Chin on their academic research were invaluable.

Much of the account of Sister Ping is drawn from court transcripts of the Sister Ping trial, case no. 94-CR-953-MBM in the Southern District of New York. The bulk of the trial took place in May and June 2005, and Weng Yu Hui and Guo Liang Qi, who were both convicted for their firsthand involvement in the *Golden Venture,* testified in return for leniency. In addition, many of the law enforcement agents involved in the case—from the FBI, INS, Coast Guard, and Hong Kong police—also testified. Since the case was on appeal as of 2007, the transcripts remained available at the federal courthouse at 500 Pearl Street. I would like to thank Patrick Radden Keefe for alerting me to their availability.

Material drawn from the court transcripts includes: the scene where Sister Ping and Weng Yu Hui meet the morning of the crash, as told by Weng; the specifics of the business dealings between Guo Liang Qi, also known as Ah Kay, and Sister Ping in a September 1991 smuggling transaction, as told by Guo; Sister Ping's line ("That's what happened in the past. We're talking business now," court transcript, page 404), as told by Guo; the fact that the captain of the *Najd II* decided to stop in Mombasa, Kenya, because he decided his share of the smuggling profit was too small, as told by Weng; the decision to crash the *Golden Venture* into Breezy Point, as recounted by Weng; the arrest of Sister Ping in the Hong Kong airport (as told by law enforcement agents).

There was a flood of newspaper accounts after the *Golden Venture* crash, but I drew some of the unique details of the boat journey itself from "Chinese Immigrants Tell of Darwinian Voyage" by Diana Jean Schemo, *New York Times,* June 12, 1993, A1.

The citation on page 122 on how every single one of the thirty-seven smuggling boats had some connection to Taiwan is drawn from unpublished figures from the U.S. Immigration and Naturalization Service, cited by Marlowe Hood in "Sourcing the Problem: Why Fuzhou?" in *Human Smuggling: Chinese Migrant Trafficking and the Challenge to America's Migration Tradition,* edited by Paul J. Smith (Washington, D.C.: Center for Strategic and International Studies, 1997), page 78.

The account of the efforts to free the *Golden Venture* passengers by Congressman Goodling, including his meeting with President Clinton, is drawn from Congressman Goodling's account in "Goodling's Efforts Led to Freedom for Chinese Refugees" by Julia Duin, *Washington Times,* March 2, 1997. Another article that proved useful in describing the *Golden Venture* detainees' time in York was Julia Duin's "Chinese Waste Away in U.S. Jails After Fleeing Population Control," *Washington Times,* December 17, 1996.

The fact that the passengers ate General Tso's chicken after their release, on page 134, is drawn from "Refugees' Golden Day" by Ying Chang, *New York Daily News,* February 27, 1997.

Chapter 9: Take-out Takeaways
Interviews were conducted at Fold-Pak's Hazleton factory in April 2006.

Chapter 10: The Oldest Surviving Fortune Cookies in the World?
Interviews with Merlin Lowe, Brian Kito, Stephen Tong, and Beverly Tong were conducted in Los Angeles in February 2007. Interviews with Gary Ono were conducted in January 2006. Information about the Umeya company in Los Angeles is drawn from Umeya's Web site, www.umeyaricecake.com.

The reference to the divvying up of territory between Twixt and Umeya on page 144 is drawn from "The Inside Story of the Fortune Cookie Craze" by Leslie Lieber, *Los Angeles Times,* June 7, 1959, page I25.

The Japanese paper is by Yasuko Nakamachi: "Tools and Skillcraft Work of the Japanese Cracker Makers in Fushimi," published in *The Annual Report Systematization of Non-Written Cultural Material for the Study of Human Societies* 1 (2004): 221–28; the report was part of Kanagawa University's Twenty-First-Century Center of Excellence Program.

Chapter 11: The Mystery of the Missing Chinese Deliveryman
Most of the reporting about the missing deliveryman was my firsthand observation done in April 2005. The police account of the 2002 Jian Lin-Chun murder is drawn from "Murdered for $25—Teens Nailed in Deliveryman Slay" by Joe McGuck, Larry Celona, Philip Messing, and Aly Sujo, *New York Post,* October 17, 2002, page 13. The murder of Jin-Sheng Liu was from "Teenager Who Lured Deliveryman to His Death Pleads Guilty" by Sarah Kershaw, *New York Times,* May 1, 2002, page B3. The account of Huang Chen is drawn from "Teen Sentenced to 51 Years to Life in Killing of Food Deliveryman," Associated Press, May 19, 2005.

Chapter 12: The Soy Sauce Trade Dispute
The interviews in this chapter were conducted with Natsuko Kumasawa in December 2006 outside Tokyo; Hiroshi Takamatsu of Kikkoman in December 2006 in Tokyo; and Masaaki Hirose and Kuniki Hatayama of Kikkoman in January 2007 in Walworth, Wisconsin.

For background information, I drew on documents filed with Codex, many of which are publicly available at www.codexalimentarius.net.

I also referred to news accounts from the time, including: "Feud Ferments Between Soy Sauce Makers" by Cindy Skrzycki, *Washington Post,* September 21, 2004, page E1; "What's Soy Sauce Without the Soy? Japan Defends Asian Seasoning's Tradition" by Kenji Hall, Associated Press, distributed September 25, 2004; "Global Food Fight? Why, Soytainly! Battle Brews over Sauce Labeling" by Kim Severson, *San Francisco Chronicle,* August 25, 2002, page A1; "Draft Codex Soy Sauce Standard Remains Controversial" by Stephen Clapp, *Food Chemical News* 46, no. 30 (September 6, 2004): 8; and "Draft Codex Soy Sauce Standard Remains in Limbo; Codex" by Stephen Clapp, *Food Chemical News* 46, no. 35 (October 11, 2004): 1.

Information on Kari-Out was drawn from interviews with the Epstein family and visits to the headquarters and the plant in 2005 and 2006, as well as the article "Outrageous Fortune: Howard Epstein's Love of Packaging Revolutionized Chinese Takeout" by Paul Lukas, *Fortune Small Business,* October 4, 2001.

Interviews at ConAgra's La Choy headquarters were conducted in January 2007 in Naperville, Illinois.

Chapter 13: Waizhou, U.S.A.
This chapter is essentially based on my firsthand experience, from the summer of 2002 to November 2004, spending time with the family in New York City and during numerous trips to Hiawassee, Georgia. A portion of the story ran under my byline as "For Immigrant Family, No Easy Journeys," *New York Times,* January 4, 2003, page A1. I am thankful to Wendell Jamieson and the late Gerald Boyd for giving me the freedom and support to pursue that article.

The information about the proliferation of Chinese restaurants draws in large part on *Chinese Restaurant News,* based in Fremont, California, and the generosity of its editor, Betty Xie. The anecdote about King Ying Low in Des Moines comes from *Los Angeles Times,* April 15, 1924, page 9.

Chapter 14: The Greatest Chinese Restaurant in the World
The information about Chinese food in Antartica is drawn from an e-mail exchange with the executive chef at McMurdo Station. The fact that NASA serves Chinese food in space in drawn from NASA's own Web site, which lists menus for its astronauts.

The visits and interviews for this chapter were conducted in the following order: Peru in

August 2006; Canada in September 2006; Japan, South Korea, and Singapore in December 2006; Los Angeles and San Francisco in February 2007; Britain, France, and Italy in February 2007; Brazil in March 2007; India, Mauritius, and Dubai in May 2007; Jamaica in June 2007; and Australia in July 2007.

Chapter 15: American Stir-fry

The interviews with Ming Tsai were conducted in March and June 2006.

Chapter 16: *Tsujiura Senbei*

The information on fortune cookies in Japan is drawn from work by Yasuko Nakamachi. The main paper, written in Japanese, is titled "Tools and Skillcraft Work of the Japanese Cracker Makers in Fushimi," published in *The Annual Report Systematization of Non-Written Cultural Material for the Study of Human Societies* 1 (2004): 221–28; the report was part of Kanagawa University's Twenty-First-Century Center of Excellence Program.

Chapter 17: Open-Source Chinese Restaurants

The insight to create a separate chapter for this stems from conversations with Jimmy Quach and Tim Wu.

The information about Chicken McNuggets on page 270 comes from *McDonald's: Behind the Arches* (New York: Bantam, 1995) by John F. Love, page 399.

Chapter 18: So What Did Confucius Really Say?

Some of the original inspiration for this chapter came from a hilarious long article by Terry McDermott: "The Sage of Fortune Cookies: A Quest to Discover Why the Ubiquitous Little Messages So Rarely Predict the Future Anymore Leads Through a Byzantine World of Secrecy and Suspicion to an Unlikely Oracle," *Los Angeles Times*, November 4, 2000, page A1.

The interviews with Mike Moskowitz were conducted in April 2006 and in January 2007 in Fort Lauderdale. The interview with Marcus Young was conducted in February 2006 in Minneapolis. The interviews and visits with Wonton Food were conducted over 2005 and 2007. The interviews with David Lee were conducted in November 2005, and with his father, Yong Lee, several months earlier, and those with Steven and Lisa Yang were conducted in November 2005 and February 2007. The visit to the Hyotanyama Inari shrine near Osaka took place in December 2006.

The information about Twixt, now part of Wonton Food, inviting the National Association of Gagwriters to submit cookie sayings on page 290 is drawn from "The Inside Story of the Fortune Cookie Craze" by Leslie Lieber, *Los Angeles Times*, June 7, 1959, page I25. The account about the salesman Faustino Corona working as a fortune cookie writer is drawn from "Postscript: Fortune Cookie Business Using the Old Noodle" by Bart Everett, *Los Angeles Times*, March 21, 1977, page OCI.

Bibliography

In addition to the specific works listed in the notes, the following sources—
some of which are also cited in the notes—proved useful in shaping my
understanding of the Chinese experience and Chinese food in America and
around the world.

Anderson, Eugene N. *The Food of China.* New Haven: Yale University Press,
    1988.

Arkush, R. David, and Leo O. Lee, eds. *Land Without Ghosts: Chinese Impres-
    sions of America from the Mid-Nineteenth Century to the Present.* Berkeley and
    Los Angeles: University of California Press, 1989.

As a Chinaman Saw Us: Passages from His Letters to a Friend at Home. New
    York: D. Appleton, 1905.

Barbas, Samantha. "I'll Take Chop Suey: Restaurants as Agents of Culinary
    and Cultural Change." *Journal of Popular Culture* 36, no. 4 (Spring 2003):
    669–87.

Bates, J. H. *Notes of a Tour in Mexico and California.* Printed for private distri-
    bution. New York, Burr printing house, 1887.

Biao X. "Emigration from China: A Sending Country Perspective." *Interna-
    tional Migration* 41, no. 3 (September 2003): 21–48.

Bonner, Arthur. *Alas! What Brought Thee Hither? The Chinese in New York,
    1800–1950.* Madison, N.J.: Fairleigh Dickinson University Press, 1997.

Chang, Isabelle Chin. *Gourmet on the Go: Delectable Chinese Recipes Adapted
    for Western Usage.* Rutland, Vt.: C. E. Tuttle, 1970.

Chang, K. C., ed. *Food in Chinese Culture: Anthropological and Historical Per-
    spectives.* New Haven: Yale University Press, 1977.

Chao, Tonia. "Communicating Through Architecture: San Francisco Chinese
    Restaurants as Cultural Intersections, 1849–1984." PhD diss. in architec-
    ture, University of California, Berkeley, 1987.

Chen, Chin-Yu. "San Francisco's Chinatown: A Socioeconomic and Cultural
    History, 1850–1882." PhD diss., University of Idaho, 1992.

Chen, Yong. "A Journey to the West: Chinese Food in Western Countries."
    Gastronomica: The Journal of Food and Culture 4, no. 1 (2004): 98–101.

Cheng, F. C. *Musings of a Chinese Gourmet.* Tiptree, Essex, England: Anchor
    Press, Ltd., 1955.

Cheng, Te Chao David. "Acculturation of the Chinese in the United States."
    PhD diss., University of Pennsylvania, 1948.

Chin, Ko-Lin. *Smuggled Chinese: Clandestine Immigration to the United States.*
    Philadelphia: Temple University Press, 1999.

Chinn, Thomas W. *Bridging the Pacific: San Francisco Chinatown and Its People*. San Francisco: Chinese Historical Society of America, 1989.

Cho, Lily. "On Eating Chinese: Chinese Restaurants and the Politics of Diaspora." PhD diss., University of Alberta, Canada, 2003.

Chop Suey Cook Book (containing authentic translations of the best recipes of leading Chinese chefs and directions for preparing various popular and healthful Chinese dishes exactly as they are prepared in the Orient). Chicago: Pacific Trading Co., 1928.

Chu, Louis. "The Chinese Restaurants in New York City." Master's thesis, New York University, 1939.

Chung, Lu Tzu. "Ethnic Enterprise in the Kansas City Metropolitan Area: The Chinese Restaurant Business, Volumes I and II (Missouri)." PhD diss., University of Kansas, 1990.

Condit, Ira. *The Chinaman as We See Him*. Chicago: Missionary Campaign Library, 1900.

Conlin, Joseph R. *Bacon, Beans and Galatines: Food and Foodways on the Western Mining Frontier*. Reno: University of Nevada Press, 1986.

Davis, Netta. "To Serve the 'Other': Chinese-American Immigrants in the Restaurant Business." *Journal for the Study of Food and Society* 6, no. 1 (Winter 2002): 70–81.

The Encyclopedia of the Chinese Overseas. Edited by Lynn Pan. Singapore: Archipelago Press–Landmark Books, 1998.

Fitzerman-Blue, Micah. "The Fortune Cookie in America." *Northwestern University Journal of Race and Gender Criticism* 1, no. 2 (Spring 2004): 15–30.

Frommer, Myrne Katz, and Harvey Frommer. *It Happened in Manhattan: An Oral History of Life in the City During the Mid-Twentieth Century*. New York: Penguin Putnam, 2001.

Gabaccia, Donna. *We Are What We Eat: Ethnic Food and the Making of Americans*. Cambridge, Mass.: Harvard University Press, 1998.

Gibson, O. *The Chinese in America*. Cincinnati: Hitchcock and Walden, 1877.

Global Human Smuggling: Comparative Perspectives. Edited by David Kyle and Rey Koslowski. Baltimore: Johns Hopkins University Press, 2001. These following articles were particularly useful: "From Fujian to New York: Understanding the New Chinese Immigration" by Zai Liang and Wenzhen Ye; "The Social Organization of Chinese Human Smuggling" by Ko-Lin Chin; and "The Impact of Chinese Human Smuggling on the American Labor Market" by Peter Kwong.

Gompers, Samuel, and Herman Gutstadt, in affiliation with the American Federation of Labor. *Some Reasons for Chinese Exclusion: Meat Versus Rice; American Manhood Versus Asiatic Coolieism—Which Shall Survive?*

Washington, D.C.: GPO, 1902. Submitted to the U.S. Senate as Document No. 137.

Guerassimoff, C. "The New Chinese Migrants in France." *International Migration* 41, no. 3 (September 2003): 135–54.

Harrison, Alice. "Chinese Food and Restaurants." *Overland Monthly,* June 1917, 527–32.

Hsia, Lisa. "Eating the Exotic: The Growing Acceptability of Chinese Cuisine in San Francisco, 1848–1915." *Clio's Scroll* 5, no. 1 (Fall 2003): 5–30.

Hsiung, Daw-jing. "Sensemaking and Culture: Examination of Two Culturally Grounded Theoretical Frameworks (Chinese, Karl Weick)." PhD diss., Arizona State University, 2004.

Jin Dongzheng. "The Sojourners' Story: Philadelphia's Chinese Immigrants, 1900–1925." PhD diss., Temple University, 1997.

Johnson, Bryan R. "Let's Eat Chinese Tonight." *American Heritage* 38, no. 8 (1987): 98–103, 105–07.

Jones, Idwal. "Cathay on the Coast." *American Mercury,* August 1926, 453–60.

Joselit, Jenna Weissman. *The Wonders of America: Reinventing Jewish Culture, 1880–1950.* New York: Hill and Wang, 1994.

Karnow, Stanley. "Year in, Year out, These Eateries Just Keep Eggrolling Along." *Smithsonian,* January 1994, 286–95.

Krich, John. *Won Ton Lust: Adventures in Search of the World's Best Chinese Restaurant.* New York, Kodansha International Inc, 1997.

Kwong, Peter. *Forbidden Workers: Illegal Chinese Immigrants and American Labor.* New York: New Press, 1997.

Kwong, Peter, and Dusanka Miscevic. *Chinese America: The Untold Story of America's Oldest New Community.* New York: New Press, 2005.

Lao, Chi Kien. "The Chinese Restaurant Industry in the United States: Its History, Development and Future." Master of professional studies monograph, School of Hotel Administration, Cornell University, 1975.

Lee, Calvin B. T. *Chinese Cooking for American Kitchens.* New York: Putnam, 1959.

Lee, Rose Hum. *The Chinese in the United States of America.* Hong Kong: Hong Kong University Press, 1960.

Leong, Gor Yun. *Chinatown Inside Out.* New York: B. Mussey, 1936.

Levenstein, Harvey. *Paradox of Plenty: A Social History of Eating in Modern America.* New York: Oxford University Press, 1993.

Li Li. "Cultural and Intercultural Functions of Chinese Restaurants in the Mountain West: An Insider's Perspective." *Western Folklore,* October 1, 2002, 329–46.

Lim, Imogene. "The Chow Mein Sandwich: American as Apple Pie." *Radcliffe Culinary Times* 3, no. 2 (Autumn 1993): 4–5.

Lovegren, Sylvia. *Fashionable Food: Seven Decades of Food Fads.* New York: Macmillan, 1995.

Lu, S., and G. A. Fine. "The Presentation of Ethnic Authenticity: Chinese Food as a Social Accomplishment." *Sociological Quarterly* 36, no. 3 (Summer 1995): 535–53.

Mariani, John. *America Eats Out.* New York: William Morrow, 1991.

McLeod, Alexander. *Pigtails and Gold Dust: A Panorama of Chinese Life in Early California.* Caldwell, Idaho: Caxton Printers, Ltd., 1947.

Miller, Hanna. "Identity Takeout: How American Jews Made Chinese Food Their Ethnic Cuisine." *Journal of Popular Culture* 39, no. 3 (June 2006): 430–65.

Pann, Lynn. *Sons of the Yellow Emperor: The Story of the Overseas Chinese.* London: Secker & Warburg, 1990.

Pieke, Frank N., et al. *Transnational Chinese: Fujianese Migrants in Europe.* Palo Alto, Calif.: Stanford University Press, 2004.

Roberts, J. A. G. *China to Chinatown: Chinese Food in the West.* London: Reaktion, 2002.

Shaw, William. *Golden Dreams and Waking Realities* (1851); quoted in Jack Chen, *The Chinese of America.* San Francisco: Harper and Row, 1980.

Spang, Rebecca L. *The Invention of the Restaurant: Paris and Modern Gastronomic Culture.* Cambridge, Mass.: Harvard University Press, 2000.

Spier, Robert F. G. "Food Habits of Nineteenth-Century California Chinese." *California Historical Society Quarterly* 37, no. 1 (March 1958): 79–84.

Takaki, Ronald. *Strangers from a Different Shore: A History of Asian Americans.* Boston: Little, Brown, 1989.

Tam, Shirley Sui Ling. "Images of the Unwelcome Immigrant: Chinese-Americans in American Periodicals, 1900–1924." PhD diss., Case Western Reserve University, 1999.

Tan, Pun Chung. *America's Overseas Chinese Restaurant Industry.* Taipei, Taiwan: Orient Cultural Service, 1971.

Tang, Charles F., with Robert Goldberg. "Chinese Restaurants Abroad." *Flavor and Fortune* 3, no. 4 (Winter 1996).

Tow, Julius Su. *The Real Chinese in America; Being an Attempt to Give the General American Public a Fuller Knowledge and a Better Understanding of the Chinese People in the United States.* New York: Academy Press, 1923.

Tuchman, Gaye, and Harry G. Levine. "New York Jews and Chinese Food: The Social Construction of an Ethnic Pattern." *Journal of Contemporary Ethnography* 22, no. 3 (October 1993): 382–407.

Twain, Mark. *Roughing It.* Berkeley: University of California Press, 1972.

Waggoner, Susan. *Nightclub Nights: Art, Legend, and Style, 1920–1960.* New York: Rizzoli, 2001.

Wong, Nellie C. *Chinese Dishes for Foreign Homes.* Shanghai: Kelly and Walsh, 1932.

Wu, David Y. H., and Sidney C. H. Cheung, eds. *The Globalization of Chinese Food.* Honolulu: University of Hawaii Press, 2002.

Yu, Renqiu. "Chop Suey: From Chinese Food to Chinese American Food." *Chinese America: History and Perspectives* 1 (1987): 87–99.

Yung, Judy. *Unbound Feet: A Social History of Chinese Women in San Francisco.* Berkeley: University of California Press, 1995.

Zelinsky, Wilbur. "You Are Where You Eat." In *The Taste of American Place: A Reader on Regional and Ethnic Food,* edited by Barbara G. Shortridge and James R. Shortridge. Lanham, Md. Rowman & Littlefield, 1998.

Zhang, Jie. "Transplanting Identity: A Study of Chinese Immigrants and the Chinese Restaurant Business." PhD diss., Southern Illinois University at Carbondale, 1999.

Zhao, Jianli. "Strangers in the City: The Atlanta Chinese, Their Community, and Stories of their Lives." PhD diss., Emory University, 1996.

ABOUT TWELVE

TWELVE

TWELVE was established in August 2005 with the objective of publishing no more than one book per month. We strive to publish the singular book, by authors who have a unique perspective and compelling authority. Works that explain our culture; that illuminate, inspire, provoke, and entertain. We seek to establish communities of conversation surrounding our books. Talented authors deserve attention not only from publishers, but from readers as well. To sell the book is only the beginning of our mission. To build avid audiences of readers who are enriched by these works—that is our ultimate purpose.

For more information about forthcoming TWELVE books,
you can visit us at www.twelvebooks.com